Chicagoland

HISTORICAL STUDIES OF URBAN AMERICA

Edited by Kathleen N. Conzen, Timothy J. Gilfoyle,
and James R. Grossman

Also in the series:

Parish Boundaries: The Catholic Encounter with Race
in the Twentieth-Century Urban North
by John T. McGreevy

Modern Housing for America: Policy Struggles
in the New Deal Era
by Gail Radford

Smoldering City: Chicagoans and the Great Fire, 1871–1874
by Karen Sawislak

Making the Second Ghetto: Race and Housing
in Chicago, 1940–1960
by Arnold R. Hirsch

Faces along the Bar: Lore and Order
in the Workingman's Saloon, 1870–1920
by Madelon Powers

Streets, Railroads, and the Great Strike of 1877
by David O. Stowell

The Creative Destruction of Manhattan, 1900–1940
by Max Page

Brownsville, Brooklyn: Blacks, Jews,
and the Changing Face of the Ghetto
by Wendell Pritchett

My Blue Heaven: Life and Politics in the Working-Class
Suburbs of Los Angeles, 1920–1965
by Becky M. Nicolaides

In the Shadow of Slavery: African Americans
in New York City, 1626–1863
by Leslie M. Harris

Building the South Side: Urban Space and Civic Culture
in Chicago, 1890–1919
by Robin F. Bachin

Places of Their Own: African American Suburbanization
in the Twentieth Century
by Andrew Wiese

Downtown America: A History of the Place
and the People Who Made It
by Alison Isenberg

Block by Block: Neighborhoods and Public Policy
on Chicago's West Side
By Amanda I. Seligman

The Elusive Ideal: Equal Educational Opportunity
and the Federal Role in Boston's Public Schools, 1950–1985
By Adam R. Nelson

City of American Dreams: A History of Home Ownership
in Chicago, 1871–1919
by Margaret Garb

Ann Durkin Keating

Chicagoland

CITY AND SUBURBS IN THE RAILROAD AGE   *The University of Chicago Press | Chicago and London*

Ann Durkin Keating is professor of history at North Central College. Coeditor of *The Encyclopedia of Chicago* (University of Chicago Press, 2004), she is also the author of *Building Chicago: Suburban Developers and the Creation of a Divided Metropolis* (1988, 2002) and *Invisible Networks: Exploring the History of Local Utilities and Public Works* (1992).

The University of Chicago Press, Chicago 60637
The University of Chicago Press, Ltd., London
© 2005 by The University of Chicago
All rights reserved. Published 2005
Printed in the United States of America

14 13 12 11 10 09 08 07 06 05   1 2 3 4 5

ISBN: 0-226-42879-6 (cloth)
ISBN: 0-226-42882-6 (paper)

LIBRARY OF CONGRESS CATALOGING-IN-PUBLICATION DATA
Keating, Ann Durkin.
   Chicagoland : city and suburbs in the railroad age / Ann Durkin Keating.
      p. cm. — (Historical studies of urban America)
   Includes bibliographical references (p.   ) and index.
   ISBN 0-226-42879-6 (cloth : alk. paper)
      1. Suburbs—Illinois—Chicago Region—History—19th century. 2. Suburban life—Illinois—Chicago Region—History—19th century. 3. Railroads—Illinois—Chicago Region—History—19th century. 4. Chicago Region (Ill.)—History—19th century. 5. Chicago Region (Ill.)—History, Local. 6. Chicago Region (Ill.)—Buildings, structures, etc. I. Title. II. Series.
   F548.68.A1K43 2005
   977.3'1—dc22
                                                                    2005002198

∞ The paper used in this publication meets the minimum requirements of the American National Standard for Information Sciences—Permanence of Paper for Printed Library Materials, ANSI Z39.48–1992.

The publication of this book was supported by a grant from the Graham Foundation for Advanced Studies in the Fine Arts.

To my parents, John and Dorothy Durkin,
who have shared with all of their children a deep and abiding affection for Chicago

Contents

Acknowledgments

Chicagoland rests on the work of hundreds of local historians and preservationists who have worked to save buildings, local stories, and archives across the region. Small professional staffs and corps of volunteers uncover new sources, investigate local sites, raise funds, spearhead restorations, lead tours, and raise public awareness. They understand the vibrancy of history that relies not just on archival sources, but on historical sites and buildings.

Harold M. Mayer and Richard C. Wade's *Chicago: Growth of a Metropolis,* in print now for more than thirty-five years, shares a recognition of the critical role that buildings can play in understanding history. Through photographs and maps, Mayer and Wade traced the physical development of the Chicago region. Mayer and Wade's volume remains a model for local historians, but also a challenge to look beyond a single suburb or neighborhood. They still remind readers that the region's parts "grew out of the same historical roots; its present problems and prospects are interwoven; and all of its people will share a common future."[1]

Chicagoland emerges from these complementary approaches to history. I have devoted many years to exploring, studying, discussing, and writing about Chicagoland. Studying at the University of Chicago with Kathleen N. Conzen, Michael P. Conzen, and Neil Harris helped hone my understanding of metropolitan landscapes. In the twenty years since graduate school, my interests have been continually refreshed by the work of historians in Chicago, especially at the Urban History Seminar at the Chicago Historical Society.

After joining the history department at North Central College fifteen years ago, I found myself working with nearby local historical societies. For many years, I cochaired a local history symposium with my colleague B. Pierre Lebeau. The symposia brought together local and academic historians to consider topics that included the Civil War, the railroad, and agriculture. Our department also developed courses in local history, as well as student internships with area historical societies. I appreciate very much conversations on local and academic history with both current and past members of my department: Barbara Sciacchitano, B. Pierre Lebeau, Jeffrey Charles, Susan Traverso, Bruce Janacek, and Brian Hoffert.

This book is also a result of more than a decade of discussions about the region's history with James R. Grossman and Janice L. Reiff, my coeditors on the *Encyclopedia of Chicago*. As well, my encyclopedia duties included reading hundreds of histories of neighborhoods and suburbs across the region. *Chicagoland* was profoundly shaped by these local histories.

As I have worked on *Chicagoland,* I incurred many debts. I want to thank Joseph C. Bigott, Robert Bruegmann, Dennis Cremin, Michael H. Ebner, James R. Grossman, Suellen Hoy, Lamar Riley Murphy, Janice L. Reiff, Amanda I. Seligman, and Ellen Skerrett for reading, listening, and responding to various parts of this project. Joe Bigott also shared photographs of sites and maps. I gratefully acknowledge the support of the Graham Foundation for Advanced Studies in the Fine Arts, which enabled me to commission photographs for the book. Leslie Schwartz graciously took up the task of traveling the region, taking photographs of familiar and unfamiliar sites. I also want to thank North Central College for summer stipends and grants to help pay for the historical photographs and maps. Dennis McClendon, Chicago CartoGraphics, designed the maps for the book, and he also provided many important suggestions drawn from his wide knowledge of the region's history.

The Chicago Historical Society, the Newberry Library, the Indiana Dunes National Lakeshore of the National Park Service, the Skokie Historical Society, the Wilmette Historical Society, and the Glenview Park District all helped with images in this book. I want to thank especially the many staff members at the Chicago Historical Society who aided me at various stages in this project. I cannot adequately thank my husband John and my children Betsy and Jack for shared hours in the car navigating the region, for their many photographs of area sites, and for the encouragement they have provided. I can only be grateful to be in their debt (and to have their company). Finally, a special thanks to Robert Devens, Elizabeth Branch Dyson, and Carol Saller; the editors of the Historical Studies of Urban America Series; and the University of Chicago Press for making this project a book.

I have written *Chicagoland* with the public historians and volunteers who explore, maintain, and interpret the history of the Chicago metropolitan region in my mind's eye. My hope is that they will find here a wider lens for their work.

Chicagoland

1

Regionalism in the Railroad Era

Thousands of people and tons of goods traveled through the Dearborn Street Station in Chicago's South Loop in 1900. This red-brick structure was one of six major rail terminals in downtown Chicago, which together linked Chicagoans in a railroad region. A century later, only the Dearborn Street Station remained (fig. 1.1). Once the headquarters of the Atchison, Topeka and Santa Fe Railroad, this 1885 structure now stands between two new residential neighborhoods: Printer's Row to the north and Dearborn Park to the south. Its nine-story clock tower stands as a visible reminder of an era when railroad clock towers regulated the ebb and flow of regional circulation of people and products.[1]

The confluence of railroads and rail stations promoted intensive urban development. Skyscrapers soon dwarfed the railroad clock towers and came to embody Chicago's meteoric rise: structures like the Monadnock Building, once the world's tallest office building at sixteen stories (fig. 1.2).[2] Over time the Monadnock emerged as one of a group of buildings, including the Rookery, Auditorium, Reliance, and Carson Pirie Scott, that have made Chicago's downtown architecture world-famous. These buildings together formed a commercial core for the region. The Loop, nicknamed for the elevated rapid transit line that encircled it after 1897, had taller and larger buildings than in any other part of Chicagoland.[3]

Downtown held the most valuable property in the metropolitan area well into the twentieth century as more and more rail lines centered there. Decisions made in the offices of new skyscrapers increasingly directed the economy of the region. Shoppers flocked to the growing number of department and specialty stores, while cultural and political institutions established roots in the city center.[4] Downtown Chicago served as the hub of an expanding metropolitan region which included Chicago and the rest of Cook County, as well as the ring of counties beyond Cook along the railroad lines.

1.1 Originally designed by Cyrus L. W. Eiditz in 1885, the Dearborn Street Station (also known as the Polk Street Station), 47 W. Polk Street, served as a passenger and freight terminal until 1970. Although a 1922 fire led to considerable change in its facade, it stands today as the last nineteenth-century station in the Loop. The station was added to the National Register of Historic Places in 1981. Eventually, the station was redeveloped as a retail galleria. (Leslie Schwartz)

The Loop rose to prominence as the region's population grew from less than 40,000 in 1840 to more than two million in the Chicago metropolitan area in 1900. By the early twentieth century, the Loop was the locus of decision-making for the regional economy.

The Railroad and the Region

Steel framing created the vertical heights of the Loop, while steel rails framed Chicagoland's meteoric economic expansion. Chicago grew rapidly after the 1848 arrival of the railroad. In the 1850s and 1860s, Chicago interests created a rail system that controlled more than 21,000 miles of rail line across the United States (one-third of all the tributary railroads in the country).[5] Chicago grew as a commercial and industrial center with an expanding hinterland.

The railroad shaped development in other cities around the United States as well. Unlike New York or Boston or Philadelphia, however, Chicago did not begin the railroad era as a substantial city. Chicago had a population of less than 30,000 in 1848 when the first railroad arrived in town. Only a small percentage of the buildings, sites, and settlement in the region predates the railroad.

Because of the railroad, the core settlement at Chicago (today the Loop) came to dominate the regional landscape. While skyscrapers become emblematic of the transportation, financial activity, and cultural amenities increasingly found in the central city, the railroad also transformed the rest of the region. Farmers, manufacturers, workers, and commuters all reoriented their understanding and use of metropolitan space, based on the geometry and schedule of railroad operation.[6]

By the early twentieth century, the rail transportation system comprised hundreds of miles of track within the region; a half dozen downtown passenger stations; dozens of outlying stations for freight, passengers, and perishables; and numerous rail yards and repair shops. "System" might be too strong a word for this transportation network, as by the early twentieth century, twenty-two different trunk lines operated within the region, each with its own internal systems of stations, freight yards and rail line.[7]

Beyond the city center, roundhouses and yards serviced the rail lines rolling in and out of the region. One of the few remaining roundhouses stands to the west of Chicago at the Fox River in Aurora. After 1855, workers for the Chicago, Burlington, and Quincy Railroad constructed and maintained railcars and engines from a stone roundhouse and various specialty shops which at one point covered seventy acres (fig. 1.3).[8] The roundhouse remains an impressive structure today. It is 264 feet in diameter and contained track and stalls for forty engines. Of rough-hewn area limestone, this massive one-story structure is

1.2 The Monadnock Building, 1889–93, 53 W. Jackson between S. Dearborn and S. Federal Streets, was built in two parts. The northern portion of the building was designed by Burnham & Root, the southern by Holabird & Roche. The structure has remained in use as an office building. In this view, looking south on Dearborn probably in the early twentieth century, the federal courthouse is on the near right and the Dearborn Street Station is in the distance. (Chicago Historical Society, ICHi 18909)

1.3 The Aurora Roundhouse was completed in 1855 by the Chicago, Burlington, and Quincy Railroad, and is arguably the oldest roundhouse still standing in North America. At 205 N. Broadway, at least 250 locomotives were built in its forty stalls between 1871 and 1910. The structure continued to function as shop space until 1974. The roundhouse is an American Society of Mechanical Engineers Historic Landmark, as well as on the National Register of Historic Places, and serves today as a restaurant. (Leslie Schwartz)

punctuated every six or seven feet with a window. Behind each of these windows was a stall large enough for a steam engine.[9] The open center of the building provided room for a turntable, so that engines could be moved into and out of stalls with ease.

The railroads provided links between downtown skyscrapers and outlying local depots, which remain one of the most ubiquitous nineteenth-century commercial buildings in Chicagoland. Perhaps in no other metropolitan area in the United States are train stations such a central part of the landscape. They served, and continue to serve, as entrance and exit for settlements across the region, as well as visible legacies of the railroad age.

Hundreds of neighborhoods and suburbs in Chicagoland began around rail stops in the second half of the nineteenth century. Places as different as Pullman, Kenilworth, Ravenswood, North Chicago, Grayslake, and Oak Park all began around train depots. Each took that rail connection and developed in ways that would have been both predictable and unpredictable.

Many of the small one- or two-room stations served both passengers and freight. While some are still in use today, local historical societies maintain others as historic sites. In Itasca, the local historical society has preserved the station once used primarily for farm produce. In Brookfield, the historical society restored the original train station, once the front entrance to an 1890s real estate speculation which drew Sunday crowds who enjoyed the picturesque setting, band music, and free picnics (fig. 1.4).[10] In Norwood Park, recent renovations have restored the Arts and Crafts design of the station, which remains in use, more than a century after the suburb was annexed to Chicago (fig. 1.5).

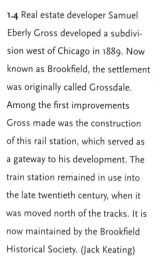

1.4 Real estate developer Samuel Eberly Gross developed a subdivision west of Chicago in 1889. Now known as Brookfield, the settlement was originally called Grossdale. Among the first improvements Gross made was the construction of this rail station, which served as a gateway to his development. The train station remained in use into the late twentieth century, when it was moved north of the tracks. It is now maintained by the Brookfield Historical Society. (Jack Keating)

1.5 In 1868, the Norwood Land and Building Association purchased 860 acres of farmland and hired a designer to plan a suburban retreat along a rail line running north from the city center. The investors built a rail station, which was replaced in 1907 with the current structure. (Chicago Historical Society, ICHi 22681)

While the history of each of Chicagoland's outlying suburbs and neighborhoods is unique, many share a foundation story around these local depots. Rail lines provide literal and figurative links between the more than 250 historical societies that are dedicated to tracing and preserving their local stories in Cook, DuPage, McHenry, Lake, Will, and Kane counties in Illinois; and Lake and Porter counties in Indiana.[11] *Chicagoland* gathers these stories together to tell a regional history.[12]

Varieties of Railroad Suburbs in Chicagoland

Working from extant depots and other remaining structures, as well as the histories behind them, basic suburban types of the railroad age emerge.[13] I have identified the origins of 233 nineteenth-century and early twentieth-century settlements: 41 percent began as farm centers, 30 percent as industrial towns; 15 percent as commuter rail suburbs, and 14 percent as recreational/institutional centers. All but the commuter suburbs are found along rail lines across the Midwest, both in and outside the metropolitan region.[14]

Although they were the most common kind of settlement in railroad-age Chicagoland, farm centers have remained nearly invisible in discussions of metropolitan development.[15] At least ninety-six incorporated suburbs and Chicago neighborhoods trace their earliest history back to agriculture, including Skokie, South Holland, Warrenville, and Gross Point.

These farm centers emerged as Chicago did, to serve the growing urban population. Initially crossroads towns, the centers provided trade and services for farmers, who needed easy transportation into the city center for their fresh produce, The centers included key component parts that are found over and over again across the metropolitan area: a train depot (or crossroads), churches, a school, and businesses that often included blacksmiths and taverns.

Farmers lived and worked on farmsteads, but as market farmers they raised crops and animals for sale. They were tied to the region through their agricultural produce. In particular, dairy and truck farms were closely linked to Chicagoland, providing the region with fresh food. Many farmers sent milk and/or produce into the city every day (during production seasons). They did not often go into the city themselves, but obtained finished products, newspapers, and other materials from the city.

Industrial towns were the second most common form of settlement in nineteenth-century Chicagoland (30 percent). Harvey, West Chicago, Summit, and Pullman all began as industrial towns. They developed around rail lines, which they used to ship goods in and around the region. Most industrial workers lived near work sites. Like farmers, they did not regularly travel beyond these workplaces and surrounding neighborhoods and towns. Instead, raw materials and finished products were shipped along the adjacent rail lines. Outsiders seldom had reason to visit these towns, which often gave them an insular quality. Their structures included a factory (or other work site), a freight rail stop, worker housing, and community institutions.

Commuter suburbs used their rail connections in very different ways from farm centers and industrial towns. They constituted 15 percent of settlements in the region founded by the early 1900s. Hyde Park, Irving Park, Rogers Park, Hinsdale, and Winnetka all began as commuter rail suburbs. In these suburbs, men traveled daily into the city center to work while women crafted a world centered around houses rather than paid employment. (A small core of shopkeepers and service providers also lived and worked in these suburbs.) Despite the daily movement of commuters, these suburbs were nearly as insular as industrial towns. There were few reasons for outsiders beyond family to visit. The key buildings included train stations, speculative plats, and houses set on landscaped lawns. These components were a common landscape replicated along rail lines in metropolitan areas across the United States.

Recreational/institutional centers accounted for 14 percent of the regional settlements by 1900. Forest Park, Evanston, Wheaton, Dunning, and Lake Villa were among settlements regularly visited by outsiders, who generally arrived and departed along the rail lines. Accommodations (day or overnight) and transportation exceeded the needs of the community population because each had to serve the visitors whose expeditions constituted the lifeblood of the economy. These sites played a particularly important role in regionalism because farmers, industrial workers, and commuters might all come to know some of these towns. Places in this category included resorts, county seats, college towns, and settlements near penal, defense, or charitable institutions.

Patterns across Chicagoland

Comparison of a specific structure or site (extant or not) to the regional patterns puts a local place in a regional context. While each of the initial settlement types can be found across the region, interesting patterns emerge from mapping all of the initial settlements with their types indicated (fig. 1.6). Some areas of the region are distinguished by a preponderance of settlements with the same initial impetus.

To the north of Chicago along Lake Michigan, a group of commuter suburbs developed along the Chicago and North Western Railway, which began service in the 1850s. Eight commuter suburbs—collectively referred to as the North Shore ever since then—extend north: Evanston, Wilmette, Kenilworth, Winnetka, Glencoe, Highland Park, Lake Forest, and Lake Bluff. In addition, Rogers Park, now a neighborhood in the City of Chicago, began as a commuter suburb just south of Evanston. Commuters shared trains and the common landscape along the rail lines in and out of Chicago. These suburbs also competed with each other for residents and investment.[16]

A concentration of industrial towns characterizes the Calumet region at the south end of the City of Chicago and surrounding suburbs. At least nine settlements in the wider Calumet region (including areas running east to Gary, Indiana) began as industrial towns, including Harvey, Pullman, South Chicago, and Riverdale. These towns grew around factories, taking advantage of the many rail lines as well as access to the Lake Calumet Harbor, in the closing decades of the nineteenth century. These communities competed with each other for factories as well as residents. Steel, oil refining, and railroad equipment were among the key industries that located in this region. Workers followed, building homes and communities.

Yet another group of similar suburbs is found to the northwest of downtown Chicago along the western boundary of Lake County and the eastern boundary of McHenry County, often described as Chain of Lakes. Along the Fox River and the small lakes in this region, recreational towns developed. Interurban and rail transportation provided access to Chicagoland residents, and these areas attracted day visitors and cottagers to their scenic waterways. Fox Lake, Cary, Round Lake, Lake Villa, and Antioch are among the settlements which for many years provided boating, swimming, and pleasant spots for summer and winter recreation. They competed with each other for visitors, although advertisements for one establishment or community could draw more visitors to the region generally.

All of these settlement types (agricultural, industrial, commuter, and recreational) share

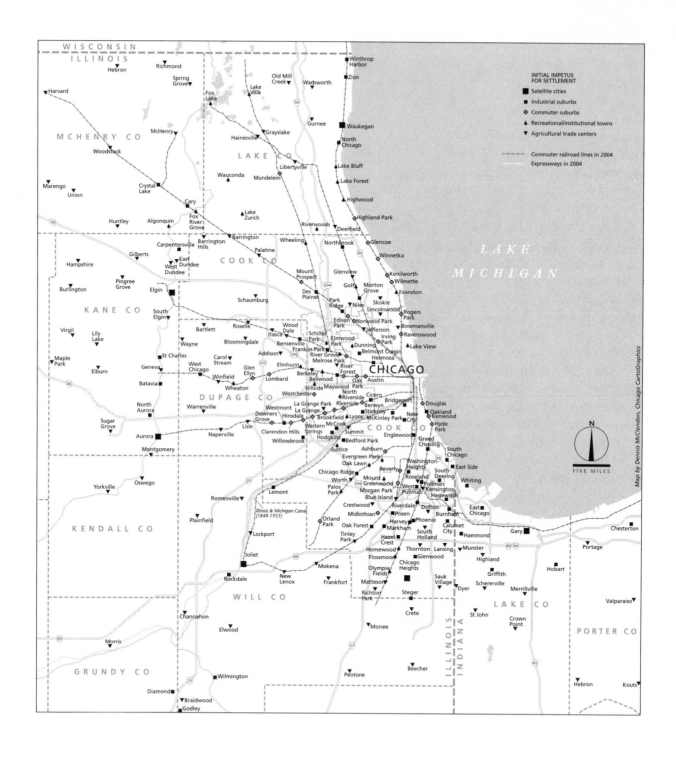

similar economic origins, which often made them competitors in the region for businesses and residents. Developers and business owners used advertisements which highlighted the advantages of their subdivisions and establishments over other similar places in the region. Regionalism emerges not only in the common sites and structures in the region, but in the relationships between places. Each of these settlement types was connected to the wider region through a railroad linking it to the city center.

This did not mean, however, that commuters to the downtown provided the most common link within the nineteenth-century region. Only residents of railroad suburbs were commuters. Farmers and industrial workers were not commuters, and more than two-thirds of the nineteenth-century settlements were either farm centers or industrial towns. Residential suburbs constituted only 15 percent of the initial settlement types.

Farmers, industrial workers, and downtown commuters, therefore, shared a region, but their paths seldom intersected. Farmers sent their produce into downtown and ventured out occasionally to recreational and institutional sites. Industrial workers lived near factories and ventured out from industrial towns and neighborhoods only in their leisure time. Residents of railroad suburbs were the only workday commuters, traveling the rail lines into and out of the city center.

The following chapters will explore each of these settlement types in greater detail. We can walk (or more likely drive) into any Chicagoland town settled in the nineteenth century and explain basic parts of the landscape around us using these four patterns. If these features are no longer visible, we can still dig for evidence of them in maps, photographs, and documents.[17] We can uncover regional connections in local history.

More than the Sum of Their Parts

Although farmers, workers, and commuters had very different regional experiences in the nineteenth century, the Chicagoland region as a whole shared a commonality defined by the physical proximity of their communities. Choose any swathe of the Chicago metropolitan area and one is likely to find a mix of commuter suburbs, industrial towns, farm centers, and institutional/recreational towns.

Sometimes from the start, and sometimes later on, farmers, workers and commuters were neighbors. Perhaps once separated by farm fields, these settlements have come to adjoin each other. This makes for a necessarily complex pattern in any given part of the metropolitan area—farm centers neighboring industrial towns abutting vacation spots next to commuter suburbs. The patterns were much like that of a kaleidoscope, where the individual pieces, corresponding to specific suburbs and neighborhoods, were in constant interaction with each other.[18]

At the same time that communities interacted and grew, they changed in response to

1.6 (opposite) NINETEENTH-CENTURY AND EARLY TWENTIETH-CENTURY CHICAGOLAND SUBURBS. At least 233 settlements in Chicagoland were founded during the nineteenth century. Basic categories for initial foundation include (in descending order of prevalence): farm centers, industrial towns, commuter rail suburbs, and recreational/institutional centers. While many settlements evolved into very different kinds of places, the initial purpose of a town continues to affect a wide range of patterns right down to the present. (Dennis McClendon)

wider economic, social, and political forces. We continue to live with the physical legacies of these settlement types and the interactions between historical settlements and settlers. We can see the forces of regional change by looking at the ways in which change has taken place within any one community in the region. But we cannot discern the broader dynamics of those forces without venturing beyond the community and into the region.

A metropolitan area, then, is more than the sum of its parts. It is a geographic area defined both by basic settlement types (which change over time), as well as by interrelationships between the settlements and residents living within these different landscapes. For instance, many Chicago settlements began as farm centers. Today, there are few farms, and many former agricultural centers have become residential suburbs. Many former industrial towns struggle with brownfields and unemployment, while only a few successfully attract new businesses and jobs.

A Historical Region

Chicagoland does not create a regional perspective; it restores it to Chicago's history. The idea of Chicago as a region has a long history. Many observers in the nineteenth and early twentieth centuries viewed Chicago as a region encompassing far more than the confines of the city center and its adjoining neighborhoods. A historical region and glimpses of its evolution unfold through examination of an 1851 map created by James H. Rees, through an 1874 book written by Everett C. Chamberlin, and through the 1909 plan of Daniel H. Burnham and Edward H. Bennett.

A Region before the Railroad

James Rees's 1851 map shows the logic of regional development before the railroad. Rees, a land agent who negotiated real estate transactions and supervised property, provided information that he thought would be valuable to investors (fig. 1.7). The map highlights all the rivers and creeks in the metropolitan area, including Salt Creek, Thornton Creek, the Little Calumet River, and Aux Sable Creek.[19] Rees also identifies marshy areas, as well as those with trees. This careful attention to natural features helped nonresident investors make sense of the landscape.

Rees also plotted the many roads that crisscrossed the region by 1851. The roads from what would become downtown Chicago, including the Vincennes Trace and the Sauk Trail, had once served as the connecting links between Indian villages. At least five plank roads, which angled outward from Chicago to the north, northwest, west, southwest, and south, operated unsuccessfully as toll roads into the 1850s.[20]

The Rees map situates the settlement at Chicago in a regional context, since Chicago was

1.7 (opposite) James H. Rees was a land agent who published this map of Cook, DuPage, and parts of Kane, Kendall, and Will counties in 1851. Rees plotted county and township dividing lines, as well as subdivided towns and Indian reserves. Among the natural features that he noted for potential land purchasers were the rivers and streams of the region, groves of trees, and swampy areas, as well as schools, post offices, mills, and taverns. The map's detail shows Lemont Township in Du Page County. Prominent are the Des Plaines River and the Illinois and Michigan Canal, which cut the township in two. Athens (now Lemont) is the platted town visible along the canal. Near the top, a crossroads settlement called Cass includes a P.O. (post office) and S.H. (school house), as well as a tavern. The names of area farm families dot the map. Along the western edge of the township, a sawmill was located along a stream running into the Des Plaines River. Several curved outlines mark wooded areas, while a shaded area in the middle right of the township indicates the location of a low, marshy area. (Chicago Historical Society, ICHi 13574)

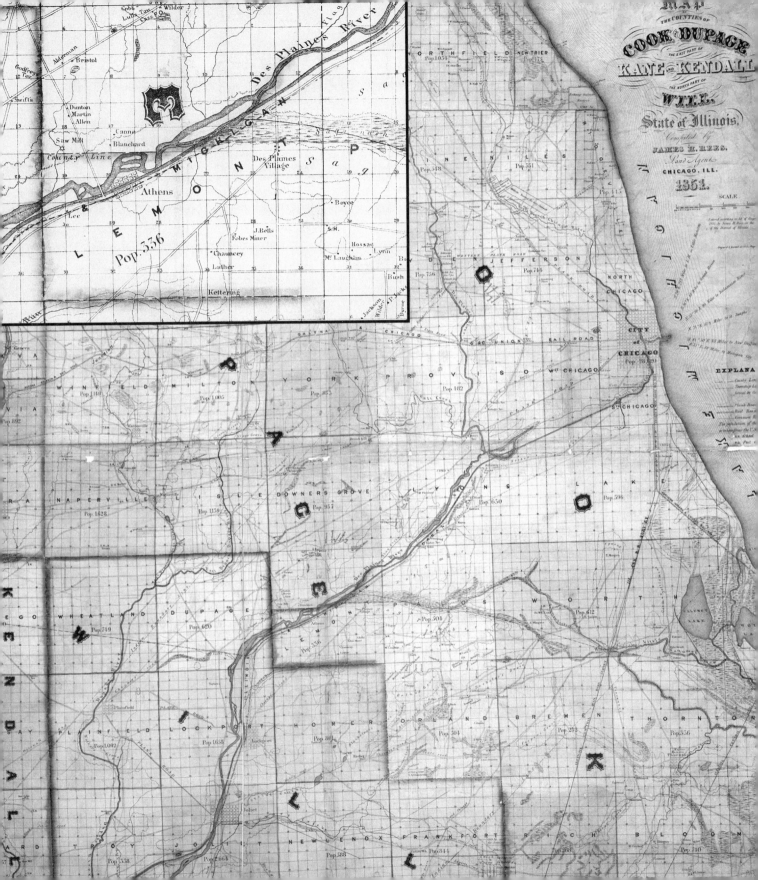

just one of fifteen sites subdivided into town lots. All of these sites were linked to water: Chicago, Dundee, Elgin, St. Charles, Geneva, Batavia, Aurora, Oswego, Plainfield, Naperville, Joliet, Lockport, Lemont, Blue Island (Worth), and Thornton. A sixteenth town, Waukegan, platted in Lake County in 1841, can be added to this group.[21] While the 1851 map leaves little doubt as to the primacy of Chicago, it presents places like Thornton, Joliet, Aurora, and Elgin as either competitors to Chicago or parts of a nascent urban network. Many in the Chicago area assumed that there would be more than one center. Residents of Naperville, Lockport, Thornton, and Waukegan had some hope of capturing a substantial share of the region's trade even into the 1840s. However, the federal investment, as well as that of New York businessmen, at Chicago shifted growth increasingly to Chicago itself. These other cities could hope only for satellite status in the orbit of Chicago.

Rees's map details a great deal more than these platted towns. By the early 1840s, virtually all of the land in this area had been claimed, with much of it under cultivation. A close look at the map shows the names of specific families living in the metropolitan area in 1851. Many of the names remain familiar: Meacham, Talcott, Higgins, Wheaton, Downers, and Cass are all farm families of this era whose names now mark roads and places.

Agriculture simultaneously dispersed families across the metropolitan area and fostered the development of farm centers. While the platted towns certainly provided many advantages, crossroads, mills, and taverns also defined an emerging urban system. Rees marked many of the mills and taverns that he found in his surveys. In many older metropolitan areas, these crossroads taverns and mills became the nucleus of urban places. In Chicago, they were quickly forgotten as the railroad transformed the metropolitan landscape.

Chicago and Its Suburbs

Between 1851 and 1873, the railroad transformed Chicagoland. By the time Everett C. Chamberlin published *Chicago and its Suburbs*, in 1874, the railroad had reoriented the region. His guidebook, aimed particularly at real estate investors, was organized the same way, and included only railroad towns.[22] Chamberlin did not present these towns in alphabetical order, but grouped them by the rail line on which they were located and in geographic order beginning with the town closest to the downtown.[23] Five lines receive the most attention: the Illinois Central line running south; the Rock Island running southwest; the Chicago, Burlington, and Quincy line and the Chicago and North Western line running west through western Cook and DuPage counties; the Chicago and North Western line northwest from the city center; and the Milwaukee Road running north along the lakeshore (fig. 1.8).

Chamberlin calls all of the settlements "suburbs," highlighting the wide range of settlement types fostered by the railroad. Included are farm centers like Arlington Heights, around which Chamberlin described "some of the finest orchards and vineyards in the

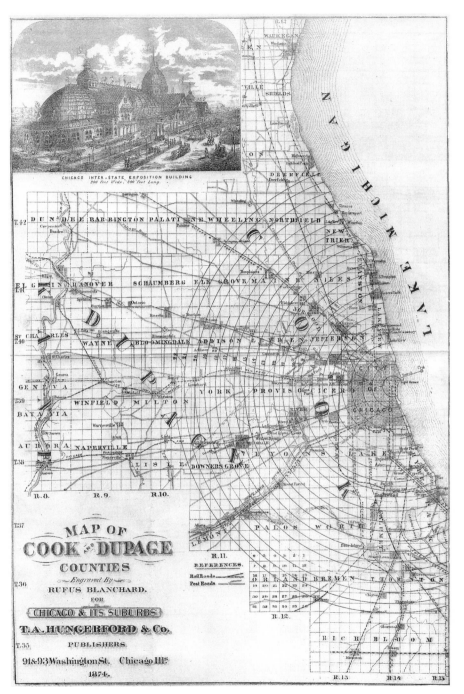

1.8 Everett C. Chamberlin, like James H. Rees, was a Chicagoland real estate agent. In 1874, he published *Chicago and Its Suburbs,* which provided more than 450 pages of description promoting the region and its potential for growth. Chamberlin included this map of Chicagoland just inside the book's cover. (Chicago Historical Society, ICHi-36142)

State. Cherries, apples, pears, berries, grapes, and the like abound in profusion; while the dairy and vegetable business is carried on to a considerable degree."[24]

Also represented among Chamberlin's "suburbs" were industrial towns like South Chicago, which received over ten pages of discussion, maps, and advertisements. These suburbs are centered in the south, especially around the Calumet region. Many were located where multiple rail lines intersect. D. S. Taylor's subdivision in South Chicago is advertised as a site for "manufacturing and residence."[25] Here both rail lines and a river portended quick growth. Chamberlin noted that harbor and water improvements made it ideal for industrial development.

Chamberlin also identified settlements whose growth was tied to institutional or recreational sites. Englewood was a "rapidly-improving suburb" whose major advantage was the Cook County Normal School, where public school teachers received their training. In 1873, the Normal School enrolled more than 450 students from across the county, who studied in a large, three-story building set within a twenty-acre park.[26] Hotels at Riverside, Norwood Park, and Maywood were identified as places which anchored new settlements, offering potential residents an opportunity to experience the area before making an investment.

Chamberlin highlighted commuter suburbs along most of the lines in and out of Chicago. Some lay within what is now the City of Chicago, including Norwood Park, Morgan Park, Ravenswood, Rogers Park, and Kenwood. Those further afield included Riverside and Lake Forest.

Chamberlin identified a region centered at Chicago but surrounded by railroad suburbs that ranged as far as Milwaukee. For him, "suburb" described the subservient relationship which these outlying communities played in the metropolitan story. Chicago was far more dominant than on Rees's map, where Chicago was one of a group of towns. The largest and most important, yes, but one of a group.

1909 *Plan of Chicago*

When Daniel H. Burnham and Edward H. Bennett planned for Chicagoland more than thirty years later, they worked within a developed region. Hundreds of settlements, mostly along the rail lines in and out of the city, defined the metropolitan area (fig. 1.9). In their 1909 *Plan of Chicago*, Burnham and Bennett noted that there existed "between this city and outlying towns within a certain radius vital and almost organic relations."[27]

They identified areas sixty miles from the Loop "as having definite relations with the city." They choose sixty miles because it was as far as "the present suburban electric lines extend, or the automobilist may cover in a drive of two hours."[28] The logic of the region was being reshaped again by the interurban and car.

The interurban, the streetcar, and the automobile fostered residential development be-

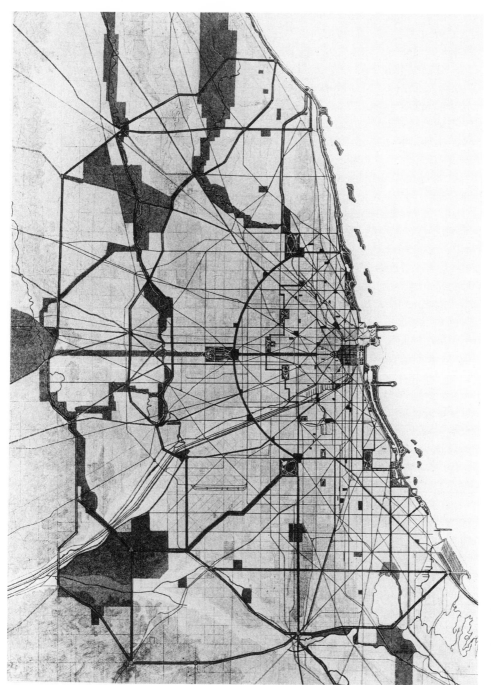

1.9 Daniel H. Burnham and Edward Bennett worked on the 1909 *Plan of Chicago* under the sponsorship of the Commercial Club of Chicago. The plan included whole sections on improvements in regional transportation. This map shows the "exterior highways encircling and radiating from the city." The system was largely in place by 1909. (Chicago Historical Society, ICHi-13284)

tween the rail lines, offering more residential choices: "The steam and trolley railways and the automobile have opened to the city workers all varieties of life, and have made possible to a large proportion of people" the comforts of suburban living.[29] At the same time that interurbans and automobiles would offer metropolitan residents more residential choices, Burnham and Bennett continued to envision water and rail transportation as the basis for industrial and commercial development. But they wanted more and more of this commerce shifted to transshipment points away from the downtown region. This was a process already well underway by 1909, with developments in the Calumet region and to the southwest of the city, where a major industrial district had been launched.[30]

Burnham and Bennett placed the Loop as the most important landscape in the metropolitan area, as a business and recreational center for a region filled with industrial, commercial, recreational, and residential sites. Burnham and Bennett recognized that the age of warehouses and factories in the downtown district was nearing an end. They envisioned that the rail yards which then lined the Chicago River would be abandoned "for freight purposes, just as the fortifications of Paris and Vienna have been transformed from absolute utility to useful purposes of an entirely different nature."[31] In place of warehouses and factories, Burnham and Bennett envisioned park and recreational uses.

Over the course of the nineteenth and early twentieth centuries, the overall logic of the region was shaped and reshaped by geographic and economic forces. Rees shows an agricultural region, with a series of farm centers dominated by Chicago. Access to water and road transportation, as well as good farmland, defined geographic advantages. By 1873, the railroad fostered a new logic for the region. Chicago was predominant as the beginning and end point for virtually all railroad lines. The farm centers, industrial towns, recreational/institutional centers, and commuter suburbs explored in this book are all part of Chamberlin's region in which the railroad looms large.

By 1909, the emerging importance of highways is visible. Burnham and Bennett did not plan for an end to the railroad era, but they did propose highway development particularly to expand residential options. They emphasized the movement of industry and shipping out from the urban core, setting the stage for what would, by the late twentieth century, be called a "postindustrial" city.

Rees's map, Chamberlin's map, and the *Plan of Chicago* together show the importance of a regional perspective before, during, and nearing the end of the railroad era in Chicagoland. They also provide snapshots of change over time. In 1851, the region was defined by an agricultural hinterland which utilized roads and water. The emergence of a rail network in the 1850s and 1860s fostered a spike in regional development. Places along railroads had better access to the center of the region. By 1909, regional planners were looking at the land between rail lines as prime for residential development, while encouraging the further decentralization of industrial and transshipment points.

Regionalism and the Railroad Age

Rees, Chamberlin, and Burnham conceptualized and described a wide region which evolved over the course of the nineteenth century. All three make clear that regionalism is not imposed on the past; it is of it. Everett Chamberlin especially shows that regionalism was of the railroad era. *Chicagoland* rests on this historical regionalism. This book intentionally focuses on the regional world beyond the Loop, in order to explore a metropolitan past encompassing Cook, DuPage, Lake, and McHenry counties, parts of Will and Kane counties in Illinois, and Lake and Porter counties in Indiana.

Chamberlin also makes clear that suburbs are not just commuter enclaves. For him, suburbs included all settlements along the rail lines out from the city center. His was not a political definition of a suburb as a local government set apart from the city. Instead, Chamberlin included places that were both within and outside the city limits. Adapting Chamberlin's perspective, I have deliberately focused on the various kinds of suburbs beyond the city center, including farm centers, industrial towns, and recreational areas as well as commuter enclaves.

I have also downplayed the distinction between suburbs and urban neighborhoods. While understanding the importance of local government, I think separating many city neighborhoods from their suburban neighbors masks the similarities in their histories. Instead, I have deliberately compared the development of urban neighborhoods with farther-flung settlements in the region.

When I began work on this project, I was interested in finding a word to describe metropolitan Chicago. I wanted a word that would keep the regional focus front and center. Too often Chicago is taken to connote just the Loop or the central city. By the early 1930s, "Chicagoland" was used by journalists and social scientists to describe the Chicago metropolitan region. The *Chicago Tribune* embraced the word to refer to the City of Chicago and its immediate hinterland, in order to expand its circulation and advertising reach. Here it helps to shift our range from urban or suburban to regional history.[32]

Reading Sites and Buildings

Chicagoland uses the built environment as an important historical source. I began by looking for visible reminders of the railroad age. Perhaps most familiar were the downtown skyscrapers, which have made Chicago famous as a center of modern architecture. However, I found thousands of other structures built in the railroad era: depots, houses, churches, factories, schools, other public buildings, and commercial structures. Some have been preserved by local historical societies or architectural history groups. Others remain in use.

I sought not the unusual and unique, but buildings that are typical to Chicagoland. Their importance lies not in their groundbreaking architecture or size, but in their number and wide-ranging placement across a region. Historic structures and sites help us to visualize commonalities across a region. While buildings have not been preserved systematically, they can be used to illustrate a regional history.[33]

Together these buildings provide an opportunity to see (and even traverse) regional history, not just read about it.[34] These are quite literally building blocks—the bricks and mortar and street plans which ultimately lie beneath the patterns with which Chicagoans live—that can show the layering of history so readily apparent in downtown Chicago in other parts of the regional landscape.

Historical evidence is all around us. *Chicagoland* rests on the notion that history, particularly social history, can help us to better understand the sites and structures that compose our everyday landscape.[35] A significant number of the important sites and structures in Chicagoland have been destroyed or modified beyond recognition. These sites have not been omitted from discussion. Instead, I have used archival, cartographic, and photographic evidence to explore places no longer visible in the landscape. My hope is that the reader learns what buildings and forms were once common—regardless of whether they are now common or rare.

Historic Preservation

Chicagoland is not straightforwardly a book about historic preservation, although I have tried to tell as much of that story as possible in the captions for the photographs. Local historical societies and architectural groups choose to preserve certain structures because they help accomplish some educational, political, economic development, or aesthetic goals. Many of the more than 250 local historical societies in the metropolitan area are involved in preservation efforts.[36] Especially since the 1960s, dozens and dozens of structures have been preserved through the combined support of these societies, along with park districts and local governments.[37] Virtually all are preserved because of their local significance. Much of the restoration has been done by local volunteers, with important aid from local governments (especially local park districts). The interpretation of these sites often relies on a local perspective—but the sites can also be used to inform or illustrate a regional history.

In the final chapter, I will try to address some of the issues related to the historic preservation of Chicagoland. I see this as a first step toward thinking about preservation historically and regionally. Perhaps from this effort, local historical societies, agencies, and preservation groups can begin to think about the buildings and sites of regional historical significance, not just significant downtown buildings or architect-designed residences in affluent suburbs.

Because my starting points are buildings and sites, *Chicagoland* can be seen as a guidebook. I have included an appendix with suggested tours for those who want to explore further the Chicagoland region. Buildings and sites, and the general patterns they represent, offer a starting point for thinking about what a metropolitan area is and how it changes over time. I hope that this book encourages readers to think about regions and their landscapes, as well as about regional issues, including planning and preservation.

These buildings and sites enable us to tangibly see the ways that the past affects the present and more assuredly argue that what we have done and what we do now will affect the future. With a basic narrative, maps, and a look at extant sites, we can read the history of urban development on the current landscape. History is not just in books—it is around us.[38]

Chicagoland before the Railroad

In the late 1820s and early 1830s, two Indian villages lay along the Des Plaines River near Lincolnshire in what today is Lake County about twenty-six miles northwest of downtown Chicago. Along present-day Half Day Road, Mettawa's village was east of the Des Plaines River, while that of Aptakeesik was to the south on the west bank of the Des Plaines. Both villages were named for their leaders, each a distinguished Potawatomi. Both had easy access to the trail between Fort Dearborn and Little Fort (Chicago and Waukegan), as well as ready access to the Chicago River (within a half mile of the Des Plaines River in the vicinity of the two villages).

Around ninety people were living at Mettawa's village in 1826. A few years later, Yankee Colbee C. Benton ventured north from Chicago with an Indian guide. Traveling on horseback in late summer, Benton was impressed with the prairie that seemed to go on "as far as the eye could see." He commented on traveling across the prairie "covered with a great variety of the most beautiful flowers, some on stalks higher than I could reach from my horse."[1]

Benton rode northward along the Des Plaines River through a heavily timbered area before reaching Mettawa's village. He described the village as "situated in a little grove of timber on the prairie. . . . The land is excellent about it, and they raise good corn. The village is small, consisting of four or five wigwams." He met Mettawa, whom he described as "about sixty years of age," and "a very sensible looking person."[2]

One envisions a farm village with excellent transportation access. Abundant water and timber graced the region. Mettawa's villagers were farmers, who raised "good corn." The village by 1833 consisted of four or five extended families living in five wigwams. The wigwams

2.1 There does not appear to be an extant image of either Mettawa or Aptakeesik, despite the fact that both led Potawatomi villages in Chicagoland into the 1830s. We are left without an image, but perhaps can envision their appearance from this drawing of Potawatomi men's clothing found in Henry Schoolcraft's *History of the Indian Tribes of North America*. (Chicago Historical Society, ICHi-36141)

were likely bark-covered structures constructed by Native Americans across this region. These wigwams afforded both interior rooms and porches for work and living space in clement weather.

By 1904, the Potawatomi village was long gone, but amateur archeologists still found rich evidence of Indian occupation. Arrowheads, pottery shards, and other stone tools were found in abundance.[3] And the site itself in 1904 still had the gentle banks of a narrow river which wound its way through a partially wooded landscape. One hundred years ago, local residents with an interest and a trained eye could find evidence of Mettawa, his villagers, and other Native Americans (fig. 2.1).

Today, however, the physical manifestation of Mettawa's village, or any other Indian village, is no longer easily seen in our landscape. There are no towns or cities in our region that date their foundations directly to an Indian village. No buildings from these Indian villages have survived to the present. The absence of this physical legacy, as well as the lack of more than a handful of written accounts, leaves the Native American history of this region far too easy to dismiss (fig. 2.2).

It also makes it easy to accept a mythology that Native Americans neither disturbed nor shaped their landscapes. In reality, Indians across North America shaped and exploited their natural environment. Native Americans did controlled burning of forests to aid in hunting, cleared fields for farming, and blazed trails and portages across this region over hundreds of years.[4]

A Potawatomi Region

To begin an exploration of Chicagoland around 1800 is not to begin at the beginning. People had already been living in this region for thousands of years. There had already been hundreds and hundreds of years of Native American history and more than a hundred years of contact with Europeans and Africans.[5]

2.2 There is little in the landscape marking the villages which Mettawa and Aptakeesik headed. But the names of a current community (Mettawa) and road (Half Day Road/Aptakeesik Road) serve as reminders of an Indian past. The site of Mettawa's village today is part of the Lake County Forest Preserve at Wright Woods along the east bank of the Des Plaines River north of Half Day Road near Lincolnshire. (Leslie Schwartz)

Control of what became Chicagoland changed a number of times, particularly in the years after European colonization. Illini, Miami, Fox, and finally Potawatomi and their allies lived in the region. No one group had long controlled this area. Colonizers too came and went, French then British then American.[6]

When Fort Dearborn was established in 1803, marking the official arrival of American colonization in Chicago, the area remained under Native American control.

For centuries, Indians in Chicagoland were farmers. With the introduction of corn from the Southwest more than 2,500 years ago, Native American groups became farmers and village life flourished.[7] By 1810, these farmers were primarily Potawatomi who had moved west into the Chicago area from the lower end of Lake Michigan near the St. Joseph River. They moved to sites along the Calumet River and the western shore of Lake Michigan, from northwest Indiana to Door County, Wisconsin. Native Americans lived across the Chicagoland region from what is now Gary to Milwaukee.[8]

Thousands of Native Americans lived in this region by the early nineteenth century. They traded and moved freely through the villages. Most were Potawatomi, but Ottawa and Ojibwa were also among them. As one historian has explained, Indian villages were "always composed of people from more than one tribe, even though they generally identified with only one particular tribe."[9]

Many of the villages were along rivers in the wider region, including the St. Joseph River in what is now Michigan and Indiana; the Elkhart and Iroquois rivers in what is now Indiana; the Milwaukee River in what is now Wisconsin; the Fox River in what is now Wisconsin and Illinois; and the Des Plaines River in what is now Illinois. The villages were organized by the river system, indicating the central importance of these waterways for transportation. In many ways, a comparable contemporary list would organize suburbs and neighborhoods around their nearest expressway. Water transportation routes were a vital part of Native American life in the early nineteenth century, just as expressway access is today.

In the first three decades of the nineteenth century, this was a Potawatomi region, more than a Chicago region. But proximity to the site of Chicago became more important because American colonial administration centered at Fort Dearborn from its construction at the mouth of the Chicago River in 1803. The U.S. Indian agent and the official U.S. trader were stationed at Fort Dearborn and played an increasing role in the life of the Potawatomi.

By 1826, there were thirty-eight Potawatomi villages under the jurisdiction of U.S. Indian agent Alexander Wolcott across western Michigan, southern Wisconsin, and northern Indiana and Illinois. According to Wolcott, the population of the villages ranged from 15 to 210. Wolcott noted no villages along the Chicago River. There were four villages on the Des Plaines River, including Mettawa's and Aptakeesik's, with populations ranging from 28 to 109. Nine villages lay further west along the Fox River, with populations ranging from 28 to 169.[10]

Four to six wigwams could easily accommodate the population of many of these villages. The village populations were largest in the spring, summer, and fall, when residents were actively cultivating farm fields of corn, squash, and beans. In winter, villages split into smaller hunting bands. American officials often identified these villages by the name of a prominent resident or chief, such as Waubansee, Mettawa, and Aptakeesik. They were not mythic figures from an Indian past, but part of a generation of Potawatomi who had to confront a threat which would ultimately destroy their villages and way of life.

Roads and Portages

Mettawa's and other Indian villages were linked not only by waterways, but by a network of trails. Henry Rowe Schoolcraft, an American passing through the area in 1820, described the many intersecting paths leading off to Indian villages in all directions from the Sauk Trail.[11] Schoolcraft envisioned Chicago as a place full of possibility: "To the ordinary advantages of an agricultural market town, it must, hereafter, add that of a depot, for the inland commerce, between the northern and southern sections of the union and a great thoroughfare for strangers, merchants, and travellers."[12] A few years later, another American traveler made his way to Chicago and found a "number of trails centring at this spot," indicating the area's importance as a crossroads not just for his group, but for regional residents and visitors both before and after him.[13]

These diagonal roads constitute one of the most important landscape legacies of the era before 1833. Many of the diagonal streets that today traverse whole sectors of the metropolitan area began as Indian trails and paths.[14] Examples are Green Bay Road, which roughly followed an interior path along the lakeshore all the way into Wisconsin; the Vincennes Trace (State Street) connecting southwestern Indiana to the Chicago area; and the Sauk Trail (near Lincoln Highway), which ran from west of this area through the south end of the metropolitan area as it continued eastward to Detroit. Dozens of lesser trails connected Indian villages and trading sites, crisscrossing the metropolitan area. Grand, Elston, Archer, Milwaukee, and Ogden avenues were among the other streets which angled out from the Chicago River and the portage area.

Without question, the most famous trail in the region was the portage route that traversed a continental divide that ran roughly north to south across the metropolitan area between the Chicago River and the Des Plaines River. Of course other portages existed. Mettawa's village provided a relatively short land connection between the west fork of the North Branch of the Chicago River and the Des Plaines River, while connections between the Calumet, St. Joseph, and Kankakee rivers in the southern and eastern part of the region provided other connections between the Mississippi and Great Lakes drainage systems.[15] However, none of these portage routes is easily found in the landscape today because canal construction, channelization, and landfill have eliminated most of the marshy wetland areas which comprised the portage areas.

One of the reasons that the portage between the Des Plaines and Chicago rivers at Mud Lake is so famous is because of the early written description provided by Louis Joliet and Jacques Marquette. The arrival of Europeans in this region, marked by Marquette and Joliet's 1673 trip, is now celebrated at the Chicago Portage National Historic Site, west of Harlem Avenue and south of 47th Street, in the Cook County Forest Preserves.

Since the marshlands (bordered by Mud Lake) and the west fork of the South Branch of the Chicago River were eliminated by later development, the portage is no longer apparent. The marked site is an open field just east of the Des Plaines River, dominated by an enormous metal sculpture of Marquette, Joliet, and an unidentified Indian companion pulling a canoe (fig. 2.3). At least three times life size, the sculpture dominates the scene. It dwarfs the natural landscape which surrounds it and celebrates the domination of European colonizers over the natural environment as well as over the Native Americans.

The sculpture also reminds us of the divide between written and unwritten history, as well as between the history of the colonizer and that of the colonized. Louis Joliet and

2.3 The Chicago Portage National Historic Site was established in 1952 on the west side of Harlem Avenue between 47th Street and the Stevenson Expressway (Interstate 55) in the Portage Woods of the Cook County Forest Preserve. The steel sculpture was designed by Ferdinand Rebechini. (Leslie Schwartz)

Jacques Marquette made this trip together only once. The importance of this portage lies not in their trip across it, but in the geography of the region. But Joliet and Marquette wrote about their experiences and their words remain long after the natural landscape has been inexorably altered. So we mark the presence of Marquette and Joliet in 1673, not that of the people who lived in the region year in and year out. While clearly of great significance as a portage site, the Chicago portage was not the sole passageway between the Great Lakes and the Mississippi River systems. In fact, Marquette and Joliet used another portage route far north of this area: through the Fox and Wisconsin rivers in present-day Wisconsin.[16]

The unidentified Native American in the sculpture ought to represent knowledge about the portage and area trails. Joliet and Marquette were the interlopers, moving in territory they did not know. But the Native American is not leading the way. Marquette stands at the front of the sculpture and Joliet looks forward, while the Native American provides only his physical strength. There is no place for the knowledge and leadership of an Indian like Mettawa here.

By 1800, hundreds of Native Americans would have led traders and colonizers along the portage routes in Chicagoland. Other roads into and around the region developed to serve Indian groups as they moved between settlements and for trade. Indians moved across the metropolitan area at a rate which seldom exceeded twenty miles in a day, a pace that let them see the region on the edge of woodland and prairie, much of it marshland between two great water systems.

Trading Posts

The Potawatomi who lived in this area in the early nineteenth century had regular contact with American, French, and British traders, missionaries, and government officials.[17] Many of the non-Indians married local Indian women to solidify trading relations, as well as to establish their own families. From these intermarriages emerged a distinctive culture—neither European, American, nor Indian.[18] By 1804, the Potawatomi "were already bending under white influence. . . . Considerable intermarriage had occurred: dark-skinned daughters of mixed marriages were often trained and educated in French-Canadian homes, while sons were encouraged to enter the trade with their fathers."[19]

There is one extant fur trading outpost from the 1820s to be found in this region: the Bailly Homestead (figs. 2.4 and 2.5), located within the bounds of the Indiana Dunes National Lakeshore just north of Chesterton, Indiana. Joseph and Marie Bailly arrived from Michigan in 1822 to build a homestead and trading outpost. Joseph Bailly was born in Quebec in 1774 after the British had taken control of Canada. He made his way westward to engage in the fur trade. His wife Marie grew up in the Detroit area, first in a French settlement with her father, and after his death, in an Ottawa village where her mother had relatives. After the War of 1812, Joseph Bailly became an American citizen and contracted to trade in the Calumet Region.

Before the Baillys chose to locate in the Calumet region, the U.S. government constructed a post road connecting Detroit to Chicago, which assured the Baillys that there would be regional traffic traveling close by. There was at least one Potawatomi village just to the east near Lake Calumet. The Baillys anticipated trade with local Indian residents, as well as with travelers.[20]

The site that the Baillys selected is on a high bluff overlooking the Little Calumet River, just north of the Kankakee Marsh. About thirty-six miles from downtown Chicago, the site was, and is, a place to see and be seen. There was ready access both to Lake Michigan and

2.4 Part of the Indiana Dunes National Lakeshore created in 1976, the Joseph and Marie Bailly Homestead is interpreted and administered by the National Park Service. The park service rebuilt the several log buildings that comprised the trading post in the 1820s. (Indiana Dunes National Lakeshore, National Park Service)

2.5 The Bailly House, built in the 1830s, also stands on the site overlooking the Little Calumet River. (Indiana Dunes National Lakeshore, National Park Service)

southward through the Kankakee Marsh to the Illinois River. Joseph Bailly traveled north into Michigan as well as south and west into Illinois as he traded with Potawatomi across the region. Because Joseph Bailly was away much of the time, it was Marie Bailly who managed the trading outpost. It was Marie who utilized her Ottawa heritage in working with her Potawatomi neighbors. She greeted visitors, negotiated trades, and managed the post. A traveler from New York in December 1833 described Marie Bailly as "a very respectable-looking Indian female, the wife, probably, of the French gentleman who owned the post."[21] Marie Bailly was in many ways, the typical wife of a fur trader in this region, adept in both Indian and colonial worlds.

Several features of the Bailly Homestead were characteristic of trading posts. Easily visible on its bluff, the site stood near a portage and trails, as well as the newly built post road. It was also proximate to Indian villagers.

The Baillys built a compound of six log structures which served as their home and trading center as well as storage buildings for the mink, muskrat, and other animal pelts they purchased in exchange for blankets, guns, and cooking pots. The reconstructed buildings now at the site are all one-room structures, none larger than twelve by twelve feet. They stand in an open field not far from the bluff. In 1833, the same New York traveler who described Marie Bailly also described the outpost: "The trading establishment consisted of six or eight log cabins, of a most primitive construction, all of them gray with age, and so grouped on the bank of the river as to present an appearance quite picturesque."[22] Soon after this visitor, the Baillys built a substantial frame house.

Bailly's Homestead stands as one of the very few physical links to the era when Potawatomi dominated the population and the American government protected a colonial outpost at Fort Dearborn. Other trading outposts were run in present-day Lyons, at Waukegan, and at Plainfield.[23] However, the site at the mouth of the Chicago River supported the largest non-Indian population in the region—as many as a few hundred people.

The oldest structure at the mouth of the Chicago River in 1800 was the house built by Jean Baptiste Point DuSable, a free black man, and his Potawatomi wife Catherine after the Revolutionary War in the early 1780s. They built a one-and-a-half-storied house in the French colonial style with a long veranda facing southward to the Chicago River. Commemorating the spot today is Pioneer Court on the east side of Michigan Avenue between the bridge over the Chicago River and the Tribune Tower.

Unable to own land in this Indian territory, DuSable nevertheless probably farmed here, for he owned a horse mill, millstones, and a bake house.[24] By 1803, John Kinzie had purchased these improvements, at about the same time that construction was begun on Fort Dearborn just south across the Chicago River from the DuSable house. The Kinzie family came from St. Joseph, Michigan, to take advantage of the opportunities afforded by the new American presence in the area. John Kinzie traded across the Potawatomi region from Milwaukee to St. Joseph to Peoria to villages on the Kankakee and Fox rivers, and in 1804 he sensed that the site around Fort Dearborn would be an important center for his Potawatomi clients.

The first Fort Dearborn stood near what is now the mouth of the Chicago River from 1803 until it was burned by Native Americans in 1812 during the U.S. war with the British. The structure looked quite similar to its counterpart at Fort Wayne, which served as its model. Rebuilt in 1815, the second Fort Dearborn served as a focal point for what has been described as a community of middlemen involved in the fur trade and "their employees—clerks, voyageurs, and engages of French, British, American, Indian and mixed extraction" (fig. 2.6).[25]

Just to the southeast of the fort, near what was then the actual mouth of the river (due to a sandbar which sent the river southward before emptying into Lake Michigan), Jean-Baptiste Beaubien also worked as an Indian trader. Like Joseph Bailly, Beaubien was a Frenchman married to a local woman of mixed race. Across the river, near Kinzie's house, stood the house of Alexander Wolcott, the U.S. Indian agent in the 1820s. Near the Wolcott house lived the Porthiers, Ouilmettes, Robinsons, and Mirandeaus, all mixed-race families who worked for the traders and at the fort.

The settlement at Fort Dearborn was a distant outpost of a colonial empire moving west-

2.6 In 1820, Henry Schoolcraft sketched the settlement which he found at Chicago (the basis for this 1857 engraving). The buildings were constructed by African Americans and European Americans, while the people visible here are Native Americans approaching the settlement in large, open canoes. To the left (south) of the Chicago River was the second Fort Dearborn; to the right (north bank), the house built by Catherine and Jean Baptiste Point DuSable (by 1820 owned by the Kinzies). (Chicago Historical Society, ICHi-05626)

ward. The military had to import food and supplies from the East. Several trading outposts brought colonial traders and their families into the region. The small garrison at Fort Dearborn had to import basic foodstuffs from the East. This outpost was an island in a larger region that was claimed by the American government but that was in fact controlled by the Potawatomi and their allies.

The Potawatomi villages in the Chicago region took advantage of the numerous connections between the Great Lakes and the Mississippi River. They were not insulated from the world beyond these portages: indeed, their connections radiated far beyond the bounds of today's Chicago metropolitan area. Native Americans lived and farmed along the rivers—the Chicago, the Des Plaines, the DuPage and the Calumet. They interacted with traders and colonial government officials in large measure on their own terms.[26]

Removal and Resettlement

Until 1833, Potawatomi and allied Indians constituted the majority of residents in the Chicago area. After 1833, Chicago became the center for westward migration, as the Potawatomi and their allies were forced out of the area. No longer an island in an Indian region, the settlement at Chicago became part of a newly emerging U.S. region.[27]

The Grand Treaty of 1833 began a process which led to the removal of the Potawatomi and their allied tribes west of the Mississippi by the federal government, in order to open the land for sale to American farmers. The Native Americans packed up as much of their villages and improvements as possible and took them westward, first to Iowa and then to Kansas.

The buildings that were abandoned were left to ruin. Cornfields that had been cultivated by Native Americans were now under the control of a new wave of farmers, who soon would bring their surplus to market at Chicago along the roads and paths developed by their predecessors.

Therefore the farm fields and trails by which Native Americans had transformed this region were quickly appropriated by the new settlers and lost their distinctive Indian origins. There is no denying that the disdain that many of the region's new settlers held for Native Americans and their societies made it even easier to appropriate, but not acknowledge, the valuable improvements which the Potawatomi left behind as they were forced westward.

In some ways, the landscape was not much affected. Natural waterways and trails defined town sites, just as they had for the Potawatomi. Indian trails were quickly identified and used by eastern migrants as they moved into the area. New farmers sought out locations near streams or rivers which provided drinking water, transportation, and power. Butterfield Creek, Poplar Creek, Hickory Creek, and Indian Creek are among the waterways which today are often ignored except during floods, but which were most important to these new farmers, as well as their Indian predecessors.

2.7 Kennicott's Grove National Historic Landmark, 1421 Milwaukee Avenue, is owned and managed by the Glenview Park District. The Kennicott family arrived in the Chicago area in 1836 and built this Gothic Revival house in 1856. Descendants of the Kennicott family lived on the property well into the twentieth century. Threatened with redevelopment, the site was designated as a National Historic Landmark in 1973 and has been owned by the Glenview Park District since 1976. (Glenview Park District)

Initially, the new migrants also sought land near wooded groves. They expected that the best soil would be wooded, and they needed the timber to construct buildings and fences. Many farmsteads were identified by proximity to a wooded area: Hickory Grove, Walker's Grove, Blackstone Grove, Orland Grove, Bachelor's Grove, Elk Grove, Plum Grove, and Babcock Grove.

To the north along the Milwaukee and Chicago Plank Road (now Milwaukee Avenue) in Northfield Township is a remnant of one such farm. The Grove, a National Historic Landmark operated by the Glenview Park District, lies adjacent to old Indian trail to Milwaukee near the Des Plaines River (fig. 2.7). The property is a 123-acre site containing prairie, oak woodland, and wetland.

In 1836 Dr. John Kennicott and his family came from New Orleans and named the area "The Grove" in honor of a stand of oaks, some of which still grace the site today.[28] Kennicott keenly observed the flora and fauna of the three natural environments around him, all of them key to the region's development: prairie, oak woodland, and wetland. He devoted much of his career to experimenting with different kinds of plants and crops to see which grew best in this area, as well as writing about his findings for a growing audience of regional farmers.[29]

One son, Robert Kennicott, was one of the region's first naturalists and led collecting expeditions for the Chicago Academy of Sciences as well as the Smithsonian Institution, while another, Charles Kennicott, was among a group of amateur archeologists investigating the vestiges of Native American occupation in this region. The Kennicotts were American ex-

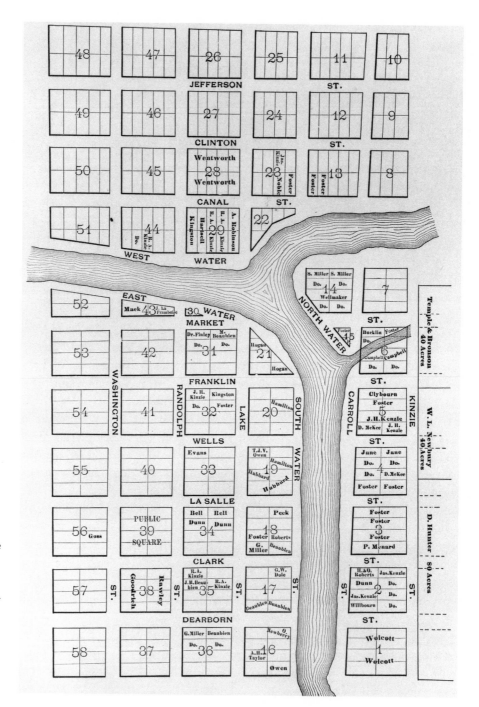

2.8 The Illinois and Michigan Canal Commissioners platted a town at the mouth of the Chicago River in 1830, marking the beginning of a new era when regional land became real estate to be bought and sold. The commissioners hoped to sell lots at Chicago, Lockport, and other canal towns as a way to finance canal construction. In Chicago, surveyor James Thompson subdivided land into streets, urban blocks, and individual lots. (*Industrial Chicago*)

plorers as much as Lewis and Clark; they were not investigating formerly uninhabited lands, but describing formerly Indian lands for an eager eastern audience.[30]

Imposing the Grid

American interest in Chicagoland was fueled by real estate speculation. By the fall of 1833, the U.S. government forced area Potawatomi to cede much of the land in the region.[31] The purchase of this land by the federal government began a shift which would ultimately lead to the removal of Native Americans from the region. Until the arrival of the U.S. government, land was not held as real estate which could be bought and sold. The Potawatomi and their allies certainly claimed and held the land across the region. However, individuals did not own or have the right to sell pieces of land. The U.S. government felt very differently about land tenure. Chicagoland was surveyed, and the township grid overlay every inch of territory. In little over a decade, a good portion of Chicagoland moved for the first time into private hands and land became real estate.[32]

Individual landownership was a fundamental principle of the early Republic. The Land Ordinance of 1785, preceding the Constitution and the Bill of Rights, authorized the survey of western lands into six-mile-square townships to facilitate this process. Congress directed that each township "would be bounded by lines running due north-south and east-west; other parallel lines would divide each township into thirty-six square sections of 640 acres each.[33]

The survey of western lands into township grids did not take place all at once in the wake of the 1785 legislation. Instead, surveys proceeded in an irregular line westward, as Native Americans relinquished their claim to lands. These surveys in Chicagoland began in the 1820s and proceeded into the 1830s. By 1840, Chicagoland had been divided into sectioned townships (fig. 2.8).

These one-mile-square sections are the base of the region as a real estate enterprise and more broadly as a metropolitan enterprise. Numbered sections and townships facilitated the ready identification and sale of land. Although the trails first blazed by Native Americans followed the natural landscape, skirting marshland, taking advantage of dry ridges, and connecting waterways and villages, the grid ignored nature, and so the roads that followed the grid often led into bogs and marshes. While right-angled streets predominate in the region today, the old diagonal roads have staying power and remain a most important legacy of centuries of Native American occupation.

Portage to Canal

One of the projects that promoted the sale of land in this region was a canal proposed to replace the Chicago portage with a ninety-six-mile permanent waterway, linking the South

The Historic Illinois & Michigan Canal Corridor in 1851

2.9 The Illinois and Michigan Canal began at the South Branch of the Chicago River at Ashland Avenue and continued ninety-six miles to LaSalle, Illinois, between 1848 and 1914. It was part of a water-based transportation network in Chicagoland. Of the successful town plats made in the region in the 1830s and 1840s, all but one were located along waterways. The exception was Woodstock, founded as a centrally located county seat for the newly created McHenry County. (Dennis McClendon)

Branch of the Chicago River with the Illinois River, from Bridgeport to Peru. This canal became the most significant manmade structure dating from the 1830s and 1840s in Chicagoland (fig. 2.9).

In some ways, the canal dramatically signaled the start of an American era in which nature would be reshaped and exploited. One early historian of the region noted with some pride that "if there is anything which marks the pioneer of the West . . . as a peculiar people it is the prematureness of their enterprise in all public works."[34] However, in spite of the fact that the canal was a massive public work, this was a public works project grounded in the natural environment and an understanding of that environment which was inherited by new migrants from their Native American predecessors.[35]

Efforts to build the canal began in 1816 (before Illinois was a state and while this region was still firmly controlled by the Potawatomi and their allies), but it was not until 1836 that construction was begun. Work was halted following the 1837 crash, and the canal, sixty feet wide at the surface and six feet deep, was finally completed in 1848.

2.10 Dug by hand, the Illinois and Michigan Canal was generally sixty feet wide and six feet deep. Stretches of the canal property were used for the Stevenson Expressway (Interstate 55). In 1974, a sixty-one-mile Illinois and Michigan Canal State Trail was created, which became the base for the Illinois and Michigan Canal National Historic Corridor. Seen here is a contemporary view of the canal at Lockport, adjacent to the Gaylord Building. (Leslie Schwartz)

The Illinois and Michigan Canal linked the Great Lakes to the Mississippi River in much the same way that the Erie Canal had linked the Atlantic Ocean with the Great Lakes in 1825. The canal was an immediate success, encouraging the expansion of business at Chicago and environs. In its first year of navigation the "waters of the canal were covered with craft of every kind, and the locks were in constant motion." Tolls amounting to $87,890 were collected that first year, when it was open 224 days.[36]

Looking at the canal today, it is perhaps difficult to envision the profound influence which it had on regional development. Later transportation improvements, including a larger canal, railroads, bridges, and roads, physically overshadow the Illinois and Michigan Canal. At Lockport, the canal is not full of water six feet deep; nor does the waterway measure sixty feet wide as it did at its opening in 1848. Instead a stream meanders several feet below the sides of the canal. Originally built with limestone sides whose straight angles must have stood in contrast to a natural watercourse, today the canal has a softness which blends into the natural surroundings (fig. 2.10).

2.11 The Gaylord Building, 200 W. 8th Street, Lockport, was constructed in 1838 as a storehouse for the Illinois and Michigan Canal. Greek Revival and Italianate additions were made to the building in the later part of the nineteenth century when the structure went through various owners and usages. Now owned by the National Trust for Historic Preservation, the Gaylord Building is operated by the Canal Corridor Association and contains offices, exhibit space, and a restaurant. (Leslie Schwartz)

The importance of the canal to the region is perhaps better understood by examining the Gaylord Building, which abuts the canal at Lockport (fig. 2.11). This massive limestone structure was built in 1838 by the Illinois and Michigan Canal Commissioners to house provisions and supplies. It is one of the largest buildings remaining in the region from the 1830s. The structure has a weighty Romanesque design with rounded windows deeply embedded into cream-colored limestone quarried further north along the canal at Summit.[37]

In 1838, the fate of the canal was uncertain. Funding was in disarray and only a small part of the canal itself had actually been completed. Constructing such an impressive building quite likely sent a message to investors and naysayers alike that the canal would indeed be built. The Gaylord Building advertised the importance of the canal as much as large, solid bank buildings reassured depositors.

It also helped to signal physically the dramatic population shift taking place in the region during these years. The new migrants certainly understood the importance of Chicago's strategic natural location, just as the Potawatomi had. However, these new migrants intended to reshape the natural environment. The Illinois and Michigan Canal was the most ambitious part of plans that also included harbor improvements at Chicago, road paving, and continued building.

New Buildings

As Chicagoland shifted from Potawatomi and their allies to European Americans during the 1830s and 1840s, new residents used the trails, farm fields, and village sites of their predecessors. But they also built frame houses and taverns with features from American and European architectural styles, particularly the Greek Revival. Frame buildings with columns and glass windows replaced French-styled houses and wigwams, as Yankee settlers from upstate New York and New England replaced Potawatomi farmers and French traders. In many cases, the architectural features were modest: front doors surrounded by a row of small leaded glass panes; long, low windows; or porches with columns. But these features were new and heralded as a new American style.[38]

Ironically, one of the first structures built with Greek Revival features in the region was built not by migrants, but by a family of French Indian traders. At Wolf Point, where the main stem of the Chicago River split into the North and South branches, Mark and Monique Beaubien belonged in many ways to the Potawatomi era. Long engaged in the fur trade, the couple came to Chicago in 1826 on the advice of Mark's older brother Jean, who operated a trading post just southeast of Fort Dearborn. Initially, Mark and Monique lived in a small cabin and engaged in trade with area Indians.

In 1831, the Beaubiens built a substantial frame structure, soon known as the Sauganash Hotel, with Greek Revival features (fig. 2.12). They catered to the new American travelers and settlers who came in increasing numbers after the end of the Black Hawk War in 1832. Juliette Kinzie, a young bride recently arrived from Connecticut in 1831, described the Sauganash Hotel as "a pretentious white two-story building, with bright blue wood shutters, the admiration of all the little circle at Wolf Point."[39] The symmetry of the door and window placement, as well as the casements of glass surrounding the front door of the Sauganash, were typical of the Greek Revival style popular across New York and New England.

The Sauganash Hotel contrasted with the few buildings then at Chicago. The oldest house, built in the 1780s by Jean Baptiste Point DuSable near the mouth of the Chicago River, was built in the French colonial style. By 1831, it was owned by Juliette Kinzie's in-

2.12 Mark and Monique Beaubien built the Sauganash Hotel in 1831 at Wolf Point (now the southeast corner of Wacker Drive and Lake Street in downtown Chicago). The Sauganash Hotel operated until 1851 when it burned down (over a decade before, the Beaubiens had sold the hotel and purchased another in Lisle). (Andreas, *History of Cook County*)

2.13 The Beaubien Tavern stood at its original site between Fender and Keller Streets on Ogden Avenue in Lisle into the 1980s. When the tavern was threatened with destruction, the Lisle Heritage Society and the Lisle Park District moved it about a mile to the southeast near the Lisle Train Depot. Renovations over the 1990s have saved this historic structure at 1825 Short Street in Lisle. (Leslie Schwartz)

laws and was in a state of disrepair. One wonders whether Kinzie would have been so quick to label the Sauganash as "pretentious" if it had belonged to her in-laws.[40]

In 1843, Mark and Monique Beaubien exchanged their Chicago tavern for a structure owned by Richard M. Sweet in Lisle Township east of Naperville along the southwestern road from Chicago (now Ogden Avenue). Beaubien would continue to move in and out of Chicago and the Naperville area over the next two decades. During the late 1840s and early 1850s, Beaubien's tavern stood at the toll stop about a day's journey out of Chicago on the Southwest Plank Road.

Although the Sauganash Hotel was torn down long ago, the Beaubien Tavern still stands in west suburban Lisle (fig. 2.13). A simple frame structure, the Beaubien Tavern probably had two rooms on the first floor and a roughly finished second floor where guests could spend the night. Still, the four small panes of glass above the front door are a nod to the Greek Revival styles of the day. Early settlers could get a drink—or two—of whiskey, purchase basic supplies, and catch up on area news.

The construction of the Sauganash Hotel led a building boom across Chicagoland. In 1833 alone, 150 new buildings were constructed in Chicago, with probably at least as many more in the region as a whole.[41] Most of the structures had few finished features. But a close look at their windows and doors uncover features of the nationally popular Greek Revival style.

The only extant structure from 1833 stands today on the Far Northwest Side of the City of Chicago. The Noble-Seymour-Crippen House is the oldest structure within current city limits (fig. 2.14). Set on high ground, the Noble House afforded an expansive view of the area and was close to several of the roads in and out of Chicago, including the Milwaukee Plank Road and Talcott Road (just to the south of the house).[42]

The single-story section of the building (facing south toward Talcott Road) was built in 1833, while the two-story Italianate section was added in the 1860s. The original portion of the house has the long, narrow windows characteristic of many Greek Revival homes. The windows open directly onto a porch.

The Mark Noble family arrived in Chicago in 1831 from England and lived at the Fort Dearborn settlement for a year. In 1833, the Nobles bought land in what would be Norwood

2.14 The Noble-Seymour-Crippen House, 5624 N. Newark, in the Norwood Park neighborhood on Chicago's northwest side, is the oldest extant building in Chicago. The Noble family built the southern single-storied part of the structure in 1833 with long windows in the building's main room. Designated a Chicago Landmark in 1988, the building remained in private hands until the 1990s, when it was purchased by the Norwood Park Historical Society, which continues to own and operate the site. (Betsy Keating)

Township and built a one-story frame house large enough for the whole family. The Nobles may have dragged the lumber for their home from the Des Plaines River, where the family had an interest in a lumber mill.

There was attic space that probably served as sleeping quarters for members of the family. A cellar could have been used as a kitchen. Mark Noble, Sr., was a Methodist Episcopal, a man of "great practical sense," and an "earnest Christian," who regularly held prayer meetings in his family's home.[43] In 1835, area Methodists had a regular preaching circuit that included the Noble House as well as Yorkville, Oswego, Aurora, St. Charles, Winfield, Elk Grove, Wheeling, Plum Grove, Libertyville, Deer Grove, Crystal Lake, and Dundee.[44]

More than 300 more buildings were constructed in Chicago between 1834 and 1837.[45] Caroline Palmer Clarke, a migrant from upstate New York, described what she saw at Chicago in 1835: "The buildings are now mostly small, and look as though they have been put up as quickly as possible, many of them are what they call here Balloon houses, that is built of boards entirely."[46]

The house that Clarke built with her husband Henry is perhaps the best-known restored house extant from the 1830s (fig. 2.15). Henry Clarke made a fortune selling hardware to Chicagoans as they built a city. The Clarkes built a Greek Revival–style house on a twenty-acre lot at Michigan and Sixteenth Street. The house itself is easily double the size of the other homes preserved from this era. It has a large portico with four pillars and a cupola.

Like the Noble House, the Clarke House first floor includes long windows that drop all

the way to the floor and open onto a porch. But the windows are considerably larger than those of the Noble House, and the facade is almost twice as large. At the Clarke House, a glass transom and decorative molding frame the front door.

The first-floor rooms at the Clarke House stand large and gracious. The entrance hall, with a finely finished staircase, outsizes most of the rooms in the other homes discussed here. High ceilings on the first floor add to the spaciousness of the formal parlors and dining room. This house, while not the oldest home in Chicago, remains a remarkable physical testament to the success of Chicagoans in building a city that was integrated into the U.S. fabric.[47]

The Clarke House, the Noble-Seymour-Crippen House, and the Gaylord Building indicate that not all new settlement took place in the immediate vicinity of Fort Dearborn.

2.15 Henry B. and Caroline Clarke built their Greek Revival house in 1836 at what is today S. Michigan Avenue and 16th Street. In 1871 the house was moved to 4526 S. Wabash; and in 1977, to its current location at 1855 S. Indiana Avenue. It is seen here sometime in the nineteenth century. It was restored in 1981 by the City of Chicago and is now maintained by the Chicago Architecture Foundation, which is headquartered in the nearby Glessner House in the Prairie Avenue Historic District. (Chicago Historical Society, ICHi-01166)

Like their Potawatomi predecessors, eastern migrants chose sites convenient to water routes and roads, much as the Potawatomi had done.

At the same time, these structures clearly represented the shifting population in the region in the 1830s. The eastern migrants rejected the abandoned housing of the evicted Potawatomi, even as they absorbed their fields and transportation network. They built in new styles, boldly proclaiming the arrival of new residents. Greek Revival features, so popular in the 1820s and 1830s in New York and New England, helped newcomers make this landscape their own.

Ironically, only a handful of the structures built in the 1830s still stand. The 1830s newcomers' stamp on the regional landscape was in many ways more ephemeral than that of their Indian predecessors. In fact, the Noble and Clarke houses are examples of a largely lost generation of building in Chicagoland.

New Towns

While most of the structures no longer stand, the real estate speculation that fueled the regional economy in the 1830s and 1840s left a lasting legacy in town plats. The Illinois and Michigan Canal Commissioners platted the town of Chicago in 1830, with the hope that quick land sales would finance canal construction. Lemont (Athens) and Lockport soon followed.

By 1850, a speculative urban system emerged based on at least seventeen towns platted alongside waterways and roads. Chicago's strategic location at the head of the canal was among the advantages that put it ahead of other new towns in the region. All but one of these seventeen sites were on area waterways: Chicago, Dundee, Elgin, St. Charles, Geneva, Batavia, Aurora, Oswego, Plainfield, Naperville, Joliet, Lockport, Lemont, Blue Island, Waukegan, and Thornton. Woodstock, platted in 1841 as the county seat for a new McHenry County, is the only town platted not along Lake Michigan or a river.[48]

While the 1840 population statistics leave little doubt as to the primacy of Chicago, places like Thornton, Joliet, Aurora, and Elgin were either growing competitors with Chicago or parts of a nascent urban network. Chicago's population was 4,470, while Lemont (Athens) stood at 1,662 and Thornton, 306.[49] Many early settlers in the Chicago area assumed that there would be more than one center. It was not immediately evident that Chicago would in fact be the central place in this region. Joe Naper, a founder of Naperville, had some hope of capturing farmers from the west before they reached Lake Michigan. Lockport, headquarters for the construction of the Illinois and Michigan Canal, vied for merchants and settlers. Waukegan, already known as "Little Fort" for several generations, had a better natural Lake Michigan harbor. It was the Corps of Engineers, New York investors, local boosters, and finally the railroad that set Chicago on a path to dominance in the metropolitan region.

Farm Centers of the Railroad Age

In 1857, Lake County farmers near Libertyville constructed a modest white frame structure for the education of area children. A tall, single-story building with a small belfry, the Wright School served Libertyville area children for a hundred years. One student in the 1910s remembered that the school operated in sync with agricultural rhythms: closed for spring planting and fall harvest, open during the summer growing season. The school also served as a social center for the community, hosting parties and other local festivities, until 1957, when only a few farm families still sent their children. Today the building is again used as a classroom, part of the Prairie Crossing Charter School (fig. 3.1). Relocated alongside a historic barn, the Wright School serves as the entranceway to an innovative conservation community, where developers are "attempting to preserve the natural history of the area," as well as "attempting to preserve the human history."[1]

Similar small frame structures dotted the regional landscape a century ago. While most of these schools have been torn down, a number of historical societies and public agencies have preserved a few of the buildings as remnants of our rural, seemingly simpler, past.[2] Elementary school groups make regular field trips to these sites. They come to see what it would have been like to be in school in their local area over one hundred years ago when most of the families worked as farmers.

These schoolhouse sites celebrate the local community spirit of early residents. They also celebrate the history of local education as it moved from single classrooms serving under a hundred students to large multischool districts serving thousands of students. But taken more broadly, the schoolhouses represent the role that farmers played in creating the landscapes, infrastructure, and institutions across Chicagoland.

3.1 The Prairie Crossing Charter School, 1571 Jones Point Road, Grayslake, was known originally as the Wright School, which operated from 1857 to 1957. In 1995, the school was moved north to its current location at the entrance to the Prairie Crossing development, a conservation community established in 1992. Today the Wright School serves as a kindergarten classroom for a public charter school. (Leslie Schwartz)

3.2 (opposite) FARM CENTERS OF NINETEENTH-CENTURY AND EARLY TWENTIETH-CENTURY CHICAGOLAND. More than one-third of the communities in the Chicago metropolitan area (ninety-six incorporated suburbs and Chicago neighborhoods) trace their earliest history to agriculture. Some are crossroads towns, while others developed around rail depots. (Dennis McClendon)

The old Wright Schoolhouse reminds us that farmers needed and built more than farmsteads. Alongside farmhouses and outbuildings, all but the most basic subsistence farmers also required taverns, mills, towns, churches, schools, and other institutions. And farmers in Chicagoland since the 1830s have produced for the market, so they needed good transportation and services. Chicagoland is covered with the legacy of this agricultural landscape.

It may seem odd to devote a chapter to farming in a book on metropolitan Chicago, but it is in fact a dominant regional landscape. At least 96 communities (incorporated suburbs and Chicago neighborhoods) trace their earliest history back to agriculture (out of 233 Chicagoland communities founded in the nineteenth century). Early farmers were market producers who supported and needed market towns. Some of these towns were founded as crossroads settlements, while others grew around railroad depots (fig. 3.2).

At first, crossroads towns near waterways developed to meet the needs of these market farmers. By the 1850s, a nascent town system had developed, linking these towns to each other and to Chicago. With the arrival of the railroads just before the Civil War, a new market pattern emerged. Rays out from Chicago along the rail lines had much heavier development than areas between. Farmers near rail stops could turn to dairying and vegetable farming for ready sale in Chicago.

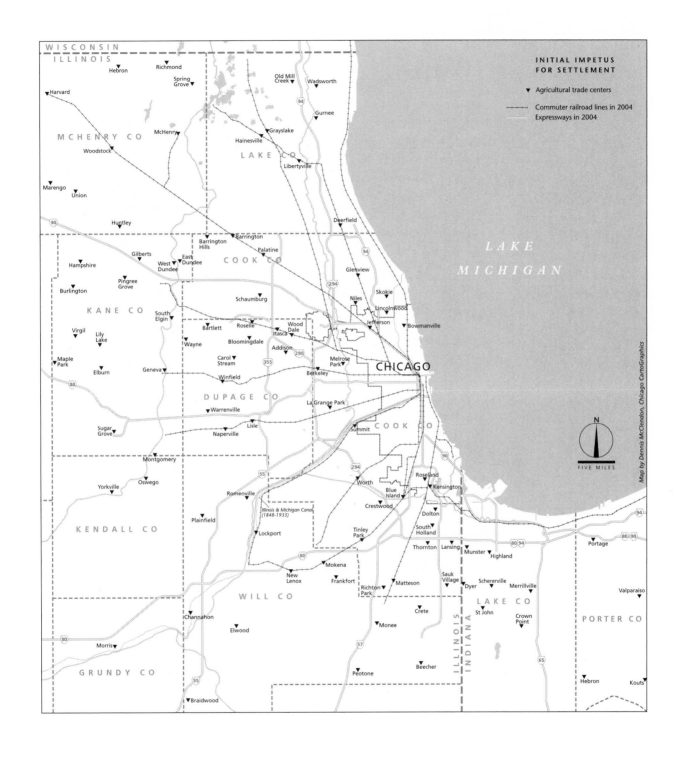

INITIAL IMPETUS
FOR SETTLEMENT

▼   Agricultural trade centers
╌╌╌ Commuter railroad lines in 2004
─── Expressways in 2004

WISCONSIN
ILLINOIS

Hebron
Richmond
Spring
Grove
Harvard
Old Mill
Creek
Wadsworth
Gurnee

94

McHenry
Grayslake
Hainesville
MCHENRY CO
McHenry
LAKE CO
Woodstock
Libertyville

Marengo
Union

Huntley
90
Deerfield

Barrington
Barrington
Hills
Palatine
94

Hampshire
Gilberts
West
Dundee
East
Dundee
COOK CO
Glenview

Pingree
Grove
Schaumburg
294

Burlington
Niles
Skokie
Lincolnwood
KANE CO
South
Elgin
Bartlett
Roselle
Jefferson
Bowmanville
Virgil
Lily
Lake
Wayne
Itasca
Wood
Dale

Maple
Park
Bloomingdale
Addison
290

Elburn
Geneva
Carol
Stream
355
Melrose
Park
CHICAGO
Winfield
Berkeley
DUPAGE CO
Warrenville
La Grange Park

88
Sugar
Grove
Lisle
Naperville
Summit
COOK CO

Montgomery
55

Yorkville
Oswego
Romeoville
Worth
294
Roseland
90
Kensington
Blue
Island
Crestwood
Plainfield
Illinois & Michigan Canal
(1848-1933)
Dolton
80 94
Portage
80 90
South
Holland
Lockport
Tinley
Park
Thornton
Lansing
Munster
Highland
KENDALL CO
80
New
Lenox
Mokena
Frankfort
Richton
Park
Matteson
Sauk
Village
Dyer
Schererville
Merrillville
Valparaiso
WILL CO
Crete
St John
Crown
Point
PORTER CO
Channahon
Monee
Elwood
57
LAKE CO
Morris
65
ILLINOIS
INDIANA
GRUNDY CO
55
Beecher
Hebron
Kouts
Peotone
Braidwood

LAKE
MICHIGAN

N
FIVE MILES

3.3 Just a little over a decade after the transition from a Native American world, the town of Chicago had more than 8,000 people living within its bounds as it supported a rich agricultural hinterland. This engraving was originally part of an 1845 city directory. Looking east over pasture and farmland to the city (and the lake in the distance), reminds the viewer that Chicago was part of a region from its earliest days. (A. T. Andreas, *History of Cook County* [1884])

Farmers founded schools, local governments, churches, and other institutions which continue to influence the daily lives of Chicagoans. Extant courthouses and rural churches, as well as one-room schoolhouses, stand as physical markers of the farmers' world.

Agriculture and Regional Growth

An engraving of the Chicago skyline for an 1845 city directory illustrates Chicago's emergence as a western center for agricultural commerce (fig. 3.3). At Chicago, a solid band of settlement follows the river. The structures are mostly one and two stories, with the spires of the town's churches rising above. The dark plumes of smoke represent Chicago's burgeoning industries, while church steeples illustrate the city's many institutions, religious and secular. In the distance, ships' masts indicate the harbor area of the Chicago River, and to the far right can be seen the entrance to the harbor at Lake Michigan. A real estate speculation in 1830 was becoming a reality fifteen years later.

The 1845 engraving places Chicago in its agricultural hinterland, with cattle grazing in the forefront of the image. Also depicted are a number of wagons, loaded with farm produce, approaching the city from various directions.[3] Americans were settling not just at Chicago, but in the region as a whole. Chicagoans no longer had to import food from the East. Instead, they consumed the produce of an expanded hinterland, and shipped the growing surpluses to eastern markets.

Farmhouses

Many farmers arrived in the region via Chicago. Some moved on immediately, often reuniting with family, friends, and former neighbors who preceded them westward. Others spent several years in the city, earning money and learning about the region.

The Peck Homestead in Lombard illustrates how families located in the region, built houses, and established farms (fig. 3.4). Sheldon Peck and his family traveled from Onondaga County, New York, on the Erie Canal westward to Chicago in 1833. Peck had been a farmer and a portrait painter in upstate New York. The Peck family came to the area to purchase better farmland. After living at Chicago for a few years, the Pecks moved west overland to an area known as Babcock's Grove, near to old New York neighbors. Now Lombard, their farm was about twenty miles from Chicago along the St. Charles Road.

The Pecks built a one-and-a half-story frame home in 1837. Originally constructing only two rooms, the family soon added a large third room. A long porch, supported by columns, distinguishes the front of the structure. The building was constructed in large measure by the Peck family themselves.

Many early farmers, like the Pecks, acquired milled lumber and built houses which resembled those they had left in the East. As market farmers, families like the Pecks used wide planks, not logs, in their house construction. Few were log cabin dwellers. However, the woodwork is simple with little ornamentation. There is no fine finished work on doors, windows, or frames.[4]

This house served not only as a residence, but also as a center for the Babcock Grove settlement. Sheldon Peck sponsored the first area school in one of the large ground-floor rooms. Peck also continued to paint portraits, including those of other early farmers like Bailey and Clarissa Hobson, who lived to the west in what is now Naperville. The Pecks did not live an isolated existence, but one shaped by farm neighbors near and wide.

Travel back and forth to Chicago most likely continued. One neighbor remembered: "It was no uncommon thing for a man to take his plow share and mould board, weighing some sixty pounds, upon his back and trudge away to Chicago, a distance of twenty-four miles,

3.4 The Sheldon Peck Homestead, 355 E. Parkside, Lombard, was owned continuously by the Peck-Metz family from 1837 until 1996 when it was donated to the Lombard Historical Society. The Village of Lombard purchased the land from the Peck-Metz family in that same year. The house was restored to its 1830s appearance and is maintained by the Lombard Historical Society. (Leslie Schwartz)

3.5 and **3.6** (right and opposite) Garfield Farm, 2N016 Garfield Road, LaFox, was owned by the Garfield family from 1841 until 1977. In that year, Elva Ruth Garfield founded a museum on the site to teach about America's prairie farm heritage. Today, the site is jointly owned by two nonprofit organizations: Campton Historic Agricultural Lands and the Garfield Heritage Society. (Leslie Schwartz)

to get it sharpened." Farmers who passed along the road in front of the Pecks' house might spend the night a mile or so further west at Stacy's Tavern.[5]

The Peck House now sits on a busy suburban thoroughfare in Lombard, across the street from a large water park and surrounded by residential subdivisions. The farm fields are long gone, but the Lombard Historical Society has restored and now maintains a piece of the western suburb's early history.

Many local historical societies have enthusiastically worked to preserve the former homes of farmers. These farmhouses range from the Pecks' 1830s house to a four-square homestead built in the 1920s. The wide geographical distribution of these farmhouses underscores the broad agricultural base on which Chicagoland rests, as well as the powerful draw which our rural past has for preservationists.[6]

Virtually all of these farmhouses have been restored to a specific year or decade. Restoration work involves many choices—only some of which are determined by a clear historical record.[7] While some sites have excellent background on the specific building over time, other restorations have to rely on general accounts of the era and are not site-specific. Even when specific sources exist, preservationists make a myriad of choices about room configurations and interpretation. For instance, local historians at the Lombard Historical Society chose to restore one of the rooms of the Peck Homestead as a school, to facilitate school tours. Interpretation of these restored farmhouses is shaped by both necessary limitations as well as the suburban perspectives of the restorers. Interior restoration often focuses on furniture styles, appliances, and domestic work. This leads to an emphasis on work done primarily by women in these houses: cooking, cleaning, canning, gardening, washing, and child care.

An implicit comparison is often made between contemporary suburban houses and the historic farmhouse. This female domestic landscape fits neatly into stereotypes from the residential suburban boom after World War II. Women predominated in the suburban landscape (even historically) and men worked elsewhere. Nothing could be further from the truth when considering the agricultural landscape.

This perception arises in part because frequently barns and other outbuildings have been leveled, leaving the farmhouse out of its original context as a part of a larger farmstead. The sphere of men's work is no longer visible. Indeed, some of the preserved farmhouses in the region have been removed from their original sites, out of the path of development. The Peck farmhouse looks out not on barns and fields, but on suburban houses and businesses. Without the outbuildings and farm fields, much of the work of both men and women remains overlooked.

Farmsteads

Because of the great value of farmland, whether in active production or redeveloped for suburban use, few farmsteads have been preserved in this region. This makes interpreting the agricultural landscape a tricky business. Without the farmsteads, the modern observer can ignore both the work done on farms and the farm products which were moved to market. Without the farms themselves, farmhouses can be interpreted easily as an insular domestic landscape.

Among the few farmsteads preserved in Chicagoland is the now 281-acre Garfield Farm, five miles west of St Charles in Kane County, which provides a fuller picture of this agricultural landscape than is possible from looking only at extant houses (figs. 3.5 and 3.6). The

3.7 and **3.8** (above and opposite) The Chellberg Farm is now within the Indiana Dunes National Lakeshore. Maintained since 1976 by the National Park Service, the Chellberg Farm is one of only a handful of living history farms in the region. (Indiana Dunes National Lakeshore, National Park Service)

Garfield family traveled west from Vermont in 1841 to claim 440 acres of land west of the Fox River. They built a substantial brick house in 1846 which also served as a tavern through the 1850s. Today, an 1842 hay barn and other outbuildings, as well as the presence of farm animals, provide some sense of the farms which once dotted the metropolitan landscape.[8]

The work was hard, done in freezing cold and intense heat. It was also rigidly divided according to gender. The men in the Garfield family built and maintained structures, tilled fields, harvested crops, planted orchards, repaired equipment, and took care of large farm animals. Their mothers, wives, and daughters worked in the house, as well as outside tending a kitchen garden and chickens and geese.

The pair of oxen kept at Garfield Farm remind us that most of the early work was done with little machinery. Oxen, horses, and manual labor powered the early farms in Chicagoland.[9] At first farmers raised corn, potatoes, and wheat, as well as cattle and pigs. Beef cattle and some hogs were also raised for market. Into the 1850s, farmers used free prairie to range stock which was marketed nearby or in Chicago.

Chicagoland farmers, like the Garfield family, initially raised the same crops as their counterparts across the Midwest. Wheat was sown with an eye toward sale in the market.[10] The Garfield family may have brought their surplus crops by a nearby road into Geneva or thirty-five miles further into Chicago. The Garfield family also participated in the market economy by opening their home to travelers, primarily farmers, who were using the road in front of their farm. The Garfield Tavern operated into the 1850s until the railroad rearranged travel across the region.

Beginning with the Galena and Chicago Union Railroad in 1848, rail lines soon radiated out from Chicago. With the arrival of these first railroads, the logic of trade changed abruptly. Farms thirty miles or more from Chicago, previously a day's journey or more from the city, might now be just over an hour by train from the city center.

Many farmers took advantage of this transportation and switched to the potentially more lucrative dairying, truck farming, or haying. They provided food for Chicago residents, as well as for the thousands of horses living there. This distinguished them from farmers further away from the railroad and beyond the metropolitan area, who continued with the production of grains and stock. This transition did not take place all at once, because the rail network in and out of Chicago did not appear overnight. Instead, over the course of the second half of the nineteenth century, new rail lines changed the dynamic of farming around them.[11]

For instance, Anders and Johanna Chellberg arrived in Chesterton from Sweden in 1863, joining a growing group of Swedish immigrants in northwest Indiana. By 1874, the Chellbergs were able to buy eighty acres from the Bailly family (discussed in the previous chapter), who had operated a fur trade outpost in this area in the 1820s. The Chellbergs had to break the sod on the land they purchased before they could begin farming. They built a substantial brick home, which still stands, from locally made bricks (figs. 3.7 and 3.8). The two-story portion of the house was built in 1884. They joined other Swedes in the area in founding the Augsburg Evangelical Lutheran Church and a local school.

The Chellbergs raised cash crops such as wheat, oats, and corn. They also had some hogs for sale. When it came time to bring their produce to market, they did so over rural roads through the end of the nineteenth century, much as farmers had been doing since the 1830s.

But with the arrival of the South Shore Electric Railroad in 1908, production shifted, as it had across Chicagoland with the introduction of nearby railroads. The Chellbergs began to keep a dairy herd and brought the milk daily to the train for delivery to a dairy in East Chicago, Indiana. The family produced milk for commercial consumption through the 1930s. To meet a seven o'clock train, the Chellbergs got up hours earlier to feed and milk the cows, cool the milk in big cans, and drive the wagon loaded with the cans to the train. While it was very hard work, this generation of Chellbergs built a one-story addition to their brick farmhouse which included a kitchen, porch, and a room for a milk separator.[12]

The experience of the Garfields and Chellbergs suggests the effects of farmers' participation in a wider regional economy. They very quickly claimed and worked most of the usable farmland in the region. Farmers grew not only the crops needed for their families, but also enough to bring to market. Their choices concerning the location of their farms, as well as crops to grow and animals to raise, were intimately tied to wider trends in the region and in the country as a whole.

Crossroads and Taverns

The success of farmers spurred the development of market centers across the metropolitan area. And while the farm fields have today largely been overwhelmed by residential subdivisions and strip malls, many of these market towns remain central to the economic, political, and social geography of the region. While a few disappeared with the farmers, many more survived to serve suburban residents.

Two very different kinds of market towns emerged in this region over the course of the nineteenth century. The earlier system emerged at crossroads, while a second system grew around dozens of rail stations.

The initial market towns were founded along roads and waterways. Taverns were often the first substantial structures built where roads intersected with other roads or waterways. During the 1830s and 1840s taverns emerged along virtually every road in and out of Chicago at intervals as close as just a couple of miles.[13] Myrick's Tavern (Chicago), Doty's Tavern (Lyons), Anderson's Tavern (Niles); the Halfway House (Plainfield), Burroughs Tavern (Evanston); the Warren Tavern (Warrenville), the Pre-Emption House (Naperville), and the Beaubien Tavern (Lisle) are among the dozens established by 1850. Most sold liquor, but they were much more than taprooms. With land travel limited to around twenty-five to thirty miles per day, taverns provided overnight accommodations for farmers and other travelers within the metropolitan area.[14] The first stockyards in this region emerged in the back lots of taverns. Taverns also served as meeting places for settlers as they organized local government, held elections, and founded religious congregations and schools. In addition, the owners of taverns often hosted local celebrations and parties.[15]

3.9 Stacy's Tavern, 557 Geneva Road, is maintained by the Glen Ellyn Historical Society under the ownership of the Village of Glen Ellyn. Built in 1846, the structure received a historical marker from the Illinois State Historical Society in 1967 and was placed on the National Register of Historic Places in 1974. (Leslie Schwartz)

Stacy's Corners was one such settlement that grew at the intersection of Lake Street, St. Charles Road, and Wheaton Road about a mile west of the Peck Farmstead and about twenty-two miles west of Chicago in DuPage County (fig. 3.9). Founded by Moses Stacy and run by his family, the tavern served as the anchor for this crossroads community. Stacy opened his home to travelers in 1837, and to meet a growing demand for accommodations, constructed a purpose-built inn in 1846.

The two-story frame structure had a ladies' parlor, taproom, and kitchen on the first floor, and bedrooms for the Stacy family and guests on the second floor. The family had very little private space, and even their bedrooms were not segregated from chambers rented to guests. Family life was intimately interwoven with the operation of the tavern.

Built without fireplaces, Stacy's Tavern had new-style stoves in three downstairs rooms. Within two years, the family constructed a substantial addition which roughly doubled the size of the building. The space served as a dining room on the first floor and additional sleeping quarters above. Guests paid fifty cents for supper, lodging, breakfast, and hay for two horses, and the Stacy family prospered as Chicago and its hinterland expanded.[16] Female travelers congregated in a parlor filled with the best furniture located off the main entrance to the tavern. It is easy to envision ladies using the tea service, doing needlepoint, and engaging in conversation in this room. Directly behind this parlor, with a separate entrance, was the taproom. The room today is sparely furnished, as it was in the mid-nineteenth century. Hard cider and later beer were no doubt consumed as men congregated around a stove in the winter months. Both men and women sat at long tables in a dining room, where the Stacy family served basic fare.[17]

The ladies' parlor embodied regional residents' aspirations to American customs and manners. Someone went to the time and expense of furnishing china, challenging the notion that this was a frontier. At the same time, the simple long tables and chairs in the dining room were no doubt built by the Stacys or area craftsmen. Overall, the public rooms at Stacy's Tavern provided a center for a crossroads community that would eventually be subsumed into present-day Glen Ellyn.[18]

Mills

Access to a mill was an important part of the success of many early farmers in this region. Gary's Mill in Warrenville, Miller's Mill north of Niles Center, the Gray-Watkins Mill in Montgomery, and Naper's Mill in Naperville are among a group of gristmills that served grain farmers by the early 1850s. Other mills were located along the Chicago, Des Plaines, DuPage, and Fox rivers, as well as the largest creeks in the region. In 1851, ten mills along the Fox River between Dundee and Oswego served farmers along the western border of Chicagoland.[19]

One of the few extant mills stands today in eastern DuPage along the Salt Creek in what is now Oak Brook. When it was built, the Graue Mill stood between the crossroads of Brush Hill and Cottage Hill (fig. 3.10). Graue Mill is an imposing brick structure of four stories, with a water-power wheel nearly two stories in height. Built in a simple style with large rectangular windows on every floor, the mill used an undershot wheel, which turned huge millstones inside the building. These millstones then ground wheat or corn into flour.[20]

The Frederick Graues emigrated from Ger-

3.10 Frederick Graue completed his mill on Salt Creek in 1852, and family members operated it until 1912. Located now at York and Spring roads in Oakbrook, the DuPage County Forest Preserve District owns the property, which has been administered since 1950 by the DuPage Graue Mill Corporation. The site is both on the National Register of Historic Places and a Historic Mechanical Engineering Landmark. In 2002, the Graue House next to the mill opened as a visitors' center for the site. (Leslie Schwartz)

many via the Erie Canal in 1833. Family members claimed and farmed extensive acreage in what would become York and Addison townships. Frederick Graue began construction of the mill in 1847, but it was not completed until 1852. The Graue family operated the mill for more than sixty years on Salt Creek just north of its intersection with the Southwest Plank Road (Ogden Avenue). The site provides a sense of the great size of the water wheels used to operate mills by the middle of the nineteenth century.

Early economic concentration took place near area mills and taverns, which themselves were located in close proximity to roads and waterways. These concentrations might have developed into a regional town system, were it not for the railroad. Instead, the railroad changed the logic of development, leaving many of these towns to stagnate until suburban growth in the late twentieth century.

Milk Stops

Mills like the Graue Mill were among the largest structures in the metropolitan area before the Civil War. The substantial investment they required underscores the early profitability of grain. But with the arrival of rail lines after 1848, many farmers abandoned grain for dairying and truck farming. This shift meant that fewer and fewer mills were needed to serve area farms.

Instead, milk stops (stations with regularly scheduled early morning trains to cart milk into the city—instead of later trains for commuters), as well as cheese and condensed milk factories, multiplied along new rail lines (fig. 3.11). Milk and farm produce could easily be shipped into Chicago. A second wave of farm centers in Chicagoland developed around railroad stations in the second half of the nineteenth century. For instance, at Lisle, about twenty-four miles west of Chicago in DuPage County, a milk stop emerged at the rail station after the Chicago, Burlington, and Quincy Railroad began service through the area in the 1860s.

Each morning, area farmers brought their milk in large metal containers to the Lisle station, located between the established towns of Naperville and Downers Grove (fig. 3.12). At first just a flag stop, by 1874 the area could support a depot—a large structure, with more room for milk cans and farm produce than for people. Newspapers, mail, and manufactured goods came out from Chicago on the trains that brought in milk. The depot provided a public space for meetings much as the taverns did for crossroads towns.[21] Slowly around depots like Lisle, market towns emerged to serve area farmers, with grocery stores, blacksmiths, and churches.

In Geneva, another eleven miles further west of downtown Chicago along the Fox River, farmers could bring their milk after 1874 to a butter and cheese dairy and creamery. Located on the west side of the river in a large limestone building, the Geneva Rock Springs Cream-

3.11 In 1873, the Chicago, Milwaukee, St. Paul, and Pacific Railroad completed its line between Chicago and Elgin, passing through the northern part of DuPage County and spurring the development of farm centers, including Bensenville, Roselle, and Itasca. By 1874, Itasca had a train station which served as a milk stop. This image shows milk containers being loaded onto a train headed into Chicago (*1874 Atlas and History of DuPage County*)

ery cooled and processed milk for local sale or for shipment into Chicago along the nearby rail line.[22] Creameries, as well as butter and cheese dairies, were found in many of the farm centers across the region in the closing decades of the nineteenth century.

While railroad towns like Barrington, Jefferson Park, Winfield, Woodstock, and Mokena grew along with agricultural trade during the nineteenth and into the twentieth century, many crossroads towns stagnated.[23] Plainfield, Niles Center, Gross Point, and South Holland remained small towns into the second half of the twentieth century, when subdivisions replaced farm fields and these towns evolved into suburban centers.

Local Institutions

Farmhouses, farmsteads, and a network of agricultural service centers were a central part of Chicagoland by 1900. In addition, farmers founded institutions which continue to influence the daily lives of Chicagoans long after the development of their farms. Public schools were among the first institutions founded by these families. Before they had the support to build even a simple school, the Pecks held classes in their home for area children. Soon one-room schoolhouses dotted the metropolitan landscape. Many of these schools became the foundation for school districts which continue to thrive down to the present.

The success of market farmers and their commercial partners led to the expansion of

3.12 The Lisle Depot Museum, 915–925 School Street, was built by the Chicago, Burlington, and Quincy Railroad in 1874. The Lisle depot was used by farmers sending milk and produce into Chicago. Only in the mid-twentieth century did commuters begin to replace milk. The station remained in active use until 1978, when it was renovated by the Lisle Heritage Society, the Lisle Park District, and the Village of Lisle as a museum. (Leslie Schwartz)

local government beyond counties and their subsidiary townships. Incorporated villages had greater powers to regulate, to provide services, and to raise taxes. In farm centers, the ability to regulate businesses and markets spurred many settlements to incorporation. Farm towns that incorporated in the nineteenth century included Glenview, Addison, Bensenville, Park Ridge, Bloomingdale (incorporated initially with Roselle), Gross Point, Riverdale, Blue Island, Thornton, South Holland, and Orland Park. Their village governments regulated businesses within their bounds, especially stockyards and establishments that sold liquor. The wish to prohibit or regulate (for a profit) the sale of liquor spurred many farm centers to incorporate.

For instance, Gross Point was a small market crossroads settlement north of Evanston in New Trier Township which first developed in the 1840s. Gross Point provided a church, cemetery, groceries, blacksmiths, and taverns for area German farmers. Residents of Gross Point organized as a village in 1874 and in 1896 built a substantial village hall with monies raised through liquor licenses and related taxes.

Churches

Farmers supported not only local businesses, government, and education. They also were instrumental in founding religious congregations. The initial network of both Protestant and Roman Catholic churches in Chicagoland came with the important support of farmers and reflected their own settlements. Churches were often located at places convenient for congregants to gather, not necessarily within a town.

St. James at Sag Bridge Roman Catholic Church stands today south of the town center in Lemont, at 106th and Archer Avenue along the Illinois and Michigan Canal (fig. 3.13). When the church was built in 1852, area residents included Irish canal workers who had turned to farming after the completion of the canal in 1848. The church, built of a local cream limestone, stands in a wooded area in the center of one of the oldest cemeteries in the region. It was deliberately located at a distance from existing settlements.

Churches anchored many of the farm towns which flourished in nineteenth-century Chicagoland. Sometimes an entire market center was dominated by the settlement of one ethnic and religious group. South Holland, in Thornton Township south of Chicago's current city limits, was settled almost exclusively by Dutch immigrants beginning in 1847. These Dutch migrants came as a group, built their homes, and began to work the land. They founded a Dutch Reformed church in 1848. While the original church does not stand, the original church bell is preserved on the grounds of the current congregation.[24]

South Holland developed along the Little Calumet River, south of the current Chicago city borders near what is now 159th Street (Route 6) and South Park. The remnants of a small agricultural town still are apparent. Along South Park, immediately north and south of the river stand a series of historic homes bearing plaques from the South Holland Historical Society. Most date to the second half of the nineteenth century, including a barn from the 1860s. Along with the Dutch Reformed Church, the Bethany Covenant Reformed Church and the Calvin Christian School are reminders of the solidly Dutch heritage of this community.

German farmers were far more numerous than Dutch in the metropolitan area. In market centers with many Germans, multiple congregations developed, reflecting the diversity of emigrating Germans, who were Roman Catholic, Jewish, and from various Protestant sects. To the north of Chicago, at the intersection of Gross Point Road, Lincoln Avenue, and

3.13 St. James at Sag Roman Catholic Church, Archer Avenue and 106th Street, Lemont, is on the National Register of Historic Places. The congregation was founded as a mission church primarily for Irish workers and contractors on the Illinois and Michigan Canal. The limestone church was constructed in 1852, when area residents worked as farmers and in local quarries. Both the church and adjoining cemetery remain in active use. (Leslie Schwartz)

what is today Oakton Avenue, the crossroads town of Niles Center developed in the 1850s. Now part of the large heterogeneous suburb of Skokie, Niles Center was a thriving farm center in the nineteenth century with a nearby mill, grocery and hardware stores, saloons, and meat markets.[25]

While this business district remains in Skokie serving the now suburban population, the three crossroads churches provide perhaps the strongest link to the old farm center. German farmers may have shared a language, but they did not share a religion. In Niles Center, however, they shared a benefactor (and a namesake). Peter Blameuser, Jr., a Catholic, donated land for both a Catholic and a Lutheran church. St. Peter's German Evangelical Lutheran was organized in 1867, and a year later the congregation built a structure which served as both a church and a school (figs. 3.14 and 3.15). Roman Catholics founded St. Peter's Roman Catholic Church in 1868, and established a school soon thereafter. The original frame building is gone, replaced by a brick church (figs. 3.16 and 3.17). Across the street from it is a Catholic cemetery, one of the few churchyard cemeteries still remaining in the metropolitan area. In 1881, St. Paul's Evangelical Lutheran Church split from St. Peter's Evangelical Lutheran Church and established a second congregation.

These three congregations are now dominated not by Germans, but by immigrants from Asia and Latin America who bring new languages to these old churches. New synagogues,

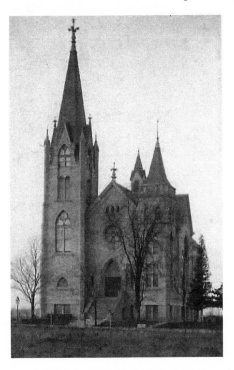

3.14 (left) German farmers in the crossroads town of Niles Center (now Skokie) built St. Peter's Evangelical Lutheran Church, 8013 Laramie Avenue (at Oakton Street), in 1868. Damaged by a lightning strike in 1901, the church was expanded during the renovation. (Skokie Historical Society)

3.15 (right) Contemporary view of St. Peter's Evangelical Lutheran Church, Skokie. (Leslie Schwartz)

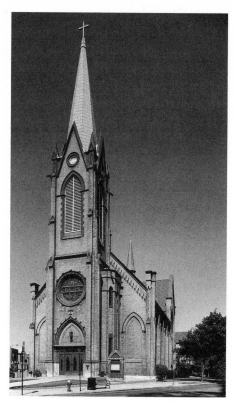

3.16 (left) Just north of the Evangelical Lutheran Church, German Catholics founded St. Peter's Catholic Church in 1868 at 8116 Niles Center Road (at Lincoln Avenue) in Niles Center. This is a postcard image taken around 1900. (Skokie Historical Society)

3.17 (right) Contemporary view of St. Peter's Catholic Church, Skokie. (Leslie Schwartz)

temples, and churches point to the contemporary religious heterogeneity. The new immigrants are high tech, professional, or service sector workers rather than farmers. But the fact that we can walk from one church to either of the others in a matter of minutes reminds us that religion shaped farming communities. It also reminds us of the agricultural crossroads towns which are today embedded in our suburban landscape.[26]

The Legacy of the Agricultural Landscape

Since the 1960s, the expressway and tollway systems in Chicagoland have led to more intensive regional development. As farmland has been replaced by roads, suburban businesses, and subdivisions, agricultural crossroad and railroad towns have been subsumed. Many of the basic institutions which nineteenth-century farmers founded and nurtured remain strong, serving new suburban residents. Milk stops on rail lines have become commuter rail stations, one-room school houses have developed into massive school districts, and tiny rural churches have become the nucleus for sprawling suburban congregations.

Suburban historical societies rightly place emphasis on the rural underpinnings of Chicagoland's history. Through the work of local historians, we have a rich collection of farmsteads, rural churches, taverns, and one-room schoolhouses. Because historical societies frequently receive their funding from local sources, especially suburban government, they may feel obligated to tell only a local story. As a result, interpretation commonly links a rural past directly to a suburban present through the history of a single community within Chicagoland.

The historical societies which preserve these rural sites certainly see themselves as outposts in an urbanizing region where farms are all but gone. This is a powerful and dangerous nostalgia—especially for people living in suburban areas who are intent on keeping city life at arm's length. Suburbanites visiting these sites learn that their community's past, like its present, can be explored in isolation, rather than in a metropolitan context.

Neither the past nor the present is so simple. Farmers in nineteenth-century Chicagoland did indeed build farmsteads and agricultural settlements. But these farmers necessarily relied on markets in Chicago to make viable their farmsteads and towns. They also provided the base for a regional economy which saw explosive growth in the second half of the nineteenth century. Their successes were instrumental to the success of the region as a whole. In turn, the success of the region spurred the development of the milk stops, farmsteads, and schoolhouses which are now preserved by local historical societies. These sites can and must be interpreted in multiple ways—for their local importance and for the ways in which they illustrate metropolitan history. Many local historians have tapped the recent rich literature in rural history which intertwines religion, ethnicity, economics, politics, and material culture, to better understand the origins of their communities.[27]

What these local historians have failed consistently to do in their interpretations of sites and buildings is to link these rural stories to the metropolitan region. In turn, academic urban historians have seldom viewed rural areas as vital parts of metropolitan areas. If urban historians took a more inclusive view, their work would provide a base from which local historians would be better armed to interpret their sites beyond a rural perspective. The nostalgia for a simple past must be tempered by the complexity of growth within a metropolitan region.

Industrial Towns of the Railroad Age

Between 4100 and 4200 S. Halsted Street, Exchange Avenue makes a short appearance, running westward half a mile to Racine Avenue. Taking a quick turn onto Exchange from Halsted, one confronts a remnant of Chicagoland's industrial past. There stands the Union Stock Yards Gate, a massive limestone structure erected in 1879, composed of one large arch bookended by two smaller arches (fig. 4.1). All around this gate once stood the pens, slaughterhouses, and meatpacking establishments which constituted the Union Stock Yards until their 1971 closure. Today the gate is surrounded instead by recent construction: single-story light-industry buildings.

While the packinghouses are gone, past visitors have penned vivid images of the sights, sounds, and smells of the Stock Yards District. Poet Carl Sandburg dubbed Chicago "Hog butcher for the world," as he described the district surrounding the gate. New Yorker Julian Street found the world beyond the gate a place filled with "the all-pervasive smell of animals."[1] In *The Jungle,* Upton Sinclair described a routinized job where each man on the line butchering hogs did "a certain single thing to the carcass as it came to him."[2] These vivid images remain, along with the Stock Yards Gate, as reminders of the past.[3]

When constructed in 1879, the gate provided a triumphal entranceway to the wildly successful consolidated stockyards which made their investors fabulously wealthy and aided Chicago's meteoric rise.[4] But when the Union Stock Yards opened in 1865, they were a suburban enterprise located in Lake Township south of the city proper amidst farm fields. Railroads provided ready transportation between farm and city and the stockyards located between them (fig. 4.2). The connection between farms, stockyards, and cities was clearly

4.1 The Union Stock Yards Gate was erected in 1879, fourteen years after the establishment of the stockyards in suburban Lake Township. Located at 850 W. Exchange, the gate was probably designed by Burnham & Root. Above the gate are the words "Union Stock Yard Chartered 1865" and above the central arch is a relief image of the steer that won the 1878 American Fat Stock Show. (Leslie Schwartz)

heard, smelled, and seen by visitors and workers. One visitor made this linkage humorously: "The hog is regarded as the most compact form in which Indian corn crop of the States can be transported to market. Hence the corn is fed to the hog on the farm, and he is sent to Chicago as a package provided by nature for its utilization."[5]

Not only ready rail access to farms and markets but also inexpensive land, an abundant regional labor pool, and a location beyond the reach of city control, encouraged the suburban development of the stockyards. One 1887 observer noted the many wooden build- ings which stood near the stockyards —possible only because the whole district was located in the suburban Town of Lake and not the City of Chicago, which had outlawed much wooden construction after the disastrous 1871 fire: "A ride out among the rows of wooden buildings still existing by the square mile in the southern suburbs, as if to tempt another great fire, leads to the 'Union Stock Yard.'"[6]

By 1890, the year after the area was annexed into Chicago, the Stock Yards District was more developed (fig. 4.3). Instead of open fields beyond the livestock pens, there now stood four- to six-story packinghouses and storage facilities where the slaughtered animals were transformed into saleable products—from dressed beef to leather to hairbrushes. In less than a quarter century, this area had become an intensive processing and production site, as businessmen and entrepreneurs built companies and an industrial work landscape.

4.2 The founders of the Union Stock Yards took advantage of the growing number of rail lines running into and out of Chicago to create a central place in the region for their industry, which was located at a distance from the city itself. This photograph of the Union Stock Yards in the late 1860s shows the suburban character of its earliest years. Open lands, not built-up city neighborhoods, surround the holding pens in the years before the construction of the Stock Yards Gate. (Chicago Historical Society, ICHi-32213)

By 1900, there were 25,000 people employed in packing and slaughtering houses. A thousand more worked in soap and candle factories, oleomargarine factories, and grease and tallow concerns.[7] Butchering livestock was broken into small, repetitive tasks and machines were introduced to reduce the proportion of skilled workers needed. Routinized tasks in overcrowded fac-

4.3 By 1890, the Stock Yards Gate was over a decade old (seen here in the distance looking west along Exchange Avenue) and surrounded by a growing industrial neighborhood. The fire hydrant and streetlights in the left foreground are visible indicators of the infrastructure developments underlying the area's move from suburban to urban. An invisible marker of the transition was the annexation of this area into Chicago in 1889. (Chicago Historical Society, J. W. Taylor, ICHi-04048)

tories and processing centers provided entry-level work for thousands of European immigrants who were drawn to Chicago in the late nineteenth century.[8]

With World War I, African Americans and then Mexican immigrants gained access to stockyards jobs. But after World War II, as trucks replaced railroads, the district began a steep decline (fig. 4.4). The owners of the stockyards, the Central Manufacturing District, closed the operations in 1971. In the following years, the stockyards were dismantled, packinghouses and warehouses leveled (fig. 4.5). In their place emerged a district that would not look out of place in any late twentieth-century suburban industrial park.

In many ways, the Stock Yards District provides a window onto the evolution of large industrial enterprises in Chicagoland. With the advent of the railroad, manufacturing and processing companies established themselves in suburban locations. Over several generations, these suburban locations became tightly knit into the urban fabric of Chicago, virtually obliterating their suburban origins. In the late twentieth century, with the decline in many of these same industries, acres of abandoned factories and warehouses were available for redevelopment.

But the rise and fall of factories and warehouses tell only part of the story of industrial Chicagoland. The separation of work and residence in the nineteenth century is marked by an industrial landscape created partially by employers and partially by workers.

Workers no longer lived on the premises of their workplaces as they did in the traditional artisanal worlds of blacksmiths, coopers, and tailors. This distinguishes the experience of

4.4 In 1954, the Stock Yards Gate was the center of a mature urban industrial neighborhood. In a ceremony marking the billionth animal to arrive at the yards, a long history is alluded to with the workers on horseback and the steam engine beyond the main gate. In a real sense, this was a high-water mark for the Chicago Stock Yards, as highways soon replaced railroads for interstate travel, and operations moved west of Chicagoland. (Chicago Historical Society, ICHi-04101)

industrial workers from that of nineteenth-century farmers, since regional farmsteads were places of both work and residence. At the same time, workers did not generally live very far from their workplaces. Because of the cost and irregularity of mass transportation (and the prohibitive cost of owning and maintaining horses), workers found housing within walking distance of their places of work. So, while work and residence were separate, they were still intertwined.

While corporations developed work sites in suburban locations, workers and speculators of necessity built new residential areas, since company owners seldom provided their workers with housing or ready access to institutions. This was true around the Union Stock Yards, as well as around the iron and steel mills, the railroad yards, the farm equipment factories, and other large enterprises.

So alongside the corporate construction of stockyards and slaughterhouses, workers built their own worlds. Southwest from the Stock Yards Gate, workers fashioned a complementary (and sometimes oppositional) residential world fittingly known as Back of the Yards. Walking down any one of the area's many side streets, one sees the other side of

Chicago's industrial landscape: worker housing and institutions. While the stockyards and packinghouses are gone, blocks of worker housing and institutions remain as remnants of the industrial era.[9]

The one-story frame cottages and two-story flats on narrow lots stand long after the stockyards are only memory (fig. 4.6). These houses were built by speculative builders, or workers themselves, beginning in 1865. During the heyday of the meatpacking industry, corner groceries and saloons were found on almost every street in this neighborhood, catering to the various ethnic groups that dotted this pedestrian world.

As well as housing, stockyards workers built community institutions. Perhaps most visible

were the many churches rising above the residential streetscape of Back of the Yards. At first mission outposts from established churches in Chicago, by the early twentieth century many congregations constructed not only large, imposing churches, but also schools, halls, gymnasiums, and communal housing for the religious.

For instance, on a four-block stretch (from 46th to 50th streets) of Hermitage Avenue, three Roman Catholic churches rise above the houses. Lithuanian, Polish, and Bohemian residents respectively built three massive stone churches in very different architectural styles between 1913 and 1915: the Lithuanian Holy Cross Church in Renaissance Revival (fig. 4.7); the Polish St. Joseph in Romanesque (fig. 4.8); and the Bohemian Sts. Cyril and Methodius in Renaissance style (fig. 4.9).[10] Each church complex took up multiple lots and stood in sharp contrast to the modest houses of the neighborhood. But it was the inhabitants of those houses and flats who constructed these grand neighborhood-defining edifices by pooling their meager wages from the stockyards and related industries. These workers were not simply employees, they were neighborhood builders.

Back of the Yards in the early twentieth century was distinctly immigrant and largely Catholic. Active discrimination on the part of stockyards employers excluded African American workers.[11] The 1904 stockyards strike, where African Americans were among the recruited strikebreakers, began a twentieth-century story in which racism would play a central role. By 1918, when thousands of black men and women were working in the stockyards, they were not welcome to live in Back of the Yards. African Americans had to commute from further afar until the closing decades of the twentieth century, after the closure of the Union Stock Yards.

4.5 After the closure of the Union Stock Yards, the packinghouses quickly shut their doors. Seen here is the wrecking of the general office of Swift and Company at 41st Place and Packers Avenue in 1971. Once leveled, this district was redeveloped for light industry, with more than 200 companies located in the area in 2003. (Chicago Historical Society, Casey Prunchunas, ICHi-24563)

4.6 Across Chicagoland in the nineteenth century, new residential areas developed alongside industrial work sites. Adjacent to the Union Stock Yards, residential streets developed into the Back of the Yards neighborhood (also known appropriately as "New City"). Much of this housing still stands today, as seen here in the 4000 block of S. Hermitage, lined with frame cottages and two-flats. (Leslie Schwartz)

Although reshaped by deindustrialization and the politics of race, much of Back of the Yards, with its housing, churches, and other neighborhood institutions, still stands, serving new residents, congregants, and customers who fashion twenty-first-century lives in buildings more than a hundred years old. In contrast, after the stockyards closed in 1971, most of the pens and packinghouses were torn down. Back of the Yards, like many other neighborhoods that developed around nineteenth-century industries, remains viable long after the stockyards went under the wrecking ball.

The Industrial Landscape of Nineteenth-Century Chicagoland

The Stock Yards District along with the Back of the Yards constitute only one of a number of industrial districts which developed across Chicagoland in the nineteenth century. Chicagoland became a processing and manufacturing powerhouse, largely by taking advantage of its rich hinterland. By the 1850s and 1860s, timber from around Lake Michigan supplied massive lumberyards along the Chicago River, which in turn supplied railroad and city builders. Livestock from farms became the base for the stockyards and meatpacking industry.[12] The steel industry grew because of the demand for rails, which linked farms across the Midwest with markets. The mail order industry emerged at Chicago because of the demand for goods from successful farmers across the region. Thus, the railroad provided a central link between Chicagoland industries and farms.

The stockyards and the meatpacking companies were among a handful of very large industries which were central to Chicago's development. By 1900, Chicago was a national leader in the production of a number of processed and manufactured goods— including iron and steel, slaughtering and meat-packing, railroad cars, and electrical equipment.[13] In turn, a handful of companies dominated each of these industries in Chicago by the early twentieth century, including Western Electric, U.S. Steel, and the "Big Three" meatpackers.[14]

This was a particularly suburban story. The need for acres of affordable land and rail access sent these large companies to the suburbs. The general outward migration of manufacturing from the city center characterizes the whole of the industrial era. Most of the companies in iron and steel, slaughter-ing and meatpacking, electrical equipment, and rail-road cars had moved to large, sprawling suburban locations by 1910.

As corporations in the largest industries were combining and consolidating into fewer and fewer individual companies between 1885 and 1920, the number of industrial firms increased more than fourfold, from 2,526 to 10,537.[15] Large companies were joined by many smaller firms who also found advantages to a suburban location. While a few large compa-nies tell a great deal of Chicago's industrial story, it is not the whole of it.

4.7 Stockyards workers built neighborhood institutions as well as housing. Holy Cross Roman Catho-lic Church, 1736 W. 46th Street, was built between 1913 and 1915 by Lithuanians living in Back of the Yards. Designed by Joseph Molitor in a Renaissance Revival style, the church is distinguished by two mas-sive towers as seen here in 1959. Still a Catholic church, the congrega-tion is now largely Mexican, with many services in Spanish. (Chicago Historical Society, ICHi-22788)

Because of the suburban appeal to both large and small companies, more than sev-enty suburban settlements in Chicagoland be- gan as industrial towns, with plants ac-tively engaged in manufacturing or process-ing (fig. 4.10). They constitute roughly 30 percent of all suburban settlements made in nineteenth-century Chicagoland (many, like the Back of the Yards, now Chicago neigh-borhoods). Some of these settlements had served as earlier, water-based industrial cen-ters, but now grew because they were near railroads.[16]

All of these communities had access to

4.8 St. Joseph Roman Catholic Church, 1729 W. 48th Street, began in 1886 as a mission congregation from Bridgeport. The church was completed in 1914 under a design by Joseph Molitor. Built by local Polish residents, the congregation maintained its Polish ties into the twenty-first century. As well as the church, the parish includes a large hall, an elementary school (which had 1,300 pupils in 1918), a gymna-sium, a convent, and a rectory. The complex takes up most of a square block. (Leslie Schwartz)

4.9 Bohemians in Back of the Yards supported the construction of Sts. Cyril and Methodius at 5001 S. Hermitage, the third Catholic church within a four-block stretch. Designed again by Joseph Molitor, this Renaissance-style church is seen here at the church's 1913 dedication. The church was closed by the Archdiocese of Chicago in the 1990s, but has been reopened as by a Seventh Day Adventist congregation. (Chicago Historical Society, ICHi-10302)

4.10 (opposite) INDUSTRIAL TOWNS OF NINETEENTH-CENTURY AND EARLY TWENTIETH-CENTURY CHICAGOLAND. This map shows the suburbs and Chicago neighborhoods whose origins lie with industry. Of these more than seventy places, most are along rail lines in and o ut of Chicago. Waukegan, Elgin, Aurora, Joliet, Hammond, and Gary were particularly large industrial centers, often referred to as satellite cities, which ringed the region by 1900. (Dennis McClendon)

rail transportation, and are found like spokes in a wheel along lines out from the city center. The features of the Stock Yards District resemble the general landscape: an industrial plant sited at an outlying suburban location with railroad connections; and adjacent residential subdivisions with houses, churches, stores, and other community institutions. In most cases this was a bifurcated landscape built by two very different groups—company owners and executives on the one hand, workers and their families on the other.

The similarities in the basic components of industrial sites across Chicagoland are often overlooked. In part, this is because a rich racial, ethnic, and religious diversity changes the veneer of these components from place to place and time to time. Signs in foreign languages advertising ethnic foods, wares, and spaces mask similar structures and functions from neighborhood to neighborhood.

Industrial Work Sites

While manufacturing and processing remain significant to Chicago's economy, the manufacturing and processing plants constructed in the nineteenth century have largely been abandoned as obsolete. The stockyards and breweries have moved out of the region, the

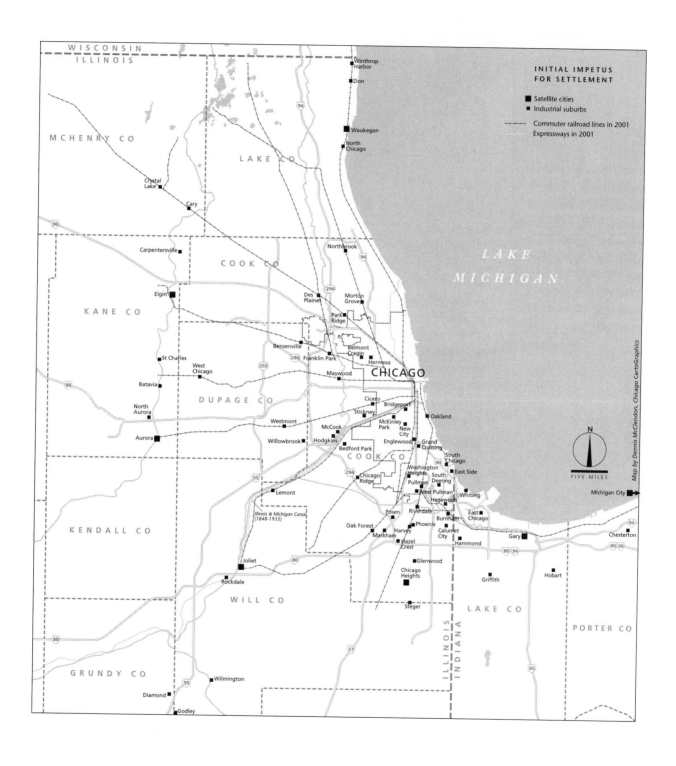

Map by Dennis McClendon, Chicago CartoGraphics

INITIAL IMPETUS
FOR SETTLEMENT

■ Satellite cities
▪ Industrial suburbs
— Commuter railroad lines in 2001
  Expressways in 2001

WISCONSIN
ILLINOIS

McHENRY CO

LAKE CO

COOK CO

KANE CO

DUPAGE CO

KENDALL CO

WILL CO

GRUNDY CO

LAKE MICHIGAN

CHICAGO

Illinois & Michigan Canal
(1848–1933)

ILLINOIS
INDIANA

LAKE CO

PORTER CO

N

FIVE MILES

Winthrop
Harbor
Zion
Waukegan
North
Chicago

Crystal
Lake
Cary

Carpentersville

Northbrook

Elgin

Des
Plaines
Morton
Grove
Park
Ridge

St Charles
Bensenville
Belmont
Cragin
West
Chicago
Franklin Park
Hermosa
Batavia
Maywood

North
Aurora
Cicero
Bridgeport
Westmont
Stickney
Oakland
McCook
McKinley
Park
Aurora
Hodgkins
New
City
Willowbrook
Englewood
Grand
Crossing
Bedford Park
South
Chicago
East Side
Washington
Heights
South
Deering
Chicago
Ridge
Pullman
Lemont
West Pullman
Hegewisch
Whiting
Posen
Riverdale
East
Chicago
Burnham
Oak Forest
Phoenix
Rockdale
Markham
Harvey
Calumet
City
Gary
Hazel
Crest
Hammond
Joliet
Glenwood
Griffith
Hobart
Chesterton
Chicago
Heights
Steger
Wilmington
Diamond
Godley

Michigan City

4.11 The manufacturing of bicycles pioneered new production techniques. Adolph Schoelinger, president of the Western Wheel Works, built a five-story factory with a pressed stone and brick front in 1890 at 201 W. Schiller. Seen here is an 1897 image of the factory taken from a catalog for Crescent Cycles manufactured by the Western Wheel Works. (Chicago Historical Society, ICHi-36140)

large-scale steel mills and railcar works out of the country. Electrical equipment has moved to new suburban plants with features required for high-technology production.

Nineteenth-century industrial sites, like farms, are often valuable properties ripe for redevelopment. Some large industrial plants, like the Union Stock Yards, were not only abandoned, but leveled and destroyed. Other have been reused, while a very few have been preserved (even partially) as historic sites.

In the last three decades, old factories and warehouses across the metropolitan area have been converted to condominiums and office and retail space. Numerous properties ringing downtown Chicago have been converted to loft residences, including the Donohue, Second Franklin, and Borland Manufacturing buildings on South Dearborn Street in an area known as Printer's Row. Along the main stem of the Chicago River, warehouse space has been transformed into offices and condominiums, including the North Pier Terminal Building and Reid Murdoch & Company (wholesalers). Beyond the central core, small factories in towns across the region have also been converted, including the Selz Shoe Factory in Elgin, the Kroehler Furniture Factory in Naperville, the Gray-Watkins Mill in Montgomery, and the Ovaltine Factory in Villa Park.

For many such buildings, real estate developers sell historic value and maintain the shells but not the original interior spaces. On Chicago's Near North Side, Cobbler Square is a residential and retail conversion of a factory which manufactured Dr. Scholl's shoes through much of the twentieth century. The factory building, with its large windows and a courtyard, provided as much natural light as possible in the interior work spaces.

This structure was constructed not by Dr. Scholl's but by the Western Wheel Works in 1890 (fig. 4.11). The name "Western Wheel Works" is etched into the stone on what was the original front entrance to the building. Over one hundred years ago, some workers in this factory stamped bicycle parts from steel using specially designed machines in large, airy open spaces, while others served as runners moving from station to station. Despite new techniques, the many German employees maintained old traditions, including regular beer at 9:30 a.m.[17] These workers lived in the surrounding neighborhood, supporting local German institutions like St. Michael's Roman Catholic Church (north of North Avenue on Eugenie) and the Germania Club (south of North Avenue on Clark).[18]

Today the structure accommodates residential units and commercial enterprises (fig. 4.12). The original use of the building is alluded to in the name of the development "Cobbler Square" and in a series of historic photographs in the lobby. Current residents who have not rushed off to downtown or Near North jobs are more apt to be sipping lattes at Starbucks (perhaps in the one located in a corner of the old Germania Club) than fortifying themselves with beer on their first work break of the day.

Only a very few factories have been deliberately preserved as historic sites, including that of the Joliet Iron Works, one of the first ironworks in the metropolitan area (fig. 4.13). Located to the north of downtown Joliet, thirty-five miles southwest of the Loop, this mile-long site is along the Des Plaines River and several rail lines. The Joliet Iron Works began manufacturing iron and steel here in 1869, about a decade after the start of the North Chicago Rolling Mill (the first regional ironworks) on the North Branch of the Chicago River.[19]

The Joliet Iron Works was successful because of the ready accessibility of coal, water, iron ore, and labor. Eventually the Union Coal, Iron and Transportation Company built a rolling mill here. Carnegie Steel purchased the plant in 1889, and it was renamed the Illinois Steel Company before it became part of U.S. Steel in the early twentieth century.[20]

Now part of the Illinois and Michigan Historic Canal Corridor, the Joliet Iron Works site is reminiscent of an archeological site: much of what remains is underground and stripped of identity. Markers reveal the purpose of the hulking piers of concrete, brick mounds, and holes in the ground (fig. 4.14). Huge brick circles are all that remain of furnaces, and elevated mounds reveal masonry which served as a base for stoves and washers. Somber concrete pilings suggest the shape of buildings that are now gone. The site, adjacent to still-operating factories, is compelling as a memorial to the long years of labor of thousands of workers.[21] But it is hard work to envision the industrial plant that once stood here (fig. 4.15).

4.12 (left) The Dr. Scholl's Company took over the Western Wheel Works building in 1904 and manufactured shoes here until the late twentieth century when the building was rehabbed as condominiums and commercial space known as Cobbler Square. (Leslie Schwartz)

4.13 (right) While no nineteenth-century steel operation still operates in the metropolitan area, a sense of the operation can be created by joining historic images of the process and the ruins of the Joliet Iron Works. Seen here is an exterior view of the converting works along the railroad tracks. (Chicago Historical Society, ICHi-35519)

Worker Housing

Around all of these plants, which at their height employed thousands of workers, seemingly instant neighborhoods and towns emerged. Graham Romeyn Taylor, a social reformer writing in 1915, noted the "wholesale scale" of home construction and other improvements around industrial plants that had moved outside of core city centers.[22] The houses in these areas were built by workers, small builders, and some larger developers. These builders stuck with simple, common designs, resulting in streets lined with urban cottages and frame flats.[23]

No historical society has preserved an urban worker cottage; there is no museum devoted to an industrial worker grocery or saloon in Chicagoland (in contrast to the many rural farmhouses, taverns, and one-room schoolhouses preserved across the region). However, this does not mean that worker housing and businesses are no longer visible in the landscape. Many neighborhoods and suburbs in the region contain housing stock still in use which date back to the nineteenth century. This part of the industrial landscape is still very visible.

Twenty-five by 125-foot lots are characteristic of many nineteenth-century worker neighborhoods in Chicago. The decisions of hundreds of land speculators to subdivide property into these long, narrow lots shaped the resulting neighborhoods in intended and unintended ways. Choosing small lots meant that the property was priced within reach of at least some workers. Workers could own and build their own modest homes or small apartment buildings.

The confines of this lot size led to the adaptation of the common rural cottage for urban use. The narrowness of these lots led Chicago builders to turn traditional frame cottages ninety degrees. Hence the gable on these urban cottages moved from the side to the front of the structure. Instead of the traditional front entrance on the wide side of the cottage, urban worker cottages had front entrances on one end of the narrow, gabled side.[24]

These frame urban cottages, often one and one-half stories, first appeared in Chicago-land in the 1860s. Many of the houses had raised basements, providing additional living space. Small developers and workers themselves built thousands of these houses during the second half of the nineteenth century as Chicago grew into a major industrial center.

This simple form is still common across the area. As well as in Back of the Yards, these cottages can be found on the North Side at Gross Park, a small subdivision north of Belmont along Ravenswood and the Chicago and North Western Railway. Gross Park was subdivided (and immodestly named) by Samuel E. Gross, a residential developer who built speculative housing across the metropolitan area. The subdivision was intended for the many skilled and semiskilled workers employed in factories along the nearby rail line. Many have been renovated but retain the classic features of the worker cottage (fig. 4.16).[25]

The worker cottages in all of these places share common features. Sometimes the front door is approached directly by a set of staircases, but often these houses have a porch which runs the width of the house. A separate entrance to the basement is regularly found under the front steps. The front door opens into three rooms opening one to another: a parlor, a sitting (dining) room, and a kitchen. Running directly alongside these rooms are two or three small bedrooms. There are no separate halls for room access. By the 1880s, access to sewers and water lines made indoor plumbing a possibility, and small bathrooms were initially installed or added later.

These urban cottages generally did not have central heating until well into the twentieth century. Coal stoves provided heat in kitchens, with other rooms heated indirectly. This meant family life revolved around the kitchen, especially during Chicago winters. Ice was delivered for iceboxes, which kept foods relatively cool.

4.16 S. E. Gross sold more than 30,000 lots and thousands of houses in twenty-one subdivisions located from Back of the Yards to the western suburbs to this 1880s, including this subdivision around a private park east of Ravenswood Avenue, just north of Belmont on Chicago's North Side, known as Gross Park. (Leslie Schwartz)

Sometimes the houses today remain much as they were in the late nineteenth century and serve similar needs for worker families. Other houses have been radically altered, as more affluent owners add square footage and amenities. One frequent exterior change has been in siding. A typical transition has been from wood to asphalt shingles to aluminum siding, but stone facing and a variety of siding colors have also helped owners change the look of their houses.[26]

Some workers managed to purchase cottages such as these by pooling family resources and with the help of ethnic savings and loans. Renting out basement rooms also helped make ownership possible. A variation on the cottage that increased rental income developed as well: a two-story and sometimes three-story flat which had the same basic layout as the urban cottage, but used the lot more intensively. Like the urban cottage, these frame flats are found across the metropolitan area—but especially in areas developed in the 1870s, 1880s, and 1890s.[27]

Worker Businesses and Institutions

Another variation in the basic worker cottage or two-flat was the transformation of a portion of the building into a store or saloon. On any street of urban cottages and flats, at least a few were built or adapted for commercial use. The commercial spaces in structures not at a corner were generally small, but were adequate for an ethnic grocery, candy store, or even a small saloon. Large display windows on the first floor distinguished the retail space from a residential flat (fig. 4.17).

In late nineteenth-century and early twentieth-century Back of the Yards, ethnic groups supported groceries and saloons near their homes, so that Poles and Czechs and Bohemians frequented different establishments. Many were located close together, sometimes even on the same block.[28]

Groceries stores catered to the food needs of immigrants from a specific region or country. Grocery store owners carried the kinds of breads, condiments, cuts of meat, cheese, and vegetables used by individual ethnic groups. Frequently the grocery store operated in a European language, not English. Many neighborhood women came to the store every day to purchase a few items and exchange news. Married women, many of whom worked at home taking care of boarders as well as families, found daily companionship at the grocery store.

Saloons, like groceries, often catered to specific ethnic groups. They were also more male-dominated. Men of the same ethnicity on the block spent hours after work, on Saturday nights, and often Sundays within these establishments drinking, talking, singing, and playing games. Larger saloons were located on corners, often extending their buildings almost the full length of the lot (fig. 4.18). The large back rooms of these corner saloons hosted neighborhood activities such as dances, weddings, and union rallies.

4.18 Saloons and funeral homes were also an integral part of many industrial neighborhoods, many remaining in business down to the present (as this streetscape in Back of the Yards shows). (Leslie Schwartz)

Examples of these structures can be found across the metropolitan area, not only in worker neighborhoods within Chicago but also in suburban industrial towns and in satellite cities. Some groceries have remained, often catering to new immigrant groups. But many have been renovated into residential space, as workers traveled to larger supermarkets in search of more selection and lower prices. Saloons officially closed in many worker neighborhoods with the passage of Prohibition in 1919, although some operated illegally.

Standing alongside the houses and small commercial spaces on the side streets of industrial neighborhoods are churches, synagogues, and other institutions built by residents over the late nineteenth and early twentieth centuries. The religious structures stand tall against the otherwise two-story neighborhood buildings.

Varieties of Industrial Sites

These basic components combined in different ways, as factories, transportation, and worker housing and institutions within any industrial area varied across Chicagoland in their characteristics of location, age, and size.

Factories located along the numerous new rail lines out from Chicago. Large companies could purchase land along any number of rail lines and create suburban towns. Oftentimes these enterprises were involved in real estate speculation as well as manufacturing or processing. Alternatively real estate speculators might plan a new industrial town and seek out companies to come to their development. These planned industrial towns included Pullman, Gary, Hammond, Harvey, Chicago Heights, Clearing, Summit, North Chicago, and Zion.[29]

Other entrepreneurs chose to site their plants in established neighborhoods or suburbs around a rail depot. Perhaps most prominent among this class are a group known as satellite cities. Satellite cities owed their existence to proximity to a large center city like Chicago, but functioned with a modicum of independence. These cities had a variety of manufacturing establishments, from extremely large plants that employed thousands of workers to small workshops with only a few employees. Waukegan, Aurora, Elgin, and Joliet were all cities of this type.[30] Established smaller towns along rail lines in and out of Chicago also attracted industry, jobs, and new residents in the nineteenth century, including Evanston, Naperville, Homewood, Chesterton, and Woodstock.

4.19 The Pullman Administration Building and Clock Tower on S. Cottage Grove Avenue just north of 111th Street served as the front façade for George Pullman's Sleeping Car Works from its construction in 1880. Solon S. Beman designed this building in south suburban Hyde Park along the Illinois Central Railroad. (Chicago Historical Society, ICHi-24181)

Finally, another group of factories and processing plants emerged along side tracks adjacent to rail lines, rather than at rail depots. In large part, these factories developed in areas where other industrial and residential development was already underway. They were followers, not leaders in the metropolitan development process.

These infill plants found usable tracts of land which may have initially been bypassed because they were not near a rail station. Many examples of this sort of development can be found within Chicago, particularly on the North Side, where industrial development rested more on smaller companies and plants than it did on either the South or West Sides.

All of these types of industrial sites share basic structures and features: good transporta-

4.20 The Pullman Administration Building remained in use until the facility closed down in 1981. Damaged in a 1998 fire, the property is now owned by the State of Illinois, which is considering development of the site as an industrial museum. (Leslie Schwartz)

tion; a factory or plant; nearby housing, groceries, taverns, churches, and other community institutions. However, each combined basic features in distinctive ways, depending on whether they were shaped by new planned industrial suburbs, by established towns, or by infill.

As suburban industrial towns grew in the early twentieth century, African Americans joined European immigrants in industrial workplaces. Waukegan, Aurora, Maywood, Gary, Joliet, Harvey, and Chicago Heights had substantial numbers of black workers and residents by the mid-twentieth century. African Americans established neighborhoods and institutions at a more convenient distance to work sites than was the case of the stockyards on Chicago's South Side.[31]

New Planned Industrial Towns

The Union Stock Yards exemplifies a new industrial town planned by a single group of investors. About the same time as the foundation of the Union Stock Yards, George M. Pullman began designing and building railroad sleeping cars in Chicago. In 1880, he purchased 4,000 acres of land beyond the then southern city limits and built a railroad car factory between Lake Calumet and the Illinois Central Tracks on either side of 111th Street. The enterprise employed thousands of workers by the late nineteenth century.[32]

Pullman hired architect Solon S. Beman and landscape designer Nathan F. Barrett to design an instant industrial town for 5,000. Beman and Barrett designed the town with a clearly identifiable front face. They planned for visitors to step off the Illinois Central train at 111th in front of the impressive Administration Building and clock tower to the north, complete with a small pond (fig. 4.19). To the south, the Florence Hotel provided elegant accommodations for visitors, high-ranking employees, and Pullman himself. Near the hotel stood a multistory arcade building that housed stores, offices, a library, and meeting rooms. Between these buildings were landscaped gardens gathered around a band shell.

Traveling to 111th and Cottage Grove today, one can still discern parts of this industrial site. To the north of 111th Street, the Administration Building, a city, state, and national landmark that was severely damaged in a December 1998 fire, still stands (fig. 4.20). An imposing red brick structure which once stood at the center of one-story production wings, the Administration Building was topped with a 120-foot clock tower which dominated the area. Arches and curved windows counterpoint the massive structure, as does its mansard roof. Missing are the acres of sheds and low buildings in which the cars were manufactured and repaired. After the closure of the Pullman works in 1981, most of the company buildings were torn down. The Administration Building remains standing, but fenced off from the rest of the community—awaiting historic preservation and interpretation.[33]

4.21 Red brick housing on the east side of St. Lawrence south of 111th Street in Pullman in 1908. All of the housing in Pullman was built by the company and rented to workers, in contrast to Back of the Yards and most other industrial neighborhoods, which were built by speculators and workers themselves. But by 1908, the Pullman Company was forced to sell this housing, and the area became much more like other neighborhoods. (Chicago Historical Society, DN-0006818)

But the car works tell only half the story of Pullman. South from 111th east of Cottage Grove are blocks of worker housing and institutions. The component parts of Pullman are much the same as in other nineteenth-century industrial neighborhoods across the metropolitan area: worker housing, churches, schools, and groceries. But no saloons. This neighborhood was built neither by workers nor by entrepreneurs catering to their needs; it was carefully planned and owned by the Pullman Company. George Pullman felt that he could do better than workers had on their own in other areas: "We decided to build, in close proximity to the shops, homes for workingmen of such character and surroundings as would prove so attractive as to cause the best class of mechanics to seek that place for employment in prefer-

4.22 Eschewing the frame cottage style, Solon S. Beman designed red brick townhouses and flats on narrow lots. Seen here is the east side of St. Lawrence south of 111th Street in Pullman in 2004. Although superficially different from the common frame cottage which workers across Chicagoland inhabited, the Pullman housing stands today like its frame cottage counterparts, long after the factories have been shuttered. (Leslie Schwartz)

ence to others. We also desired to establish the place on such a basis as would exclude all baneful influence."[34]

They built the town all at once, and the Pullman Company remained the owner of the property. In contrast to other industrial neighborhoods where one-third or more of the residents lived in houses they owned, the Pullman Company owned all of the housing in the town until an 1898 court case forced the company to divest its real estate holdings (fig. 4.21).

The housing is distinctive from that found in other worker neighborhoods in Chicago. Beman and Barrett did not restrict themselves to standard twenty-five-foot lots, urban cottages, and storefront groceries. They built a wide range of housing, from single-room occupancy "block houses" on the fringes of Pullman town to fourteen-foot-wide brick townhouses to gracious, large houses on fifty- to sixty-foot lots which fronted on 111th Street. Beman's fourteen-foot-wide brick row houses, dubbed "The Cottages," did not look much like the frame urban cottages built in other neighborhoods, but they shared basic characteristics: narrow, small rooms and few amenities (fig. 4.22).

George Pullman envisioned all of his workers attending the same interdenominational church. To that end, Beman designed the Greenstone Community Church near the center of town (fig. 4.23). He found, however, that his Roman Catholic workers were particularly unwilling to worship in a Protestant Church. Pullman then had Beman design Holy Rosary

4.23 George Pullman understood that worker neighborhoods needed more than housing to be successful. He built an arcade, a park, a market hall, a hotel and a stables south of 111th Street amidst his housing. In addition, the Pullman Company built the Greenstone Church for the entire community, across the park in this 1908 photograph. Again, Pullman built here what other workers did for themselves in other parts of Chicagoland. (Chicago Historical Society, DN-0006894)

Roman Catholic Church, at 11130 Martin Luther King Drive. While the Catholic Church shared building material and some other features with the Greenstone Church, its tower and small rose window reflected the German background of its congregation.

Pullman's planners did not wait for small entrepreneurs to build stores and groceries catering to the various ethnic residents in the area. Instead, Solon S. Beman designed a round market building in an Italian design, where workers could go to buy food and other goods. Pullman rented space in the market to small vendors. Around the market building, which today has only one of its original two stories, four arcade buildings used as rental housing still stand.

Pullman insisted that no alcohol would be sold within the limits of his company town. However, enterprising small businessmen opened saloons just beyond the limits of Pullman in the Kensington neighborhood. And after the Pullman Company was forced to sell much of its real estate in the area, saloons were among the first buildings constructed.

Industrial towns for more than one company owed their existence to speculative developers. These real estate entrepreneurs saw the opportunity to increase the value of their property by providing improvements which would attract manufacturing establishments. Sometimes the developers were connected to at least one of the companies located at the planned industrial town. Speculative developers were responsible for the establishment of Chicago Heights, Harvey, North Chicago, and Zion. Some were more successful than others, but each contained factories and worker neighborhoods developed by a first generation of employers and employees in the late nineteenth century.

Charles H. Wacker headed up a group of investors who bought 4,000 acres of land about twenty-six miles south of downtown Chicago in 1887. Located along several rail lines, including the Elgin, Joliet and Eastern Railway (Chicago Outer Belt Line), the company developed an industrial town with two parts: a section for factories and a section for worker housing. Inland Steel Company was the first industrial enterprise to move to Chicago Heights, which grew to 1,500 residents by 1895 and 15,000 by 1910.[35]

Established Towns

Entrepreneurs also sought out sites in established outlying towns. Many of these towns first developed along the navigable rivers and roads in the region in the 1830s, and several had multiple rail lines by the end of the nineteenth century. With less expensive property than at Chicago, these towns were attractive to industrial developers. Waukegan developed around a natural harbor north of Chicago near the current Wisconsin state line. Elgin and Aurora both straddled the Fox River west of Chicago. Joliet to the southwest was along the Des Plaines River and after 1848 the Illinois and Michigan Canal.

All four of these towns stand about thirty-five miles from Chicago. Before the railroad, this distance made them competitive with Chicago in their immediate hinterlands.[36] The dominance of these towns was assured when each succeeded in negotiating multiple rail lines through their towns. The completion of the Outer Belt Line in 1890 drew even more factories to these outer cities.[37] They were in a strong bargaining position because of their early success as water towns.

While their populations paled in comparison to that of Chicago (which by 1890 included the Calumet region), these satellite cities were the largest beyond Chicago in the region. With the rise of bulk processing and manufacturing, they parlayed their transportation and commercial advantages into an industrial advantage. When potential processing or manufacturing establishments sought an outlying regional location, these towns offered more than most. Company owners would not have to live in a wholly isolated community, without amenities. Their families could attend established churches, synagogues, and schools and shop in thriving (if small) business districts.

Elgin's case is illustrative. Thirty-five miles west of Chicago along the Fox River, the area was quickly

4.24 The Elgin National Watch Company, National Street and Grove Avenue, along the east bank of the Fox River. Seen here is the front entrance to the complex in 1966 just before demolition. In the background is the neighborhood that thousands of workers built over a century. Typical are frame worker cottages seen in other parts of the metropolitan area. While the watch company was demolished, the housing continues to serve Elgin residents. (Chicago Historical Society, ICHi-26799)

4.25 In 1965, the Elgin National Watch Company complex was closed and the plant was demolished the following year. One of the few remaining structures is the Elgin Watch Company Observatory just a few blocks southeast of the original main entrance at 312 Watch Street. The company donated the observatory to the City of Elgin in 1960, and it is used today by the local school district. (Leslie Schwartz)

settled by farmers in the 1830s. The town grew as a stop first on the Chicago-Galena stage, and then on the Galena and Chicago Union Railroad. Industry began with a sawmill, then a variety of dairy-related enterprises, including Gail Borden's condensed milk factory.

A watch company located in Elgin in 1866 and developed techniques for mass-producing watches. The Elgin National Watch Company soon included a department that built and maintained the machines used to make watches, another department that produced more than 250 different kinds of screws, and an assembly department where all of the manufactured pieces were turned into individual watches. They also built an observatory as part of their timekeeping mission (figs. 4.24 and 4.25).

By 1870, a workforce of 300 men and 200 women turned out 25,000 watches annually. By 1904, between 2,500 and 3,000 men and women were employed by the watch company, out of the 4,885 people employed in all manufacturing establishments within Elgin. The company built a substantial factory, with large windows and a clock tower, on spacious grounds along the Fox River just south of downtown Elgin at National Street. Operations continued at the plant until 1965.

The factory was demolished one hundred years after its founding to make way for a strip mall, now adjacent to a riverboat casino. But the worker cottages in the surrounding neighborhoods stand as a legacy of the industrial era.[38] While the watch company built dormitory housing for single workers (fig. 4.26), most employees lived in the neighborhood that emerged to the east and south of the plant. On small lots, worker cottages not unlike those seen in Chicago neighborhoods like Back of the Yards continue to serve Elgin's population.

Infill Industrial Sites

While a focus on the largest enterprises and consolidating corporations provides information on roughly half the wage earners in Chicago, it leaves out the other half of manufacturing workers who worked in smaller industries and for smaller companies in establishments that ranged from just a few people to thousands of employees.[39]

Thousands of small factories dotted Chicagoland by 1900, taking advantage of the many rail lines that ran through area neighborhoods and suburbs. In some cases, a rail station did not serve as the center for development. Instead, factories simply sited along rail lines,

4.26 The Elgin National Watch Company built dormitories for its single workers. In 1891, the company completed the National House and Gymnasium, which provided more housing for single workers, as well as recreational facilities. Most employees, however, lived in the neighborhood of worker cottages which still stand, though the plant was demolished nearly forty years ago. (Chicago Historical Society, ICHi-20416)

and used a sidetrack for their business. Other factories did not work with bulky or heavy raw materials or finished products (such as those manufacturing clothing). They did not have to pay a premium for ready access to rail service, so were more footloose in their location decisions.

In the industrial sites that developed around these smaller factories, there was no clear line between industrial workplaces and residential areas. Houses, institutions, and factories were found on the same streets. Neighborhood workers were not employed solely by one factory. They generally walked in at least a few different directions to get to work. These districts lacked the industrial solidarity of areas like Pullman, Back of the Yards, or even around the watch company in Elgin.

Factories integrated into the streetscape, rather than dominating it, are typical of neighborhoods where workers were employed in smaller establishments. The urban cottages, flats, churches, grocery stores, and saloons were joined by factories that were on street scale. Many of the industrial sites were single factory buildings that contained not only manufacturing space but also offices and warehouses.

The industrial neighborhood around St. Alphonsus Roman Catholic Church and School —which over time came to comprise a large city block bounded by Southport, Greenview, Wellington, and Oakdale—provides good examples of such streetscapes.[40] The church began as a mission from St. Michael's Roman Catholic Church on North Avenue. Both churches were run by the German Redemptorist fathers for Germans and other Catholic residents in the area.

4.27 Construction of St. Alphonsus Roman Catholic Church, 2948–58 N. Southport in Lake View, was begun in 1889. Its Gothic Revival style was designed by Shrader & Conrader for the German Redemptorist order. Over the next several decades, a massive complex was developed, including the St. Alphonsus Athenaeum begun in 1910 directly south of the church. (Chicago Historical Society, ICHi 24537)

The imposing church building was constructed over nearly a decade—between 1889 and 1897. The church's entrance stands almost a full flight of stairs above ground level and a large tower stands as the tallest landmark in the area (fig. 4.27). Constructed in a German Gothic style, the church anchors a massive complex which included both grammar and high schools, separate housing for religious men and women, a gymnasium, auditorium, and other facilities.[41]

On the streets around St. Alphonsus are many structures similar to those found in Back of the Yards (fig. 4.28). As on the South Side, speculators (or workers themselves) constructed urban cottages and frame flats on narrow twenty-five-foot lots. Sometimes workers and their families built small cottages, which they later dragged to the back of the lot when a larger house was built in front.[42]

Single-family homes were interspersed with structures that housed both businesses and residential units. On some blocks, housing stood side by side with factories. Just down the street from St. Alphonsus at 1317 Fletcher Avenue was a brewery constructed in the 1880s and purchased by the Best Brewing Company in 1891. It consisted of a brick two-story structure built on this largely residential street (fig. 4.29). In 1893, the company made a large addition which included machine, brew, mill, boiler, and engine houses.

The plant produced beer until Prohibition, when it turned to making artificial ice and malt syrup. After Prohibition, the brewery made special label beer for chain stores, including Hillmans, National Tea, and A&P Tea Companies. The brewery shut down operations in 1961. Residential units now occupy these former brewing "houses" (fig. 4.30).[43]

Saloons once marked many of the corners in the neighborhood. While the buildings remain, saloons have been renovated into other business or residential uses. Among the few saloons that remain, Schuba's, at 3159 N. Southport Avenue, was built by the Schlitz Brewery in 1903 (fig. 4.31). The Schlitz trademark is still clearly visible, displayed near the roofline of this multicolored brick building.[44]

The evolution of the neighborhood around St. Alphonsus was less dramatic than around the stockyards, in part because the factories came from a wide range of industries. Plants closed, industries shifted, and new factories opened, providing changing opportunities for area workers. Smaller factories offered different options in jobs, employers, and work settings. Skilled workers and craftsmen continued to find work, while other factory operatives worked their way into clerking in area firms whose headquarters were in the neighborhood, not in downtown skyscrapers. White-collar and blue-collar workers lived and worked side by side in this neighborhood.

As factories left the area in the second half of the twentieth century, the neighborhood languished for a time. Then new, more affluent residents began to move into the neighborhood. Some of the abandoned factories were torn down to make way for expensive townhouses and condominiums. Other factories, like the Best Brewery, were converted to housing. With the conversion of small groceries, saloons, and other small businesses, the neighborhood became more solidly residential as real estate values soared.

The Legacy of the Industrial Landscape

Manufacturing and processing employment in Chicagoland grew through the nineteenth century and well into the twentieth. Decline set in after World War II, and between 1977 and 1981 alone, the Chicago region lost 203,700 manufacturing jobs.[45] The physical patterns that developed in response to the rise of industrialization saw a similar boom and bust.

Many of the largest industrial companies located in the suburbs, at some distance from the built-up area in Chicago. Over time, many of these suburbs have evolved into city neighborhoods tightly woven into the urban fabric. More than 20 percent of the suburban communities and outlying neighborhoods founded in the region during the nineteenth century owe their existence to the processing and manufacturing enterprises. These places have had to deal with dramatic changes as industrial enterprises have scaled back and shut down.

Only a very few industrial plants have been deliberately preserved. Many more establishments have been leveled in recent decades, as public and private initiatives look to reuse industrial space which is no longer needed. Many of the preserved industrial structures are the work of real estate developers renovat-

4.28 Frame worker cottages and two flats were built across the neighborhood of St. Alphonsus during the 1880s and 1890s. A not uncommon practice was for the original small cottage to be dragged to the back of a lot, with the construction of a newer two-flat on the front of the lot. Seen here is housing in the 1300 block of W. Fletcher. (Leslie Schwartz)

4.29 This historic image of the Best Brewery shows the building while it functioned as a brewery at 1317 Fletcher Street. (Chicago Historical Society, ICHi-23887)

4.30 After shutting down operations, the Best Brewery was converted to residential use. Where once the brewery provided jobs on an otherwise residential street, now the street is almost exclusively residential. (Leslie Schwartz)

ing old factories for residential, commercial, and retail use. While the interior spaces have largely been destroyed, the exteriors stand as reminders of an earlier age.

Understanding the basics of the industrial landscape during the railroad era helps to explain why housing and institutions are where they are. In neighborhoods with small factories and a wide range of institutions and housing within a small area, reuse by different classes of people appears easier. These neighborhoods are not as isolated from the metropolitan fabric.

In areas with large-scale industrial sites, correspondingly large and homogeneous neighborhoods developed. This was perhaps the first time that a class of people lived in such an insulated world on such a large scale. In many ways, this kind of neighborhood development served as a model for the massive suburban housing boom after World War II—certainly more than elite residential suburbs. No residential commuter suburb in the nineteenth century could match the scale of a Back of the Yards or Pullman.

Catholic parishes shaped public life in these worker neighborhoods of the railroad age. While Protestant and Jewish congregations were present, Catholic parishes physically and organizationally shaped the districts around the stockyards and steel mills. The separation of Catholics into distinct ethnic parishes, then, fostered clear distinctions in these otherwise large, homogeneous neighborhoods. For much of the nineteenth and early twentieth centuries, these congregations remained isolated. Their isolation fostered intense, shared experiences among the thousands of residents in these neighborhoods who worked for the same employers and lived on the same streets.

These tightly knit neighborhoods did not initially include African Americans.

4.31 The Joseph Schlitz Brewing Company built Schuba's at 3159 N. Southport in 1903 under a design by Frommann & Jebsen. It was one of a number of saloons constructed by the brewer to increase sales and improve distribution. (Leslie Schwartz)

Employment discrimination kept blacks from most industrial jobs until World War I. Then as African Americans gained employment in the stockyards and steel mills, their white co-workers did not welcome them into their nearby established worker neighborhoods. While this meant that African Americans avoided the noxious environment around many of the largest plants, it also meant that they were forced to lose time or pay carfare everyday. African Americans were a largely unrecognized group of commuters in a region built by workers who sought housing close to work.[46]

5

Commuter Suburbs of the Railroad Age

Riverside, one of the most famous railroad suburbs in the United States, lies about ten miles southwest of downtown Chicago along the Des Plaines River. Although it is most famous for its design and architecture, the most memorable images of Riverside may well be of expansive lawns and shady trees. Despite the dominance of green, Riverside is not a natural site. It is a manmade landscape designed for an exclusive group of metropolitan residents who have used restrictive covenants, local laws, zoning ordinances, and taxes, to maintain this leafy suburban retreat.

The Riverside Improvement Company, a group of real estate investors, hired the landscape architects Frederick Law Olmsted and Calvert Vaux to design a plan for a suburb not long after the Chicago, Burlington, and Quincy Railroad arrived in the area in 1863. Olmsted and Vaux had recently completed plans for Central Park in New York City, as well as for the South Parks in Chicago. In 1869, Olmsted and Vaux completed their plan for a subdivision with curvilinear streets large lots, and a 1600-acre reserve along the Des Plaines River (fig. 5.1). Olmsted intended suburban life to be "an advance upon those [civilized refinements] which are characteristic of town life."[1]

The railroad bisected the Olmsted plan for Riverside, providing the only straightaway in it. The center of Riverside today remains its train station (fig. 5.2). It is accessible from outside the community only by winding through a series of curved streets, although it affords commuters a half-hour commute into the city by rail. Beside the train station is a water tower (fig. 5.3), representative of the infrastructure improvements made by the development company in their quest to bring the amenities of the city to country life. The developers sunk

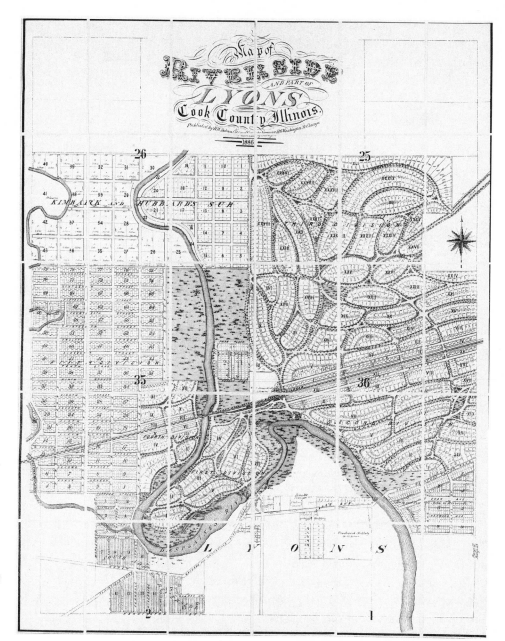

5.1 This 1886 map shows the Frederick Law Olmsted plan for Riverside. While the subdivision developed slowly, Riverside has been much studied by urbanists and landscape architects as a model for suburban design. The Riverside Landscape Architectural District was designated a National Historic Landmark in 1970. (Chicago Historical Society, ICHi-14189)

a well, laid out water and sewer mains, established gas hookups, paved roads, installed streetlamps, and built sidewalks in Riverside.[2] To facilitate maintenance of these improvements, residents organized as an incorporated town in 1875. Within a few years, they had constructed a substantial brick and stone town hall.

Understanding the need to attract local shops and businesses to accommodate the basic needs of commuters and their families, the Riverside Improvement Company built an arcade building between the town hall and the depot (fig. 5.4). This substantial brick business block helped to spur the creation of much-needed businesses like a grocery, meat market, and pharmacy.

One of the first buildings that Riverside's developers built, the Riverside Hotel, no longer stands. The hotel was designed by William Le Baron Jenney as a three-story building with wide balconies overlooking the Des Plaines River; it was constructed in 1870 (fig. 5.5). Early investors hoped that the hotel would help keep their investment afloat as a summer resort while the area developed slowly as a suburb.

Around this core of buildings, individual homeowners and investors slowly began to build homes on the 100-by-225-foot lots. While the company did not build housing, they used deed restrictions to outlaw fences and maintain a standard thirty-foot setback. Houses were built over the next century in a variety of styles, from fussy Queen Anne houses with large front

porches to the simple lines of several Frank Lloyd Wright designs. Overall, the large house on a landscaped lawn has been replicated hundreds of times so that the suburb does indeed look like a park with houses sited within it (fig. 5.6).

These buildings and features, most of them still visible in Riverside, are in fact a common landscape found along rail lines in metropolitan areas across the United States. The component parts of railroad commuter suburbs include the plan, the commuter rail line, the train depot, the village hall, the hotel, the business block, and the manicured houses set on wide, open lawns. In Chicago, at least thirty-five settlements began as railroad commuter suburbs in the nineteenth and early twentieth centuries (fig. 5.7). Many are now within the Chicago city limits like Norwood Park,

5.2 The first Riverside train station, 90 Bloomingbank, was a modest frame structure designed by William Le Baron Jenney. The station was rebuilt in 1902, according to a design completed by the company architects of the Chicago, Burlington, and Quincy Railroad. Today, it is a reddish brick building with a red tile hipped roof with wide eaves that protect commuters from the elements. In 1993, the station was designated a Riverside Landmark. (Leslie Schwartz)

5.3 The Riverside Improvement Company sunk a well and built a 108-foot water tower designed by William LeBaron Jenney in 1871. The tower was renovated in the 1910s after a fire. It was designated an American Water Landmark in 1972 by the American Waterworks Association. The Riverside Historical Society operates a museum in the adjacent water tower pumphouse. (Joseph C. Bigott)

5.4 (left) The Riverside Improvement Company Building, 1 Riverside Drive, is an early example of an arcade and the first commercial building in Riverside. It was designed by Frederick C. Withers (onetime partner of Calvert Vaux) and built in 1871 between the train station and the village hall. The ornate stonework and towers complement that of the town hall. (Joseph C. Bigott)

5.5 (right) The Riverside Hotel was designed by William LeBaron Jenney and built by the Riverside Improvement Company in 1870. It stood just a short distance southeast of the train station on a bluff over the Des Plaines River. This is a 1908 image of the 125-room hotel, which no longer stands. (Chicago Historical Society, Chicago Daily News, DN-0006799)

Austin, Ravenswood, Irving Park, and Washington Park. Others remain independent suburbs and include Lake Forest, Hinsdale, Highland Park, and River Forest.[3]

Railroad Commuting

Commuting is so central a part of our lives today that it is difficult to envision a time when we devoted far less time and energy to it. But Chicago in 1900 was such a place. Workers, small business owners, and farmers generally lived and worked near employment. Professionals, merchants, and others who held upper-middle-class jobs in the downtown district became the Chicago area's first commuters. Most industrial workers and many service sector employees continued to live very close to where they worked until the second half of the twentieth century. African American domestic workers, stockyards workers, and steelworkers were a clear exception to this pattern. Because of housing discrimination, they often lived at some distance from their places of employment.

While the idea of living away from the growing congestion of the city center had begun to form for those who could afford it, not until the arrival of the railroad could the upper middle class find refuge that would last for more than a few years in the face of Chicago's growth.[4]

Railroads provided the means for sustainable commuter settlements. Middle- and upper-class downtown workers became Chicago's first commuters as they traveled rail lines daily from outlying stops. Across the Chicago area during the years around the Civil War, commuters took advantage of the railroads' speed to move far from the built-up city center. The railroad web determined where suburbs were planted—most in the ten-to-twelve-mile range from downtown—a half-hour to forty-five-minute commute.

For the first hundred years of settlement, commuter suburbs were tied closely to the patterns of railroad development. In the 1850s, five lines ran directly north, northwest, west, south, and east from the city center. By the 1880s, more lines had been added in virtually every direction. By the late 1880s and 1890s, many of the lines that had had only one track were double-tracked. Interurbans and rapid transit lines opened even more territory to commuter settlements in the early twentieth century.

Thirty-five communities in the metropolitan area trace their origins to these elite enclaves. This is a factor that makes Chicago distinctive.

5.6 Fifty houses were built in Riverside in 1870 and 1871, but then the subdivision saw little growth until the 1890s. Seen here are two houses built in the late nineteenth century. Riverside is also home to several architecturally significant houses, including the Avery Coonley house designed by Frank Lloyd Wright and completed in 1908. (Joseph C. Bigott)

In other U.S. cities, long histories before the railroad meant that crossroads towns and older regional centers are more important. Boston's metropolitan area consists primarily of old colonial towns which have woven together. Philadelphia and New York City, which like Chicago have many rail lines, also had older, established communities which predate the rail era.

In Chicago, one can go in virtually any direction from downtown and search out a rail station—either in or outside the limits of the City of Chicago. Walking from the rail station in circles no further than three or four blocks, you are apt to encounter a small business district, a distinctive plat, and at least some homes that date to the final decades of the twentieth century—in short, a commuter enclave.

Residents who have inherited these neighborhoods or suburbs have frequently chosen to preserve some of this history—a rail station, house, or water tower—as sites for local exhibits and collections. In addition, many railroad towns now have historic districts intent on preserving the residential areas that emerged around these stations. This preserved landscape helps us to see the world of Chicago's early commuters.

Depots

Train depots served, and continue to serve, as entrance points into this landscape (many historic depots, like the one at Riverside, remain in use as commuter stations). They remind us that railroads are central to understanding where early commuters located.[5] While no more than one or two rooms, these depots often served not only passengers but the fledgling communities as well. Residents of Wilmette and Norwood Park (when it was an independent

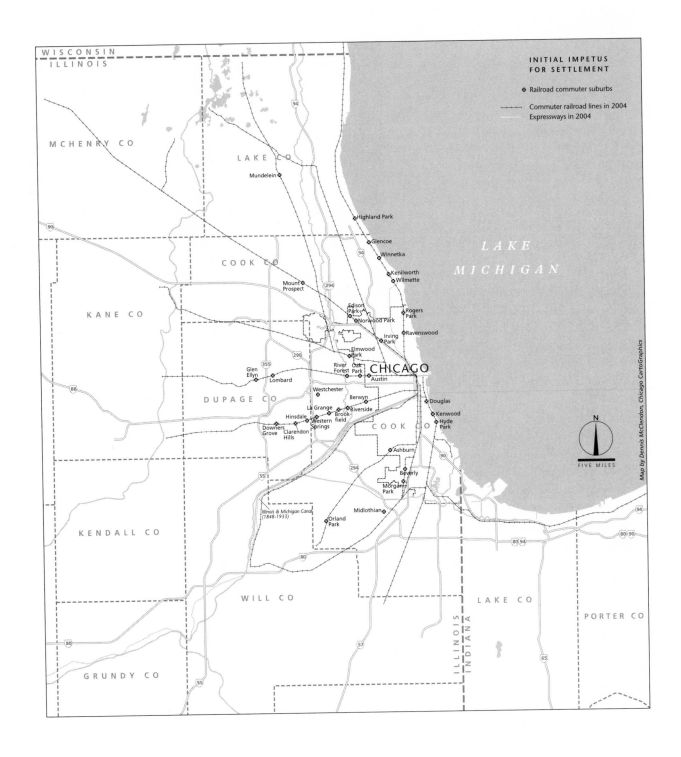

INITIAL IMPETUS
FOR SETTLEMENT

❖   Railroad commuter suburbs
        Commuter railroad lines in 2004
        Expressways in 2004

LAKE
MICHIGAN

WISCONSIN
ILLINOIS

McHENRY CO

LAKE CO

Mundelein

Highland Park

Glencoe
Winnetka
Kenilworth
Wilmette

COOK CO

Mount
Prospect

Edison
Park
Norwood Park

Rogers
Park

Ravenswood

Irving
Park

KANE CO

Elmwood
Park

River   Oak
Forest Park   CHICAGO

Glen
Ellyn

Austin

Lombard

Westchester

Berwyn

Douglas

DUPAGE CO

La Grange
Brook-
field

Riverside

Kenwood

Hinsdale
Western
Springs

Hyde
Park

Downers
Grove
Clarendon
Hills

COOK CO

Ashburn

Beverly

Morgan
Park

Illinois & Michigan Canal
(1848-1933)

Midlothian

Orland
Park

KENDALL CO

N

FIVE MILES

WILL CO

LAKE CO

ILLINOIS
INDIANA

PORTER CO

GRUNDY CO

5.8 In 1891 Joseph Sears supervised construction of the Kenilworth train station, only a flag stop the year before. The building's exterior is original to 1890. (Leslie Schwartz)

suburb) held public meetings and other gatherings in the depots, which were quite often the largest semipublic space.

A wide range of train depots have been preserved across the Chicago metropolitan area. Many of them hark back to agricultural origins and are simple and utilitarian. In contrast, developers and early residents of commuter suburbs often built more elaborate, specially designed structures. They understood that the train depot functioned as an entranceway, a front face for their communities. Travelers passing on the train were likely making judgments on the suburb beyond based on the style, color, and ornamentation of the train depot.

Kenilworth developed as an elite commuter enclave on Chicago's North Shore in the early 1890s. The town's main developer, Joseph Sears, constructed a "fine station" as one of the first improvements he made in this new residential suburb between established railroad suburbs at Wilmette and Winnetka, some fifteen miles north of Chicago along Lake Michigan.

The exterior of the station looks much as it did when first constructed in 1890 (fig. 5.8). F. E. M. Cole visited Kenilworth in 1907 and admired "the beauties of the low-lying stone depot half hidden in vines and shrubbery and gay with flowering plants." Today, nearly a century later and with cell phones, computers, portable stereos, and designer coffee, commuters still wait for morning trains at the same station.[6]

5.7 (opposite) COMMUTER SUB-URBS OF NINETEENTH-CENTURY AND EARLY TWENTIETH-CENTURY CHICAGOLAND. At least thirty-five neighborhoods and suburbs in Chicagoland began as railroad commuter suburbs. (Dennis McClendon)

Suburban Plats

Beyond the depots, real estate speculators platted subdivisions which transformed rural land into suburban
property. These plats can be understood both by examining their contours on a map and by walking or driv-
ing the streets and property represented on the maps.
Either as representations or as actual landscapes, these
plats often dramatically illustrate how commuter towns
were set off from adjoining farms and settlements. Today, while many of these plats directly abut lands with
other suburban or urban uses, their distinctiveness often remains visible.

At first, models for commuter railroad subdivisions
were urban. In particular, the urban square, houses surrounding a private park, served as an early model. Over
time, and in places like Riverside, the houses moved into
the park.

Oakenwald, one of the very first railroad suburbs in
Chicago, was the brainchild of Stephen Douglas, the U.S.
senator from Illinois.[7] With Douglas's aid, the federal
government sited the Illinois Central Railroad through

5.9 The Groveland Park Cottage, 601 E. Groveland Park Avenue, was built in the early 1870s after the resolution of lawsuits following the death of property owner Stephen A. Douglas. Douglas had originally registered the Oakenwald subdivision in 1855. (Leslie Schwartz)

the area a few years later. In 1855, Douglas made several subdivisions, including Groveland
Park, located between Cottage Grove and the Illinois Central tracks at 33rd Place. It is a small,
quiet park around which still stand single-family homes on the fifty-foot lots which Douglas
recorded. A visit there today finds the subdivision tucked between high-rise developments.
The Groveland Park Gardener's Cottage is a tiny Greek Revival brick cottage with the name of
the development in red letters across its front face (fig. 5.9). A wrought iron fence fronts the
Cottage Grove side of the subdivision, reminding the visitor that this suburban retreat has
long been overrun by more urban development (fig. 5.10).[8]

Douglas's Groveland Park took the urban grid and encircled a park. Douglas had no
doubt seen successful urban developments around small parks such as Washington Square
in Manhattan and Lafayette Square in Washington, D.C. It is reminiscent of the way in
which London developed around small parks. Other Chicago developers also understood
the value of parkland to suburban development.[9] Along the lakeshore twenty-seven miles
north of Chicago, the Lake Forest Association took a further step with its 1857 plat (fig. 5.11).
The real estate syndicate hired a landscape architect to design the community. The result is
a romantic parklike design, inspired by Andrew Jackson Downing.

5.10 At center is 649 E. Groveland Park in 1915. The home at the far left is in an Italianate style popular into the 1870s, with brick homes further to the right. (Chicago Historical Society, Chicago Daily News Photographer, DN-0065216)

Unlike Groveland Park, where rectangular lots surrounded a rectangular park, Lake Forest's plan took the park into the streets and lots themselves. The subdivision was a park with homes within it. The curvilinear streets and irregular plots marked a new form in Chicago. Until this point, the grid had been the clear basis for town plats.[10] Even today, one can see Hotchkiss's original vision of a college and a town in a park. Local government, through planning and zoning, has helped maintain the broad setbacks, winding roads, and large, single-family houses.

Lake Forest's parklike plan was followed in other nineteenth-century commuter suburbs, including Highland Park, Norwood Park, and Riverside.[11] The Hollywood subdivision in Brookfield is yet another suburban area that is off the grid. Initially the westernmost part of the Olmsted plan for Riverside, Hollywood was purchased and developed by Samuel E. Gross in 1893. Gross was a prolific developer, but most of his subdivisions maintained the grid. At Hollywood, Gross hired Carl Mendius, a draftsman, to design a subdivision on the curvilinear plan of neighboring Riverside. Gross rejected Mendius's version of Olmsted's 1869 plan, so Mendius decided to "draw the craziest sub-division plan I could cutting the area into 25 foot lots." Gross liked it and it became the plan for Hollywood, which is today eastern Brookfield. A drive along eastern Brookfield's streets quickly highlights the curved streets and odd-shaped lots. The area is distinguished by narrower streets than those found just over the Salt Creek to the east in Riverside.[12]

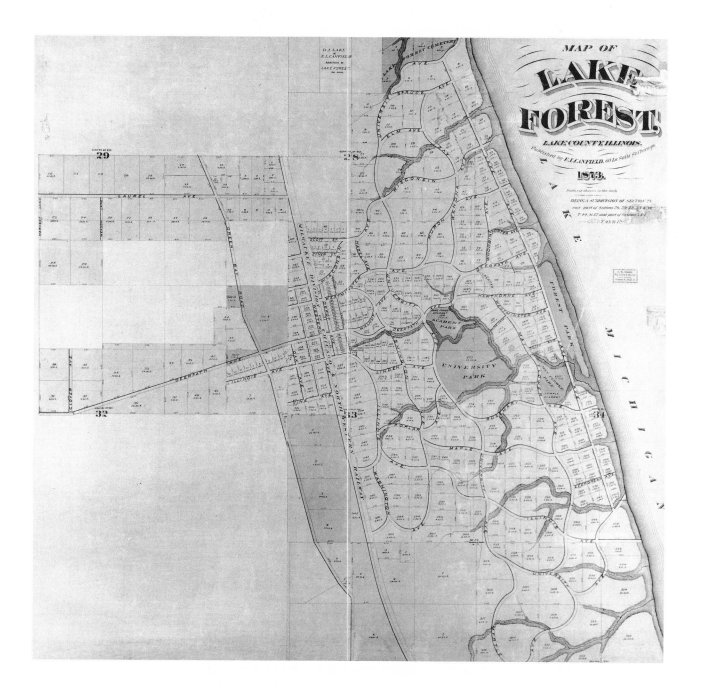

5.12 The Hyde Park House was built by Paul Cornell in 1853 at 53rd Street and Lake Michigan (1511 E. Hyde Park Boulevard). The spot was popular with summer visitors, included Mary Todd Lincoln, who stayed here after her husband's assassination. The building burned to the ground in 1879. (Chicago Historical Society, ICHi-00727)

Suburban Hotels

Development companies sometimes constructed hotels near their rail depots as a means to introducing visitors to their new suburbs. The strategy succeeded in Riverside, where affluent Chicagoans came out for summer respites and, in 1871, to escape the devastation of the Great Fire. The hotel provided a way to familiarize well-to-do Chicagoans with a new concept—a beautiful subdivision allowing those who could afford it the opportunity to live in an area near outdoor recreational activities.[13]

There is little or no evidence of these hotels in residential rail suburbs today. Many burned within a few years of construction. Others were torn down as the suburbs became more successful as permanent residences. One of the oldest suburban hotels in the region was built in 1859 along Lake Michigan by Paul Cornell, a successful Chicago businessman and real estate speculator. Cornell had purchased 300 acres of land along Lake Michigan and the newly adjacent Illinois Central Railroad between 51st and 55th Streets in Hyde Park Township, six miles south of Chicago's downtown. He negotiated with the Illinois Central Railroad for a passenger station, which opened in 1856. Cornell platted large lots for sale around the station and dedicated a small lakefront park.

Cornell built a house for his family and opened a hotel, the Hyde Park House, along Lake Michigan at 53rd Street in 1857 (fig. 5.12). The four-story frame structure included a gabled attic and porches, described further as "an elegant resort hotel, gaslit, prettily land-

5.11 (opposite) The initial plan for Lake Forest was completed in 1857 and is attributed to Almerin Hotchkiss, a surveyor who did work in St. Louis. The plan complements the many ravines in the area in a romantic style popular in cemeteries at that time, as seen in this 1873 map. (Chicago Historical Society, ICHi-16261)

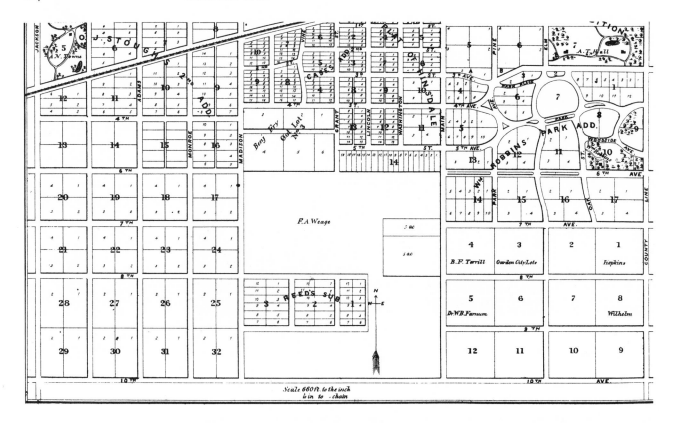

5.13 This 1874 map of Hinsdale shows the area immediately south of the railroad station. The original plat of Hinsdale, commissioned by William Robbins in 1864, had modest lots (many thirty feet wide) and centered south of the train station. Oliver Stough subdivided property further to the west of the train station with larger lots, but still on a grade. By 1874, Robbins had added an addition to the east of his initial plat which abandons the grid in places for large curvilinear lots. (*1874 Atlas of DuPage County*)

scaped, hospitably verandahed. It was the center of the community's social life and the scene of many summer festivities," anchoring the suburb that is now the established Chicago neighborhood of Hyde Park.[14]

Although hotels like the Riverside Hotel and the Hyde Park House drew only clientele who had the time and money for extended stays, and little white-collar or professional work took place in these residential suburbs, the presence of the hotels indicated that service workers were employed here—in the business blocks, hotels, and in the suburban houses themselves.

Houses

While developers were often responsible for planning the first rail depots, laying out initial plats, and perhaps building a hotel, they seldom built more than a few houses. In the nineteenth and well into the twentieth centuries, suburban houses were more frequently built by their initial owners or on a small scale by speculators intent on renting or selling.

Today this residential landscape can be explored in two very different ways: through the stock of housing that remains in use, and through house museums. Both have advantages and disadvantages. Examination of housing still in use provides a sense of neighborhood context, while house museums provide explicit interpretation and access to interiors.

The range of extant nineteenth-century housing in railroad suburbs suggests that most railroad suburbs had a variety of residents—commuters, local businessmen, local craftsmen, and workers. The range also reflects the fact that these railroad suburbs were seldom an instant success. There was a long window of residential development in many of these towns. Developers sold lots and new residents built homes often over several generations. Empty lots were a common feature of railroad suburbs well into the twentieth century.

Because of these factors, many elite enclaves were more diverse in the past than they are today.[15] This point can be lost by looking only at the housing that remains within suburban towns. Teardowns or major additions mask a historically more diverse housing stock.

Hinsdale is one such case. Sixteen miles west of downtown, Hinsdale developed as a suburban settlement during the years immediately after the Civil War. In 1864, William Robbins donated right-of-way and a train depot to the Chicago, Burlington, and Quincy Railroad and hired H. W. S. Cleveland to plat a 480-acre tract south of the tracks (fig. 5.13). This assured the rapid rise in the value of his property, as well as the arrival of dozens of prospective land purchasers. By 1874, he had sold 320 of the 480 acres, and the population of the community was estimated at 1,500. At this time, a yearly commutation ticket to Hinsdale cost $75, and a one-way commute to downtown Chicago could take as little as a half hour.[16]

Hinsdale's range of housing types indicates that along with affluent residents were servants and skilled craftsmen needed to build and maintain these homes, as well as small businesses needed to cater to day-to-day needs of suburbanites. A close look at Robbins's 1874 plat shows that he and other early subdividers anticipated residents of varying incomes, evident from the range of lot sizes and shapes available. Frontages ranged from 30 feet to more than 300 feet (almost all larger than the 25-foot frontages common in Chicago's worker neighborhoods). The smallest lots were on the grid and to the near south of the train station. Large gridded lots were available north of the railroad tracks. Robbins's Park Addition, just to the east of his initial plat, featured front footages ranging from 50 feet to well over 200 feet.

5.14 Immanuel Evangelical Church, 302 S. Grant Street, Hinsdale (also known as Immanuel Hall), was built by William Vornsand in 1900. Many of the church members were skilled artisans employed in constructing the many large suburban houses or in other area businesses. When the church was threatened with demolition, area residents bought the structure, which was added to the National Register of Historic Places in 2000. The structure is now maintained by the Hinsdale Historical Society and the Village of Hinsdale. (Leslie Schwartz)

The most modest range of cottage houses built in the early plats are located on the smaller lots to the south and west of the train station. Many are clustered around Immanuel Church, built at Second and Grant in 1900 by German-speaking workmen (fig. 5.14). Many of the skilled craftsmen who built the more elaborate homes in Hinsdale over the course of the late nineteenth and early twentieth century lived around this wooden Gothic church (fig. 5.15).

To the east and north of these modest lots and houses, beyond the business district, are some of the largest houses and lots in the old part of Hinsdale (fig. 5.16). In 1866, Oliver Stough, who subdivided and sold lots in this area, built a large Italianate house with a large front porch (fig. 5.17). Neighboring houses are about this size or larger, most of them built before 1900. Residents in this neighborhood included an Illinois Central Railroad executive, early landholders and developers, the president of American Terra Cotta Company, a Hinsdale merchant, and a judge.[17]

Domestic tours such as these can be done in virtually any of the commuter suburbs in the metropolitan area. While the mix of housing and lot sizes varies from community to community, housing styles follow a similar progression. Early suburban homes, built in the 1860s and 1870s, followed Italianate styles. By the 1880s and 1890s, more ornate Victorian styles came into fashion, followed by Craftsman and Prairie styles. Throughout the nineteenth and into the twentieth centuries, less affluent suburbanites built simple frame cottages.[18]

All of the specific houses described in Hinsdale have been preserved privately—that is, maintained as private residences. Many have been adapted and renovated over their history, adding infrastructure connections, new windows, and other improvements. That so many

5.15 These houses, originally inhabited by skilled construction workers, stand near Immanuel Church in an area within Robbins's original plat for Hinsdale. (Leslie Schwartz)

older homes are still inhabited is a reminder that while Chicagoans' lifestyles have changed considerably since the Civil War, we still live in the same houses. We live with the past.

Going beyond this everyday living with the past, historical societies in many of these commuter suburbs have chosen to preserve one house as representative of their past. One might expect that these houses, which often serve as museums, libraries, and historical society offices, would have been carefully chosen for the historical significance of the architecture or inhabitants. This seems rarely to be the case.[19]

The houses maintained by local historical societies, with varying aid from municipal governments and park districts, are often not representative of their community's housing styles, significant residents, or key period of growth. Instead, happenstance fuels many of these important preservation efforts. Sometimes a house is preserved because it has been donated to a historical society. In Hinsdale, a local

school district donated a house that is more modest than many of the houses built there in the nineteenth century (fig. 5.18). Caroline Martin Mitchell bequeathed a large red brick Victorian mansion to the City of Naperville in 1936. Her family had been prominent residents of Naperville for more than 100 years and their house was among the most substantial in town. Neither Hinsdale nor Naperville residents have preserved a representative house.[20]

Historical societies in commuter suburbs cannot preserve a representative house because no such house exists. These commuter suburbs include a wide range of housing. Their character differs sharply from the cookie-cutter subdivisions of the post–World War II era, where houses sometimes varied only in color and minor facade changes. Nineteenth-century commuter suburbs had housing for a wide range of upper-middle and upper-class families, from modest frame structures to palatial stone mansions. The recent spate of teardowns in older commuter suburbs has replaced many smaller nineteenth-century houses with larger "McMansions." Teardowns threaten not only old houses, but the variety of housing available in railroad suburbs.

The groups who preserve these houses generally choose an era for the preservation setting. That is, the houses are stage sets for a particular period. Furniture, clothing, wall coverings, colors, appliances, and other household items have been chosen as "authentic" from a particular era. To walk into these houses is to glimpse not some abstract notion of the past,

5.16 On a large lot in Stough's addition north of the railroad tracks, Dr. D. K. Pearson built this house in 1886 at 122 N. Grant Street. Seen here in 1910, Pearson bequeathed the house to the Village of Hinsdale, hoping that it would become a public library. Instead, the village sold the property and found a more central location for the library. (Chicago Historical Society, DN-0056000)

5.17 Oliver Stough, the real estate developer who platted the property north of the Hinsdale train station, built this house for his family in 1867 on a twelve-acre site. He moved the house to 306 N. Grant Street in 1885. (Leslie Schwartz)

but a particular place and time. Taken together, these houses provide insights into changes regarding house furnishings, activities, and work. As with the preserved farmhouses, the emphasis is on women's work within houses.[21]

Houses in Hinsdale, Arlington Heights, Highland Park, Lombard, and Palatine take a visitor back to the era between 1870 and 1890. Downers Grove, Naperville, and Homewood present interiors from the beginning of the twentieth century. Des Plaines, Mount Prospect, Evanston, and Morton Grove are among the house museums that represent the 1910s and 1920s.[22] Houses in commuter rail suburbs are among the most preserved and interpreted structures in the metropolitan area.

Most of the house museums represent the middle class, with a few forays into the mansions of the wealthy. In Hinsdale, a house museum interprets the decidedly middle-class world of a downtown white-collar worker and his family. While the historical society suggests that the restoration depicts "a typical Hinsdale family" of the 1870s, it represents neither the homes of German craftsmen in west Hinsdale nor the twenty-to-thirty-room mansions on the east side of the old town.[23]

Village Halls and Business Blocks

The ability to provide heretofore urban services in a rural setting is a key characteristic of residential railroad suburbs. Commuters and their families wanted many of the services that they had gotten used to in the city center: running water, indoor plumbing, and gas lighting. While some services were provided and maintained privately, the vast majority of settlements turned to local government to install and maintain infrastructure systems. Residents in many of these railroad suburbs chose to incorporate as villages just a few years after initial settlement.[24]

Village governments not only devoted themselves to infrastructure, they also helped to cultivate the character of exclusive enclaves. By the mid-twentieth century, zoning emerged as a way of maintaining the single-family character of these suburbs. Even those railroad suburbs which have been annexed into the City of Chicago maintained some autonomy over zoning (and the contentious issue of liquor sale).

Village government may have started, as it did in Norwood Park, in the train depot, but village or town halls quickly became standard features. Some of these buildings remain in use by local governments down to the present; others have been torn down; and still others have been preserved through reuse. Kenilworth has one of the most distinctive village halls, built in Prairie Style by George Maher, who also built a number of homes there (fig. 5.19). No longer the village hall, the building serves as a community center.

Business blocks are another regular feature of rail suburbs. To the north of Kenilworth at Lake Forest, Market Square stands as an elaborate example of this kind of commercial development (fig. 5.20). Completed in 1916, this is one of the oldest planned shopping centers in the nation. It is distinguished not only by its age, but also with a design by Howard Van Doren Shaw and the fact that it is larger than most suburban shopping districts. Yet its location immediately across from the station, and its focus on a local market, are typical of business blocks built in rail suburbs across the region.[25]

5.18 The Hinsdale Historical Society looked for a suitable house for a museum for many years. In 1981, a local school district offered a house which stood on property they wanted for playing fields. Using private funds, the society moved the frame Italianate house to 15 Clay Street. Built in 1874 by a clerk who commuted to Chicago, it is neither one of the smallest nor one of the largest houses built in Hinsdale in the nineteenth century. (Ann Keating)

Suburban Churches and Clubs

With only a few exceptions, the first residents of commuter suburbs in Chicagoland were wealthy Protestants. Many supported churches and clubs which served as an extension of the domestic environment. In some communities, developers or early residents sought to avoid religious divisions by encouraging membership in a pan-Protestant union or community church. For instance, Joseph Sears, developer and early resident of Kenilworth along

5.19 The original Kenilworth Village Hall was designed by George Maher. It is seen here in 1910 just east of the Kenilworth train station. Today the building serves as a community center. (Chicago Historical Society, DN-0008570)

the North Shore, was instrumental in the foundation of the Kenilworth Union Church in 1892 shortly after the suburb's foundation. The congregation was nondenominational Protestant, in an attempt to appeal to all community residents.[26]

The Kenilworth Union Church was sited along the main east-west thoroughfare linking the train station with the lakefront (fig. 5.21). Later, other Protestant denominations were allowed to locate here as well. But the exclusive nature of this suburb kept out Roman Catholic and Jewish congregations altogether.

Exclusivity was also fostered through private clubs, especially country clubs, where control over members and guests assured homogeneity.[27] Residents of early commuter suburbs banded together to build golf courses in Riverside, Hinsdale, Evanston, and Downers Grove. Because residential suburbs were often home to middle-income as well as wealthier families, country clubs could exclude unwanted neighbors.

The Legacy of the Residential Railroad Suburb

Overall, the residential railroad suburbs remain far less changed than farm or industrial settlements in Chicagoland. Most continue to function as commuter centers. Men continue to wait outside train depots to get to downtown jobs—although women now stand on the platform as well. Public buildings are often still in use or preserved. Much of the original housing stock still is in use, while house museums preserve the world of the nineteenth-century middle-class commuter and his family. As with the farm centers, institutions organized by the first generation of residents are often still active, even if serving different constituencies.

This continuity is maintained through the vigilance of local government and other community groups. Suburban governments have considerable control over local zoning and other ordinances which regulate growth and redevelopment. Not all these measures are designed to preserve a historic legacy. Many railroad commuter suburbs have aggressively annexed territory, actively sought commercial and office development, and encouraged the gentrification of more modest older residential areas.

Suburban governments have tried to shape the significant changes within Chicagoland to their own advantage. In the late nineteenth century, white-collar workers readily embraced the convenience of commuter trains with ready access to downtown jobs. By the late twentieth century, growing numbers of these white-collar workers commuted by automobile as work sites shifted to include suburban locations. Now the Loop is only one of a series of white-collar work centers in the metropolitan area. Oakbrook, Naperville-Lisle, and

5.20 Market Square in Lake Forest was an early planned shopping center. Designed by Howard Van Doren Shaw, the center was completed in 1916 and is now on the National Register of Historic Places. (Leslie Schwartz)

5.21 The nondenominational Kenilworth Union Church was organized in 1892 as a church which could serve new suburban residents who had previously attended various denominational churches. (Leslie Schwartz)

the Lake-Cook Road corridor in Deerfield-Northbrook are all recently established office and commercial centers whose employees may live in nineteenth-century railroad commuter suburbs. Many suburban governments actively courted new white-collar businesses and their tax dollars.

Those commuter suburbs with ready access to new centers of white-collar work along the expressway systems have seen the most dynamic growth in the closing decades of the twentieth century. Rail suburbs with ready access to expressways provide an important flexibility for two-income families whose jobs and work locations can change frequently. And the added tax base provided by business and commercial enterprises has become quite attractive to railroad suburbs which at one time had very few white-collar employment opportunities.

The shift to automobile travel has also affected shopping. Railroad suburb residents are no longer a captive market for the businesses around the train station. Shopping centers and malls have gradually moved to the outskirts of established railroad suburbs where there is room for parking. At the same time, many suburban governments have aggressively redeveloped their "historic" downtowns in order to better compete with outlying shopping centers.

In recent decades, commuter suburbs have faced the phenomenon of teardowns, where smaller, less-expensive housing in a community is replaced with larger, more expensive structures. While some suburban governments have intervened to regulate the rate of teardowns, few have outlawed them altogether, perhaps because of the increased tax revenues which they generally afford.

In the nineteenth century, the residents of commuter suburbs included local shopkeepers, craftsmen, village employees of varying levels, and domestic workers as well as the upper-middle-class households supported by downtown commuters. A decline in the need for live-in help, small merchants, and local craftsmen, coupled with dramatic increases in house values, have led to the demolition of many of the modest homes which served workers within nineteenth-century railroad suburbs. They have often been replaced with far more expensive and larger houses which have led to more homogeneity in railroad suburbs like Hinsdale, Wilmette, or Glen Ellyn than was the case in the nineteenth century.

Recreational and Institutional Centers of the Railroad Age

Chicagoland camp meetings for Methodists began as summer excursions as early as the 1830s. The Methodists founded four formal camp meeting grounds in nineteenth-century Chicagoland: at Lake Bluff, thirty miles north of downtown Chicago; at Camp Berger, south of Chicago; at New Lenox, thirty-one miles southwest of downtown; and seventeen miles northwest of the Loop at Des Plaines.[1] These were among hundreds founded by Methodist groups across the country, many on the outskirts of quickly growing cities.

Used almost exclusively in the summer months, these campgrounds often located at places of natural beauty with ready access to rail transportation. Methodists journeyed to the sites to hear noted evangelists, singers, and choirs and to participate in programs of religious conversion and reflection. As one of the initial organizers of the Des Plaines Methodist Camp Ground remembered, "The need of special revival services was very great, for all the powers of darkness were many, bad and defiant. Rum, riot and ruin seemed to have full sway."[2] For several generations, camp meetings fought the perceived evils of city life from sites at an easy distance from downtown.

The Des Plaines Methodist Camp Ground stands as the only Chicagoland encampment that survived into the twenty-first century. A group of area Methodists that included many early supporters of Northwestern University founded the camp in 1860 at a scenic site along the Des Plaines River about seventeen miles from downtown Chicago. The site is south of the Des Plaines stop of the Chicago and North Western Railway, which ran through the area beginning in 1854.

In August 1860, workmen (many of them students from Evanston's Garrett Biblical Institute) constructed a tent, platform, and pulpit for a preacher. The Methodists arranged

6.1 Although many of the cottages at the Des Plaines Methodist Camp Ground were initially constructed by Chicagoland congregations, most were sold to individual families by the mid-twentieth century. Each cottager paid a ground rent to the Chicago District Camp Ground Association, which still owns and maintains the property. This 1909 photograph shows women working on porch screens of a cottage. (Chicago Historical Society, DN-0007496)

special excursion trains and upwards of 20,000 people flocked to the site. After the opening event, some made their way home on the trains or using their own horses and wagons. Others set up tents, while still others slept in the open air.

Within five years, campers constructed more permanent buildings. The campground was modeled on plans for an encampment in Martha's Vineyard, Massachusetts, in a "wheel pattern" of buildings and tents, which stood in contrast to the grid of the city. By 1870, many of the "sawtoothed bargeboard camp-meeting style cottages" which still stand at the site had been constructed (figs. 6.1, 6.2, and 6.3). Swedish, Norwegian-Danish, and German Methodists joined English-speaking Methodists at the site. Members of the Evangelical Association and the United Brethren groups joined the Methodists in their summer encampments.

While the camp was built expressly to leave behind the cares of everyday Chicagoland, the cottages were quickly named for the locations of the congregations that built them. Austin House, Auburn Park House, Geneva House, and St. Charles House were among the cottages named for Methodist congregations by 1915. They had Chicagoland suburbs and neighborhood names, but they were rearranged at the campground, next to new neighbors. One longtime camper remembered the cottages that fronted one of the parks: the Lakeview Church (North Side) was next to the South Side Englewood congregation, which was next to a house owned by a congregation in Western Springs (west suburb), which was next to the house owned by the Fifth Avenue Church on May Avenue (near the city center).[3] While the congregations remixed geographically, campers remained loyal to ethnic ties well into the twentieth century. Separate services were held by Swedish, Norwegian, German, and English-speaking Methodists. Initially, these separate services were held out of doors. Between 1876 and 1903, a large tent housed most assemblies. Then in 1903, a 1,200-seat auditorium named the Waldorf Tabernacle was built to replace the tent (fig. 6.4). Smaller meeting halls known as tabernacles were built by Swedish and Norwegian-Danish campers.

The Des Plaines Methodist Camp Ground embodies the importance of religion to nineteenth-century Chicagoland. Religion was important not just to neighborhood life, but also to the region as a whole. Religious congregations were the backbone of neighborhood institutions in farm centers, industrial towns, and commuter suburbs. But religion also provided links beyond a local area to a wider regional community. Methodists supported congregations in their neighborhoods and suburbs and also supported regional sites like the campground.

Features of Institutional and Recreational Centers

The Des Plaines Methodist Camp Ground is an unusual example of an extant and operating nineteenth-century seasonal recreational site. Despite their relative absence in the twenty-first-century landscape, these sites played a crucial role in nineteenth-century Chicagoland. They allowed residents from different neighborhoods and suburbs—and sometimes radically different social classes who might not normally live or work together—to come together.[4] Recreational travel could make metropolitan residents out of Chicagoans who seldom left their farms, industrial neighborhoods, or regular rail commutes.[5]

Outlying institutions and recreational sites varied in several key ways. Some sites, like the Des Plaines Camp Ground, were private and drew participants who shared a commitment to a particular religion, ethnic group, or special interest. In contrast, commercial sites generally drew anyone willing to pay usage fees. Finally, public institutions and recreational areas were available to residents across the region.

All of the sites were designed for visitors, who came to attend camps and schools, cel-

6.2 The Des Plaines Methodist Camp Ground is located at 1250 Campground Road, off Algonquin Road in northwest suburban Des Plaines. Over time, the association has taken over ownership of many of the cottages. In the 1960s, to commemorate the centenary of the campground, one of the cottages was renovated as a museum. Known as the Heritage House, it is open during special summer events. (Leslie Schwartz)

6.3 With cottages and the camp-ground in the background, this family enjoyed breakfast at a picnic table at the Des Plaines Methodist Camp Ground in 1925. (Chicago Historical Society, DN-0079224)

ebrate holidays, participate in sports, commune with nature, or bury their dead. Some were young, some were old. Individuals as well as extended families came. Some came because they wanted to; others were compelled by public agencies to become inmates of outlying institutions. In contrast to commuter suburbs, farm centers, and industrial towns, where visitors were infrequent, the economies of institutional and recreational centers were fueled by outsiders.

Outside of the downtown area, at least thirty-two neighborhoods and suburban areas in Chicagoland began because of recreational or institutional uses (fig. 6.5). Most were along railroads, streetcars, or interurban lines. Many were near area rivers and lakes. Camp meetings, golf courses, picnic groves, beer gardens, amusement parks, cemeteries, and religious and public institutions served as the centers of these settlements.[6]

These institutional and recreational sites provided a transitory urban system—one that encouraged (or demanded) metropolitan residents to leave their day-to-day patterns. These places were better known to a wider group than many neighborhoods and suburbs which were far better established, but isolated. They were also places that highlighted natural features of the region, unusual in a period when the natural landscape was overwhelmed by railroads, industrialization, and rapid urbanization.

6.4 The Waldorf Tabernacle built in 1903 is still in active use over one hundred years later. During July, performances take place in the tabernacle every weekend. Summer day camps and retreats also use the facility. The Des Plaines Methodist Camp Ground is privately operated, facing high maintenance costs and dwindling income. Nominated for landmark status in Illinois, the site was part of the 2003 Chicagoland watch list compiled by the Landmarks Preservation Council of Illinois. (Leslie Schwartz)

Often located along the rail lines at some distance from downtown, institutional and recreational sites also served as an advance guard in regional real estate development. Religious, ethnic, educational, and charitable institutions purchased outlying tracts for immediate use, but also viewed them as investments that would yield future dividends. Other speculators purchased outlying land and established commercial picnic grounds and amusement parks which provided immediate profits as well as potential long-term investments.[7]

Day Visitors and Picnics

Because time and means were limited, most people planned their trips with care. Picnics were one of the simplest ways that metropolitan residents could get out and explore the region during the summer. Because most workers toiled six days a week, picnics took place on Sundays and a few holidays, when railroad and later interurban and streetcar lines offered special trains (fig. 6.6). By 1860, "Sunday had already emerged as the busiest travel day for the horse railway companies" and commuter railroad lines "aggressively sought weekend business."[8]

Often picnic sites were informal—small groups on private property, with or without the owner's permission. There were also commercial picnic sites which provided accommodations for hundreds of visitors. The wealthiest Chicagoans could picnic on property that they owned, often near their second homes.

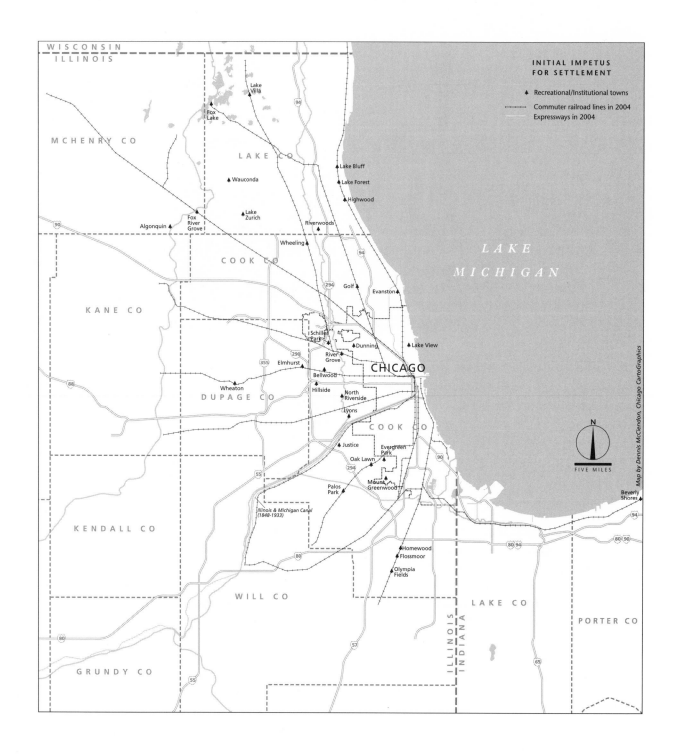

INITIAL IMPETUS
FOR SETTLEMENT

▲ Recreational/Institutional towns
━━━ Commuter railroad lines in 2004
━━━ Expressways in 2004

WISCONSIN
ILLINOIS

MCHENRY CO

LAKE CO

Lake
Villa

Fox
Lake

▲ Wauconda

Lake
Zurich ▲

Algonquin ▲

Fox River
Grove ▲

▲ Lake Bluff

▲ Lake Forest

▲ Highwood

Riverwoods

Wheeling

LAKE
MICHIGAN

COOK CO

KANE CO

Golf ▲

Evanston ▲

Schiller
Park
Dunning ▲

River
Grove

Elmhurst

Bellwood

▲ Lake View

CHICAGO

Hillside

Wheaton ▲

North
Riverside ▲

DUPAGE CO

Lyons ▲

COOK CO

▲ Justice

Evergreen
Park ▲

Oak Lawn ▲

Mount
Greenwood ▲

Palos
Park ▲

KENDALL CO

Illinois & Michigan Canal
(1848-1933)

▲ Homewood
▲ Flossmoor

▲ Olympia
Fields

WILL CO

LAKE CO

PORTER CO

ILLINOIS
INDIANA

Beverly
Shores ▲

GRUNDY CO

N

FIVE MILES

6.6 In July and August 1908, the *Chicago Daily News* ran a series entitled "The Trail of the Trolley," which detailed interesting day trips from Chicago primarily along the interurban lines. The July 31, 1908, article highlighted a trolley line out to Libertyville in Lake County, Illinois. The reporter described area farmhouses, cattle, and haystacks. Seen here are people along the Chicago, North Shore, and Milwaukee Railway (Skokie Valley Line) at the Libertyville Station in 1908. (Chicago Historical Society, DN-0006822)

The Fourth of July was a popular day for summer picnics. Across the metropolitan area, groups struck out on foot or in buggies, but mostly in rail cars to picnic sites. In 1872, the editor of the *Naperville Clarion* described how Fourth of July picnic parties made their way out from Chicago to DuPage in carriages (almost a half-day trip in itself), as well as getting off at almost every station along the rail lines. Problems arose when visitors chose to picnic on private property without permission, particularly on farmland. At the same time, many metropolitan residents took their picnics to the farms or near the homes of relatives or friends.[9]

Although it is difficult to track the identity of groups that used informal picnic grounds, Germans pioneered this leisure time activity in Chicagoland. We can imagine family, neighbors, and work groups taking advantage of trolleys and interurbans to journey out on Sundays and holidays. Some of these informal groups developed into private clubs around land used for particular sports and hobbies. Along the North Branch of the Chicago River at Belmont and in what became Palos Park, nineteen miles southwest of downtown, Germans founded sharpshooters' clubs, taking advantage of inexpensive scenic land at both sites. Germans working in a variety of settings and living in neighborhoods across the city could join one of these clubs, which offered shooting ranges as well as picnic groves for families and friends (fig. 6.7).[10]

Germans were prominent among the groups that organized singing and musical societies and purchased outlying land for summer excursions (fig. 6.8). For instance, a German

6.5 (opposite) RECREATIONAL AND INSTITUTIONAL CENTERS OF NINETEENTH-CENTURY AND EARLY TWENTIETH-CENTURY CHICAGO-LAND. At least thirty-two neighborhoods and suburbs in Chicagoland trace their origins to recreational and institutional uses. (Dennis McClendon)

6.7 This Kurz & Allen lithograph was originally printed in two colors. It shows German American men of the Pionere der Chicago Turngemeinde at ease in a variety of outdoor summer pursuits: sharpshooting, gymnastics, walking, singing, and beer drinking. (Chicago Historical Society, ICHi-14830)

singing society, the Schiller Liedertafel, located facilities in Schiller Woods about thirteen miles west-northwest of downtown along the Des Plaines River. Nearby picnic grounds and dance pavilions provided a wide range of recreational activities. The facilities were modest enough to allow for German membership from a wide class base.

Around these private clubs and near informal picnic areas with easy access to transportation, commercial picnic groves emerged which saved picnickers the trouble of toting food and beer to picnic sites. Chicagoans flocked to a series of private beaches along lakes in McHenry County and the Lake counties in Illinois and Indiana. Picnic trains regularly brought Chicagoans to Cedar Lake, Indiana, in the first decades of the twentieth century. Resorts in the Chain of Lakes region in Lake and McHenry counties catered to both those making day trips and others who could afford to rent cabins for overnight stays. Hundreds of Chicagoans traveled to the restaurants, gardens, and resorts in this area in the early twentieth century, and even more came after the arrival of the mass-produced automobile in the 1920s.[11]

By 1899, one directory listed twenty-seven picnic groves, most within forty miles of Chicago and along commuter rail lines.[12] Many of these picnic groves located along the Des Plaines River. Near the Des Plaines Methodist Camp Ground, the Northwestern Park—with ready railroad access into Chicago—provided dancing, boating, and swimming along the river for a daily fee. South along the river, access to Schiller Woods between Irving Park and Belmont came from a railroad stop known as Fairview. Picnic groves there catered to company picnics, while individuals paid fees to hike along the river or enter dance pavilions or saloons.

Ogden's Grove, Wright's Grove, Brand's Park, Hoffman Park, and Schutzenpark were among the picnic groves that dotted the metropolitan area by the early twentieth century. Many were located along rivers and streams, which provided a picturesque backdrop for summer outings. Churches, businesses, unions, and clubs sponsored special events at commercial picnic groves.

In July 1869, the Desplaines Hall Workers Club sponsored a picnic in Ogden's Grove, near North and Halsted—a site that could be reached on foot by North Side residents. A reporter in a local German-language newspaper described his arrival at the picnic grove: "Sunshine, woodland green and woodland shade, the sound of horns! on a Sunday afternoon, what more could a German heart possibly wish for?!—A good mug of beer!" The reporter found not only beer, but "cheerful groups everywhere, families and their friends taking of Sunday afternoon nectar, extra-strong coffee, and . . . Topfkuchen [a sweet bread] and buttered almond cake."[13]

6.8 Singing societies held special events at picnic groves, here the Grüsse vom Cannstatter Volksfest. (Chicago Historical Society, ICHi-21431)

Funerals and Cemeteries

While Chicagoans ventured beyond their neighborhoods for pleasant summer outings, they were also drawn out of their neighborhoods and suburbs for funerals, which often took them to outlying cemeteries. Into the twentieth century, funerals used horse-drawn hearses. With the introduction of streetcars and the railroad, funeral trains became a standard feature in the metropolitan landscape. Often, a funeral procession began on foot at the home of the deceased, continued on to a church, and then the entire party loaded onto a funeral train bound for a cemetery (fig. 6.9).

Virtually all outlying cemeteries developed along streetcar, interurban, or railroad lines

6.9 This 1915 funeral procession included pallbearers carrying the caskets of the deceased (siblings who were victims in the Eastland disaster) through the streets of Chicago's Southwest Side. By then, the funeral party often traveled by rail to an outlying cemetery. (Chicago Historical Society, DN-0064964)

after the 1850s. It was important that urban workers could make the trek to a cemetery for a funeral and later to visit gravesites. Over time, workers became familiar with neighborhoods and suburbs along the route to the cemeteries, widening their view of the region.

A funeral took industrial workers away from their neighborhoods and houses for most of a day. Taverns and restaurants developed adjacent to cemeteries and became welcome stops for food and drink, especially in the winter. For workers with limited time off, there was a practical logic to patronizing leisure parks and picnic groves adjacent to cemeteries that they wanted to visit on rare summer free days. At Justice, Hillside, and Evergreen Park, restaurants and taverns to serve mourners were joined by picnic groves, beer gardens, and dance halls by the end of the nineteenth century.

Cemeteries then had an odd, but understandable, relationship with outlying restaurants and picnic groves, whose owners could rely on a steady business from mourners. For instance, Henry J. Kolze acquired land in 1885 at what is now Irving Park and Narragansett in the Far Northwest Side neighborhood of Dunning. He built a hotel adjacent to Mount Olive Cemetery, which catered to mourners. Kolze then developed wooded acreage at Narragansett and Irving Park as a beer garden and picnic grove. Clubs, churches, and companies held picnics at the site well into the twentieth century.[14]

6.10 Home to at least five cemeteries, Forest Park (on the western boundary of Chicago) developed numerous restaurants and amusements. In 1908, the owner of a picnic grove west of Forest Park along the Des Plaines River developed an amusement park. The park featured a giant safety roller coaster, a fun house, beer garden, casino, swimming pool, and skating rink. Seen here is a 1915 photograph of a goat pulling a small cart with two girls at the park. (Chicago Historical Society, DN-0064698)

Among the hundreds of cemeteries established across Chicagoland in the second half of the nineteenth century, some were township cemeteries, serving a largely rural (and generally Protestant) population. But most were segregated by ethnicity and religion, and to a lesser degree by class. Some were private and Protestant—like Calvary, Rosehill, and Graceland cemeteries. Roman Catholics and Jews were neither welcome nor interested in burial in these cemeteries.[15]

Instead, Jews and Catholics (and often ethnic subgroups of each) purchased outlying land and developed cemeteries for their own members. While across the metropolitan area taverns and restaurants emerged to serve funerals, Chicagoans visited only those near the cemeteries they had developed. Sorting by ethnicity, religion, and class was already at work. Perhaps nowhere was this trend clearer than at Forest Park. West of Chicago, Forest Park has been home to five cemeteries since the 1870s: Jewish Waldheim Cemetery (1870), Concordia (German Lutheran, 1872), German Waldheim (German Jewish, 1873), Forest Home (Protestant, 1876), and Woodlawn (1912). Eventually, Chicagoans came to Forest Park not just to visit one of the cemeteries. An amusement park and racetrack also operated in the area by 1910 (figs. 6.10 and 6.11). The amusement park that operated there from 1907 to 1922 featured a giant safety roller coaster, a fun house, beer garden, casino, swimming pool, and skating rink.

6.11 Forest Park was also home to the Harlem Race Track. Seen here are the grandstands in 1901. (Chicago Historical Society SDN-00513)

Amusement Parks

While the World's Columbian Exposition was planned as an international event drawing millions of tourists from beyond Chicagoland, regional visitors were a vital part of the economic success of the 1893 fair. Chicagoland residents were encouraged to visit the fair multiple times. One of the favored marketing techniques for attracting a wide regional clientele was a series of special "ethnic days"—for the Irish, Poles, Germans, and African Americans—which mimicked the ethnic and religious sorting already taking place in regional picnic groves, cemeteries, and other amusement sites. Those regional residents used to socializing with others of their same ethnic group were encouraged to attend the fair on these days, but were not precluded from coming on other days.

In turn the 1893 World's Fair affected Chicagoland residents' views on summer fairs and activities. Experiencing the Midway, with new rides like the Ferris Wheel which were lit by electricity at night, exposed residents to new summer expectations. Within a few years, some of the older picnic groves began to invest in more improvements and became the first amusement parks in the region.

Perhaps most famous was Riverview, a picnic grove on the North Branch of the Chicago River at Belmont, which operated as an amusement park between 1904 and 1967 (figs. 6.12 and 6.13). Begun in 1879 as Sharpshooter's Park, the acreage was initially used by a group of Germans for a rifle range, as well as a picnic grove for the members' families. Over time, the club added a bandstand, dance pavilion, and food booths, and over the objections of some members, Riverview opened to the public as a beer garden. After 1904, the name was changed and rides and attractions added to what became one of Chicagoland's most famous amusement parks. Riverview Park, while open to the public, also sponsored various special days for religious, ethnic, and work groups, which continued to encourage a segregated use of this semipublic space.[16]

The interurban also led to the development of high culture summer venues. In 1904, investors in the Chicago, North Shore, and Milwaukee Electric Railway built a summer home for the Chicago Symphony Orchestra near Highland Park along Chicago's North Shore (fig. 6.14). Ravinia park had theater pavilions and the 1,000-seat Murray Theatre. Adjacent to the pavilion were playing fields and a picnic grove where liquor was strictly forbidden. The founders aimed at a middle-class suburban audience who could access the park by interurban, rail, trolley, or automobile.[17]

6.12 While workers could travel out from the city to visit amusement parks, there were parks and picnic groves much closer at hand. White City on the South Side and Riverview on the North Side were two of the largest amusement parks in Chicagoland in the first part of the twentieth century. Seen here are two young women on the "Pair-o-chutes" at Riverview Park in 1939. With the North Branch of the Chicago River in the background, encroaching urban development is apparent. (Chicago Historical Society, ICHi-20038)

6.13 This earlier, 1908 photograph shows Riverview's Merry Go Round, with visitors walking through the landscaped grounds. Also seen here are the lines of electric lights which illuminated the park at night. After the amusement park closed in 1967, it was demolished and replaced by an industrial park which included DeVry Institute. (Chicago Historical Society, ICHi-19797)

Very few of these private groves, beaches, and amusement parks survived into the second half of the twentieth century.[18] Some lost their attraction. While pollution declined along the Lake Michigan shoreline, it increased along the Des Plaines and Chicago rivers in the first decades of the twentieth century.[19] The pleasure of a picnic grove along the Des Plaines dropped dramatically. The pleasure was also reduced for many during Prohibition, when the inability to sell alcohol eliminated much of the profit from beer gardens and picnic groves. The automobile also made workers more mobile. They could travel farther and to places inaccessible by rail or streetcar.

Many of these areas became forest preserve property. Cook and DuPage counties had established the first forest preserve districts in the region by the late 1910s, buying some of their lands from the owners of picnic groves or amusements parks, particularly along the Des Plaines River. For instance, the Cook County Forest Preserve purchased the site of the Northwestern Park in Des Plaines. While the forest preserve district dismantled the casino and dance pavilion, it built and maintained picnic sites and trails. One observer noted, "On Sundays and holidays, hundreds of thousands of people swarm" to forest preserves.[20]

Sojourners: Summer Colonies and Camps

Regional retreats also developed devoted to sojourners who stayed for a season, a term, or a posting as cottagers, students, or soldiers. For instance, wealthy Chicagoans purchased large tracts of land for country estates. These affluent sojourners did not have to share their leisure space. By the early twentieth century, country estates could be found in every direction from downtown.

While many of these estates have subsequently been subdivided for other uses, a few remain largely intact: the Joy Morton family estate in Lisle today is the Morton Arboretum; the McCormick estates in western DuPage include the property that today is Cantigny park; and to the northwest in Libertyville, Samuel Insull built a retreat now known as the Cuneo Mansion. Wealthy families could afford to maintain multiple residences, which gave them a privileged, but nonetheless metropolitan, vantage point.

Less affluent but still privileged metropolitan residents who could afford to rent or purchase second homes supported cottage colonies across Chicagoland. Others flocked to hotels at outlying sites and commuter suburbs like Riverside or Norwood Park. Family-operated resorts developed along the west bank of the Fox River in McHenry County at the end of the nineteenth century. Run for profit, these resorts catered to middle-class families who could rent the cottages for varying periods of time. Businessmen could travel back and forth to the city during the week, or come out to stay with their families on weekends. Similar cottage resorts developed at Fox Lake and Antioch.

Middle-class and upper-middle-class families sometimes gathered to create summer colonies based on some common interest—perhaps religion, ethnicity, or pastime. Certainly this was the case with the Methodists who organized the Des Plaines Camp Grounds.[21]

To the southwest, wealthy Chicagoans built second homes in the 1890s at Palos Park. Sharing an interest in the arts, these colonists formed the Palos Improvement Clubhouse as an arts center. Into the early twentieth century, the community drew artists and performers, including Lorado Taft, Pearl Buck, and Sherwood Anderson. In the decades after World War II, this summer colony evolved into a residential suburb.

Sports drew people together as well. Sharpshooting clubs were organized by immigrant groups who purchased outlying sites for shooting ranges. The first golf clubs developed in much the same way, although they generally required a larger land purchase. The Glen View Country Club was established in 1897 at a distance from the Chicago, Mil-

6.14 A. C. Frost, the developer of Ravinia Park, was also the president of the Chicago, North Shore, and Milwaukee Railway. He created Ravinia Park to encourage leisure ridership on his electric line and also to introduce potential regular commuters to the suburbs in the area. Ravinia Park opened in 1904, as the first patrons of outdoor classical music performances passed through this gate just beyond the railroad tracks. (Leslie Schwartz)

6.15 The Homewood Country Club was one of several golf clubs located near the Flossmoor Station of the Illinois Central Railroad. Seen here are women golfers and caddies on the grounds of the Homewood Country Club in 1905. In the left background is a part of the frame clubhouse, which has since been replaced. Over time, these golf clubs built more and more elaborate clubhouses, better reflecting the affluence of their members. (Chicago Historical Society, DN-003638)

waukee and St. Paul Railroad about fourteen miles northwest of the Loop. At first trekking out on summer weekends to a flag stop, golfers eventually got a regular rail station, and the suburban settlement aptly called Golf developed. Unlike the sharpshooters, many of these golfers held professional or management positions in downtown Chicago and could link their leisure world with their daily life through a suburban enclave.

Along the Illinois Central Railroad twenty-four miles south of downtown, a group of investors established the Flossmoor Country Club in 1898. Initially, its golf course was ringed by tents and cottages which members constructed for their weekend use. The success of this club led to the establishment of other country clubs in the same area. In 1901, the Illinois Central Railroad subdivided property near the rail station adjacent to the golf course. They offered special services for golfers, and residential construction began in earnest in the 1910s (fig. 6.15). A summer cottage community was on its way to becoming a commuter suburb.[22] By 1900, twenty-six golf clubs had organized in Chicagoland. These golf clubs drew an affluent group who could afford the purchase and upkeep of summer houses and country club dues. Selective club membership meant that only those with the means and the proper credentials were able to participate. The selectivity of golf club membership rested not only on wealth, but also on ethnicity, race, and religion. Discrimination against Jews, Catholics, and later African Americans was a standard part of country club life.

In response to this kind of discrimination, a group of wealthy German Jews developed a summer retreat in 1901 along Lake Michigan in Highland Park. Among the organizers of the retreat was Julius Rosenwald, president of Sears, Roebuck & Company and a leading regional philanthropist. The retreat, known as Wildwood, initially consisted of summer cottages for families who lived closer to downtown. Wildwood cottagers established a golf course (now the Lake Shore Country Club) nearby and as the twentieth century unfolded, the summer cottages became year-round houses.[23]

The experience of Wildwood summer sojourners was both typical and atypical of that of many wealthy Chicagoland residents. A selective group, organized around shared ethnicity, religion, and leisure interests, founded a summer colony. Like many other summer colonies, Wildwood eventually became part of a permanent commuter suburb. However, this group organized in the face of overt religious discrimination.

Outlying Private Institutions

Alongside these recreational sites were a number of outlying places which emerged around public and private institutions. Like recreational sites, they revolved around visitors, not permanent residents. They included private camps, colleges, orphanages, and hospitals. Many were sited at a distance from downtown Chicago in order to take advantage of lower real estate costs.

6.16 Camps for children, particularly poor children from inner-city neighborhoods, were located across Chicagoland by the early twentieth century. Most were founded by specific ethnic and religious groups. In this July 1916 image, children run toward a camera at the Salvation Army Camp in west suburban Glen Ellyn. (Chicago Historical Society, DN-0066686)

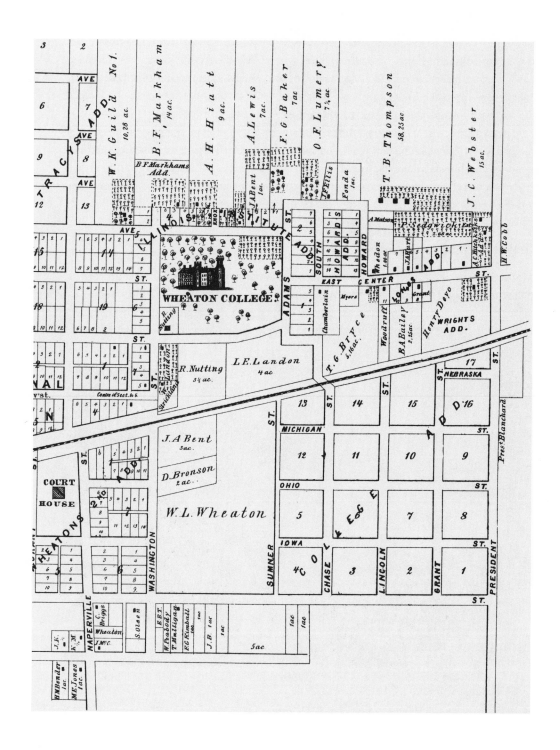

Ethnic and religious groups built camps and orphanages out beyond the built-up area in Chicago (fig. 6.16). Most members of the group needed only occasional access to these places, so organizations readily took advantage of less expensive land in outlying parts of the metropolitan area.

For instance, in the first decades of the twentieth century, Bohemians in Chicago supported the creation of the St. Joseph's Orphanage in Lisle, far from the industrial neighborhoods from which many of the children came. In Addison, Evangelical Lutherans (German) established an orphanage in 1874 for children of their denomination across the region. Along a new rail line northwest out from Chicago in DuPage County, the orphanage joined a seminary that the denomination members had recently constructed.

Institutions were also established for the ben- efit of elderly members of ethnic and religious groups, as well as by county governments. The establishment of the Scottish Home by the Illinois St. Andrew Society in the 1910s near the Des Plaines River drew retired men and women who had the leisure to enjoy the wooded setting with other Scottish and Presbyterian people.

Religious denominations founded colleges at Wheaton, Evanston, Hyde Park, Lisle, Elmhurst, Naperville, and Lake Forest along regional rail lines. These religious groups sought affordable but accessible land and often deliberately sought a location beyond the immediate temptations of the city center. The colleges spurred residential development, as well as some additional retail businesses.

Twenty-five miles due west of downtown Chicago, Wheaton was platted in 1853, just a few years after the first rail line ran through this area. Jesse and Warren L. Wheaton not only platted a town, they supported the establishment of the Illinois Institute under the supervision of Wesleyan Methodists. Blanchard Hall, later to be the central building of Wheaton College, opened that year. Blanchard Hall was built of a cream limestone mined at Batavia and hauled to the site. Illinois Institute became Wheaton College in the 1860s, and drew students, faculty, and visitors to the town (fig. 6.17).[24]

Over the course of the nineteenth century, these colleges provided jobs and a steady stream of sojourners in their towns. Local boosters sought out colleges as stable economic and cultural influences. Today, college grounds like those at Wheaton provide open spaces, generally carefully landscaped, which remain a sought-after backdrop to suburban living despite town-gown fights over parking, congestion, and student life.

Public Institutions

While many of the key governmental offices in the region were in downtown Chicago, there were a range of public institutions with outlying locations from the 1830s. County seats provided a governmental presence in outlying areas. The initial courthouses for Cook, Lake,

6.17 (opposite) Wheaton College was a central part of the early town of Wheaton. Blanchard Hall, built of the same limestone as University Hall in Evanston, served as the defining physical feature of the college and is seen here as the only building drawn on this 1874 map. (*1874 Atlas of DuPage County*)

and DuPage counties were relatively modest Greek Revival structures. All were replaced by larger stone buildings by 1860. The courthouses were designed by some of the region's first architects and were among the most costly early buildings. Settlements vied for the status of county seat. While Chicago confidently held the seat for Cook County from its creation, Naperville lost out to Wheaton as county seat of DuPage in the early 1860s. When McHenry County was carved out of Lake County in 1844, new and existing settlements competed for the status of the county seat. Alvin Judd successfully lobbied for a new site at the center point of the reshaped McHenry County, directly west along an established road from the old county seat at Waukegan. He also offered two acres to the county, beating out the bids of the established towns of McHenry and Crystal Lake.

Alvin Judd laid out Woodstock, the new site, around a public square. While public squares were common in the Midwest and South, they were an unusual form in the Chicago metropolitan area, where a crossroads or rail station more frequently served as the focal point for community development. The town has cultivated a historic look, with its carefully landscape square, the historic opera house, small restaurants, antique shops, and other specialty stores.[25]

The old McHenry County Courthouse dominates the west side of Woodstock's town square (fig. 6.18). A large, two-and-a-half-story red brick building with a white cupola, its raised first floor is accessible to the street from a substantial limestone staircase. Adjoining the courthouse is a limestone building that housed the county jail. Across the street, a hotel housed overnight visitors who were not incarcerated.[26]

Completed in 1857, the courthouse was designed by John Mills Van Osdel, who had built the Cook County Courthouse in Chicago in 1853 (fig. 6.19). The McHenry County Courthouse was very similar.[27] Cook County politicians were probably pleased when the addition of a fourth floor and larger cupola in 1858 made the Cook County Courthouse demonstrably bigger.

The courthouse was the center of Woodstock's earliest development. Farmers and businessmen from across the new county traveled there for county business, and in turn, county government provided jobs and growth. The same was true for the other county seats in Chicagoland. In and around the courthouse, much of the public life of these rural counties took

6.18 The old McHenry County Courthouse, 101 N. Johnson Street, dominates the west side of Woodstock's town square (the Woodstock Opera House stands to the south). Built in 1857 from a design by John M. Van Osdel, the building remained the county courthouse until 1972, when a new facility was built on the outskirts of Woodstock. The building was purchased by a local family in an effort to preserve it and has housed a variety of offices and meeting spaces, including a Dick Tracy museum. (Leslie Schwartz)

place, including campaign speeches, Fourth of July celebrations, and patriotic parades. Beyond county seats, public institutions devoted to keeping certain residents away from a general population (due to, among other things, a fear of contagious disease or violent behavior) were established (figs. 6.20 and 6.21). For instance, county and state governments located public hospitals at Elgin, Hinsdale, Oak Forest, and what is now the Chicago neighborhood of Dunning, locations that afforded easy transportation across the region. Similarly, the state prison at Joliet was sited at a distance from other towns but not too far from the city center.

One or more substantial structures served these institutions, with surrounding grounds. Some included their own farms, with inmates doing fieldwork. Family members and friends generally had limited access to the sites. Visitors arrived on Sundays and holidays, after sometimes lengthy treks across the metropolitan area. These institutions provided employment for some local residents, and area businesses catered to visitors. Because of this, many communities sought these institutions, despite their dangers.

Military installations were also a governmental presence in Chicagoland by 1900. There

6.19 In 1853, Chicago built a combination courthouse and city hall adjacent to its public square. John M. Van Osdel largely repeated the three-story design four years later in Woodstock. As in Woodstock, the building fronted the public square, visible in this July 4, 1855, image (from a daguerreotype by Alexander Hesler). The building was enlarged in 1858 and destroyed in the 1871 Fire. The Civic Center now stands on this site in downtown Chicago. (Chicago Historical Society, ICHi-00430)

6.20 The Cook County Infirmary and Insane Asylum, later renamed the Chicago State Hospital, was built just north of Irving Park Road at Narragansett Avenue on Chicago's Far Northwest Side beginning in 1868, initially to house both the physically and mentally ill. Seen here are several buildings in the facility in 1908. In the 1970s, the facility was renamed the Chicago-Read Mental Health Center. It was closed and redeveloped over the course of the 1990s. (Chicago Historical Society, DN-0053716)

was no active military stationed in the Chicago region between the end of the Civil War and the establishment of Fort Sheridan in 1887, after the labor unrest of the 1877 railroad strike and the 1886 Haymarket affair. Fearing more worker protests, a number of prominent Chicago businesses donated land along Lake Michigan to the federal government for a military post adjacent to the town of Highwood (fig. 6.22). Working through the Commercial Club of Chicago, these businessmen wanted contingents of the army closer at hand should labor unrest recur.[28]

Built over almost a decade beginning in 1887, the army base housed thousands of soldiers and their families by 1900 (figs. 6.23 and 6.24). A local reporter described the scene in 1908, noting that the installation was "not built in the usual stereotyped barrack style. The stiff rectangular form of structure, the uncouth quadrangles flanked by mess halls on all sides with the brick barrack grounds and the four even pavements and the general dismal prison atmosphere has been completely blotted out at Fort Sheridan. It rises on sloping hills . . . with forest trees that slope to the lake front."[29]

The village outside the military installation, Highwood (known for a time as Fort Sheridan Village), grew in response to the soldiers and their families, developing saloons and a variety of local merchants. Highwood's permanent population catered to the ebb and flow of troops. It developed as a suburban town used to strangers, a town whose economy rested on the monies they spent.

The Legacy of the Institutional and Recreational Landscape

All of the institutional and recreational sites in this chapter share common landscape features: an institution or natural amenity that drew people, ready transportation, accommodation (restaurants, hotels, and shops), and residential space for service workers which included housing and other basic businesses and institutions. Yet they were also a heterogeneous mix of public and private, permanent and temporary.

The economies of most of these places rested on business generated by visitors. Students spent money in college towns, soldiers at towns near military installations, and those with local government business in county seats. All of these institutions variably affected the development of the towns in which they were located. Large houses were more prevalent around college campuses where students sought room and board. Saloons and restaurants were common in towns with military installations as well as near cemeteries, but were prohibited in many towns with religious schools and colleges.

Taken together, the histories of these locations show the crucial role of ethnicity and religion. But class was also of great importance. Some of these sites required substantial personal or group investments and so were able to easily exclude most Chicagoans. But other

6.21 Seen here are the substantial grounds around the Chicago State Hospital. Visitors also came to the eight nearby cemeteries, and the restaurants, taverns, and picnic groves that emerged near their entrances. (Chicago Historical Society, DN-0006807)

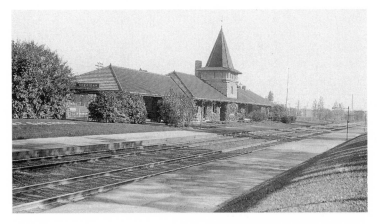

6.22 Ready access to Fort Sheridan from this station of the Chicago and North Western Railway was vital to the success of the military operation. Seen here is the Fort Sheridan Station in 1910. (Chicago Historical Society, DN-0008738)

sites developed to cater to Chicagoans of all classes, providing low-cost leisure alternatives.

Leisure and institutional activities drew Chicagoans out from their neighborhoods and suburbs. The wexlthiest Chicagoans could afford separate town and country homes, often physically separating work and leisure environments. The upper-middle classes who lived in railroad suburbs sited their homes near leisure sites, and developed country clubs near these homes.

Working-class residents of Chicagoland lived close to places of employment well into the twentieth century. Their daily lives were largely bounded by the neighborhoods which they created near job opportunities. It was leisure activities which drew working-class residents of Chicagoland out from their neighborhoods and suburbs.

These sites were a metropolitan frontier because they were the greatest distances which Chicagoland residents claimed as their own during the railroad era. They provided the outlines of future development. These institutional and recreational towns were pulled more tightly into the metropolitan fabric in the twentieth century, as the automobile and economic change shifted patterns of residence, work, and commutation.

Regional residents who had visited outlying private parks and groves provided a ready base of support for the wide band of forest preserves developed after 1920 in Cook and Du-

6.23 Holabird & Roche designed many of the buildings at Fort Sheridan, while Ossian Simonds designed the landscape. The plan included a large building which contained infantry barracks and a large water tower fronted on a parade ground. The water tower was placed on the National Register of Historic Places in 1974. The officers' quarters were large houses along loop roads on bluffs overlooking Lake Michigan. (Leslie Schwartz)

6.24 Part of Fort Sheridan was designated a National Historic Landmark District in 1984. The U.S. Army base ceased operations in 1993. While the military maintained control of more than 400 acres, an additional 415 acres was sold as surplus property. Over two hundred acres went to the Lake County Forest Preserve, with the rest of the acreage redeveloped as a luxury residential community. The barracks, stables, and officers' quarters have all been renovated for luxury residential units. (Leslie Schwartz)

Page counties. Sunday and holiday trips helped foster a regional vision which understood the value of public preserves even if they were at some distance from residential neighborhoods and suburbs.

Other places that began as leisure sites, attracting workers from across the metropolitan area, have now developed as residential or commercial centers. The trips of workers to these leisure sites during the nineteenth century opened their horizons beyond their neighborhoods to the wider region. In the second half of the twentieth century, many large industrial sites closed their doors. Workers joined their middle-class counterparts as commuters, first using mass transportation and then increasingly private automobiles to get to jobs which were now at some distance from their homes. While some workers remained in the older industrial neighborhoods, others moved to outlying subdivisions—sometimes near the picnic groves, camps, and cemeteries to which they had traveled as children in the first part of the twentieth century.

In this way, recreational and institutional sites served as a frontier for metropolitan development. Too far a distance from downtown for immediate intensive development, individuals and institutions invested in future development. They took advantage of excellent transportation to found outlying institutions and recreational sites which would be developed more intensively over time.

Regionalism through Neighbors and over Time

Regionalism emanates in part from the shared characteristics of communities with similar origins. Farm centers, industrial towns, commuter suburbs, and recreational/institutional centers: residents of each of these types of communities shared experiences, even if they remained blissfully unaware that their worlds represented aspects of a regional pattern. To sum up these patterns is to establish a rather simple regional analysis, which can be extended by exploring the competition for residents and resources among similar communities.

Regionalism also dwells in the relationships between places, particularly in the dense weave of interactions between neighboring communities. Because all settlements in Chicagoland have boundaries and neighbors, a regional view provides an opportunity to knit together both similar and different experiences across local areas into a wider history.

Together these component parts and relationships constituted a sustainable, functioning region into the twentieth century. While local histories provide the information needed to build this regional story, people did not lead narrowly local lives—their experiences were seldom bound within a single locality. Regionalism allows us to see patterns and interrelationships beyond a single locality, patterns and interrelationships which were central to the nineteenth-century metropolitan area.

Neighbors in a Region

Industrial towns, commuter suburbs, and farm centers located along rail lines across the metropolitan area. Different kinds of settlements, then, often abutted one another. The diversity of the metropolitan region is visible in almost any group of adjoining suburbs or

7.1 The earliest farm centers were located at crossroads, while later ones evolved around train stops. To the north of Chicago, a farm center named Gross Point emerged at the crossroads of Ridge Avenue, Wilmette Avenue, and Gross Point Road in the 1840s. This early twentieth-century postcard shows eight images along Ridge Avenue, including the local church, town hall, businesses, and houses. (Wilmette Historical Society)

neighborhoods. The history of interactions between neighbors is as important to understanding region as identifying common landscapes.

Sometimes these interactions have been positive, but at other times sharp disagreements highlighted the very different backgrounds, needs, and goals of people who have called this region their own. Neighboring settlements with competing visions of land use, development, and appropriate public behavior led to (and continue to lead to) compromise and conflict. Because so much of the history about the Chicago region draws on the stories of individual neighborhoods or suburbs, these interactions are often lost or viewed from a one-sided perspective.

The density of these neighborly relationships is key. A metropolitan area can be defined as a region composed of settlements which must compete with three, four, or more neighbors who have different agendas and roles in the region. An industrial town, an agricultural center, or a vacation spot could easily be located beyond a metropolitan area, where open space and farmland are the only neighbors. However, within an metropolitan area these types of settlements are influenced and changed by neighbors as well as regional development.

While it is difficult to contemplate the myriad connection possibilities within the Chicago metropolitan region, we can get a sense of the density of these connections through a close examination of small sections of the region. Two communities offer particularly striking examples of this manifestation of region: Riverside and Gross Point. Riverside was a quintessential railroad commuter suburb, and Gross Point a farm center.

Gross Point and Its Neighbors

Gross Point was one of dozens of crossroads farm centers that developed in nineteenth-century Chicagoland, located about fourteen miles north of downtown Chicago and a mile inland from Lake Michigan (fig. 7.1). German Catholics farmed area plots, came together to found a church and cemetery, and frequented the stores and services offered in a business district along Ridge Road (fig. 7.2).

Today, Ridge Road is still lined with two-story structures containing stores and offices on the first floor and apartments on the second floor. Most of these buildings date from the last two decades of the nineteenth century and the first decade of the twentieth century. The oldest commercial structure still standing is at 801 Ridge Road (fig. 7.3). Constructed around 1870, the building initially was a hotel and tavern run by John Schaefer. Taverns continued to operate here until Prohibition in the 1920s (figs. 7.4 and 7.5).

As many as fourteen other taverns operated in just a few blocks of Ridge Road at the turn of the nineteenth century. A feed store, several groceries and general stores, a meat market, a shoe and clothing store, and a blacksmith shop also provided needed services to area farmers.[1] Residents of Gross Point organized the community as a village in 1874. Revenue for village services came in large part from licenses and taxes on area taverns.[2] In 1896, the village erected a substantial hall, which included a large meeting room as well as office space.

To this point, Gross Point's story is typical of other farm centers across the metropolitan area, and indeed across the Midwest. However, the large size and grandeur of the village hall are not readily explicable from this short history. Built with income from tavern licenses,

7.2 (left) Gross Point served a largely German Catholic area. Area farmers built St. Joseph's Roman Catholic Church in the 1840s, seen here in a 1909 photograph. Most farmers lived at some distance from the settlement at Gross Point, but supported its institutions and businesses. (Chicago Historical Society, DN-0054492)

7.3 (right) As well as supporting a church, farmers in and around Gross Point supported a number of businesses, including taverns. John Schaefer's tavern was among them, built around 1870. Seen here in 1909 at 801 Ridge in Wilmette (Chicago Historical Society, DN-0054490)

7.4 (left) The old Gross Point taverns have become antique stores and decorating boutiques in west Wilmette. Seen here is Brandt Interiors, originally John Schaefer's tavern. (John J. Keating)

7.5 (right) Interior of a Gross Point tavern, undated (Wilmette Historical Society)

the village hall points to questions concerning the substantial revenue stream which these tavern licenses seem to have generated. More bluntly, was it only Gross Point residents supporting the more than fourteen taverns on a short strip of Ridge Avenue? Or is Gross Point's history dependent on actors outside its boundaries?

In fact, Gross Point's eastern neighbors developed quite differently and challenged it in a number of ways as they developed collectively.[3] The eight suburbs along Lake Michigan running north between Evanston and Lake Bluff have come to be known collectively as the North Shore. All of the North Shore communities were railroad commuter suburbs, attracting affluent families who wanted to escape city living (fig. 7.6).

Kenilworth is perhaps the most exclusive of this affluent network. Descriptions of the area by the town's initial developer and early resident Joseph Sears emphasize the natural beauty of the site, set along the Lake Michigan shoreline.[4] Nestled between two existing North Shore towns, Wilmette and Winnetka, the site seemed ideal for a wealthy retreat. Sears laid out winding streets and large lots, sponsored the establishment of local government, and supported measures such as temperance within the village.

A drive through the streets of Kenilworth today shows the success of much of Sears's dream for an exclusive enclave. Large houses stand gracefully on sprawling, landscaped lots, winding back and forth along the lakeshore. The wide, curved streets at the southwest corner of Kenilworth end at Ridge Road and the farming settlement of Gross Point. The remaining storefronts and homes along Ridge Road are typical of farming communities, but contrast today with Kenilworth's large homes and lots (fig. 7.7).

Some residents of Wilmette, Evanston, and Kenilworth—which had outlawed the sale

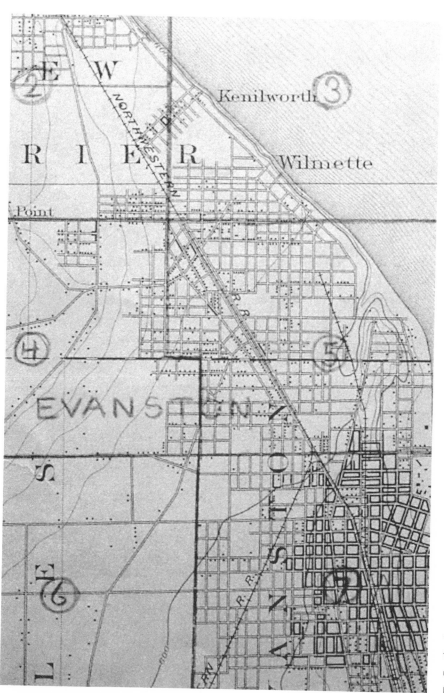

7.6 As with other settlements in the region, Gross Point had to negotiate with its neighbors. This 1897 topographical map from the U.S. Department of the Interior (the Evanston Quadrangle) shows that Gross Point's neighbors included the North Shore commuter rail suburbs of Kenilworth, Wilmette, and Evanston. (Joseph C. Bigott)

7.7 While nearby Gross Point catered to the needs of area farmers, just blocks away, gardening, not farming, predominated. Kenilworth residents worked in their yards, developing gardens filled with flowers (and sometimes vegetables). Here a village resident uses a hoe in the yard of her Kenilworth home in 1917. (Chicago Historical Society, DN-0067895)

of liquor within their boundaries—railed against the Gross Point taverns as a threat to their suburban enclaves. While these North Shore residents were concerned about the behavior of Gross Point residents, they were also concerned about North Shore residents who frequented these nearby taverns.[5]

The situation on the North Shore was further complicated by Northwestern University's original state charter. Just a few miles southeast of Gross Point, both Evanston and Northwestern University were founded by Methodists with a staunch temperance outlook (fig. 7.8). As part of the university's 1853 charter, the State of Illinois granted the institution a four-mile radius from its geographic center in Evanston where liquor would be prohibited. This limit extended well beyond the boundaries of Evanston to include what became the communities of Wilmette, Kenilworth, Rogers Park (now a neighborhood in the City of Chicago), and Gross Point.

The four-mile limit sometimes served as a rallying point for temperance-minded residents from Evanston. In the 1870s, Evanston minister Dr. M. C. Briggs began a crusade against the Gross Point taverns that were inside Northwestern University's four-mile limit.

An 1896 account described him as "a man of very positive convictions and a born fighter." Briggs was perhaps concerned about the behavior of Gross Point residents, but he was most clearly concerned with the behavior of Evanston residents, in particular Garrett Biblical Institute students who frequented the Gross Point establishments. Briggs understood that the North Shore communities did not operate in a vacuum.[6]

While enforcement of the four-mile limit was never very successful, after 1919 national prohibition led quickly to the closure of Gross Point saloons and the dissolution of the Village of Gross Point. With the dividing issue of temperance resolved, Wilmette annexed Gross Point in 1924. Appropriately, or perhaps ironically, the Gross Point Village Hall now serves as the home of the Wilmette Historical Society (fig. 7.9). Also ironic is the fact that while the one community in this group that allowed taverns lost its independent identity, the strongest temperance advocate, Evanston, is no longer a dry town.[7]

And yet, relations between Gross Point and its North Shore neighbors were not always contentious. In May 1912, the *Evanston News* changed its name to the *Lake Shore News*. Under the newspaper name ran a subhead "EVANSTON—WILMETTE—KENILWORTH—WINNETKA—GLENCOE." In the following issues, columns headed "What People Are Doing in Kenilworth" or "What People Are Doing in Evanston" carried local news for each of these communities. While Gross Point is not mentioned at all in editorial notes or on the banner, it too had a column about "What People Are Doing in Gross Point." The June 20, 1912, issue included notes on the visits of Gross Point residents to Evanston and the lakeshore.[8]

The opening of New Trier High School in 1901 highlighted both the differences among the five incorporated communities in New Trier Township and their ultimate need to work together. While residents of Glencoe, Winnetka, Wilmette, and Kenilworth supported the creation of a high school, Gross Point residents fought the ultimate eastern location for the school. But working together to create this public institution changed each of these communities. While it was unlikely that Gross Point would have supported a high school at the level demanded by their more affluent neighbors, once it was constructed, Gross Point teenagers had access to the same education as their neighbors on the North Shore (fig. 7.10). Their access to high school was shaped by their neighbors.[9]

Both New Trier High School and the Gross Point Village Hall stand as monuments of suburban cooperation. Neither could have been built by Gross Point without interactions with very different neighbors found only in a metropolitan region like Chicagoland. Communities like Gross Point dot the Midwest, but its distinctive features—imposing village hall and

7.8 Methodists founded Northwestern University at Evanston in 1854, seven years after the foundation of St. Joseph Roman Catholic Church a few miles to the northwest in Gross Point. Seen here is University Hall, built in 1869 of area limestone and still in use. Under its charter, Northwestern outlawed the sale of liquor within four miles of University Hall, which included the already thriving taverns at Gross Point. (Ann Keating)

access to one of the very best public high schools in the country—come from its regional neighbors.

Riverside and Its Neighbors

Riverside and its neighbors provide another example of the kinds of interactions that shape local community histories as well as the wider metropolitan history. Riverside is one of the most famous commuter suburbs in the metropolitan area, located about ten miles west of the Loop. Designed by Frederick Law Olmsted and Calvert Vaux, Riverside has been studied by urbanists and landscape architects since they devised their 1868 plan for curvilinear streets, large lots, and a 160-acre reserve along the Des Plaines River.[10]

7.9 In response to the temperance crusades of their neighbors, Gross Point residents organized the community as a village in 1874. The imposing village hall, built in 1896, stands near the south end of the business district at 609 Ridge Road. Ironically, Gross Point was annexed to Wilmette after national prohibition, and this building now serves as the Wilmette Historical Society. (John J. Keating)

In promotional material for the Riverside Improvement Company, in Olmsted's written descriptions and in the later work of scholars, Riverside is described as a retreat from urban life: "For years it was somewhat remote from Chicago, a village of winding roads and lovely parks inhabited by a small number of well-to-do residents of old stock."[11] But by the early twentieth century Riverside was surrounded by suburban neighbors as well as the winding Des Plaines River (fig. 7.11).

Riverside residents were very aware of their neighbors. The *Riverside News* was a regional paper that covered many communities besides Riverside, including Lyons, Brookfield, Summit, Clearing, LaGrange, Berwyn, Willow Springs, and Argo. In many issues in the early 1910s, whole columns were devoted to local news of each of these towns. In general, the news included Chicago visits and visitors, illnesses and births, deaths and marriages. Riverside was one of a group of neighboring suburban communities, not an isolated retreat.

Riverside's putative isolation was belied by its location only a few miles north of the Illinois and Michigan Canal Corridor, which later included a railroad and the Sanitary and Ship Canal along one of the region's key industrial corridors. The Argo Corn Starch Company anchored a new industrial town, known today as Summit, south of Riverside after 1910. The area drew other employers as well as hundreds of resident workers by World War I. To the east, Berwyn developed slowly in the late nineteenth century. Swedish railroad workers in the 1860s and 1870s squatted on land owned by the railroad in an area known derisively as "Upsala."[12] After Western Electric developed Hawthorne Works a few miles to the east in Cicero, Berwyn quickly developed as an area of solid worker housing. The straight streets and unusual, flat-roofed one-story houses contrasted with the curvilinear streets and architect-designed houses of Riverside.[13]

Directly to the west of Riverside, Samuel E. Gross subdivided a new railroad suburb in 1889. Initially known as Grossdale, the area competed directly with Riverside for residents, but offered generally smaller lots and more modest improvements. The eastern portion of Grossdale, later Brookfield, even included curvilinear streets like Riverside, although they were narrower and created less park space.[14]

North of Riverside, leisure activities dominated development along the Des Plaines River (fig. 7.12). In the eastern part of the village, David A. Gage, city treasurer of Chicago, purchased around 1,600 acres in the 1860s to be used as a country estate. Gage, like other wealthy Chicagoans, could afford to have two homes— one in the city and another in the countryside.

7.10 New Trier Township High School, designed by Norman S. Patton of the Chicago firm Patton & Fisher, opened in 1901 on the border between Kenilworth and Winnetka. The high school served all of the communities in New Trier Township, which included Gross Point, Glencoe, Kenilworth, Wilmette, and Winnetka. Only Gross Point, though, was not a North Shore commuter suburb along the Chicago and North Western Railway. (Wilmette Historical Society)

Sometime before 1900, a colony of summer cottages belonging to Chicago businessmen constituted the Riverside Holiness Association. The cottages, built between Des Plaines Avenue and the river, abutted onion farms, forming a community that contrasted both to the rural retreat to the east and the year-round parklike setting in Riverside to the south. The Optimates Canoe Club drew people with an interest in boating on the Des Plaines together. The Melody Mill Ballroom drew Chicagoans from across the metropolitan area for big band concerts.[15] Two retirement facilities, the Scottish Home and the British Home, provided communal accommodations along the Des Plaines River to the north of Riverside.

Riverside's oldest neighbor, Lyons, was to the south, at the confluence of the Des Plaines River and Salt Creek, and was a crossroads for four major highways: Harlem Avenue, Joliet Road, Ogden Avenue, and Archer Avenue. By the 1870s picnic groves dotted the area, as immigrants and working-class Chicagoans took advantage of the river views at prices they could afford. These picnic groves thrived on the trade of Chicagoans journeying out to Lyons on a Sunday or holiday. Hauser's was one such picnic grove—known especially for its clam chowder. Lyons picnics became known as "skillies," famous for both food and drink.

In 1907, the amusement park called Cream City opened in Lyons south of the river off Ogden Avenue (fig. 7.13). The following year local brewer George Hoffman built a dam on the river and a tower adjacent to the dam. Here he developed a picnic grove and amusement park which included boat rides on the Des Plaines River (figs. 7.14 and 7.15). The arrival

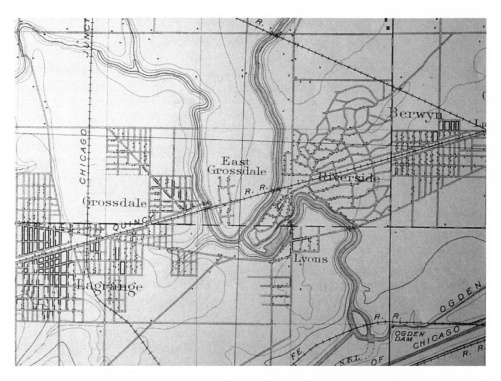

7.11 The distinctive plan of Riverside, including curvilinear streets, is clearly visible in this portion of the 1901 edition of the Riverside Quadrangle of the topography map published by the U.S. Department of the Interior. The plat is familiar to urbanists, but Riverside's neighbors probably are not, including Berwyn, with its Hawthorne Works worker housing to the east; Brookfield (Grossdale), with its smaller lots to the west; and the crossroads town of Lyons to the south. (Joseph C. Bigott)

of the interurban in 1914 made for easy travel for Chicagoans out to Cream City and other amusement parks.[16]

Only the Des Plaines River separated Riverside's residents from the bustle of Lyons' amusements. While Olmsted and Vaux may have sought to design a retreat that insulated Riverside residents from urban life, on any summer Sunday the noise and crowds across the river regularly disturbed the elite enclave.

One would expect a certain amount of antipathy between these neighbors. The Des Plaines River became something of a battleground between Riverside and Lyons residents, as well as outsiders. Riverside residents used the river to launch their own boats and as a backdrop for their homes and gardens. Lyons residents too took advantage of the river for their own recreation, but they also used the river for profit. The picnic groves, beer gardens, and boat concessions that operated on the Lyons side of the Des Plaines attracted residents from across the metropolitan area. While Riverside residents could do little about activities in Lyons and could not keep nonresidents away completely, they did seek to regulate businesses and events within their town and to maintain control of the village's public spaces. For instance, the village board of Riverside outlawed boat concessions from public property within Riverside in the early summer of 1912. The village acted after a petition from local

property holders, who stated "that the river was a mecca for all classes of Chicago folks, both desirable and undesirable." Local residents were also concerned about pickpockets and noted that the extension of the electric streetcars from Chicago to Riverside in 1910 had resulted in these new problems.[17]

The bridge connecting Lyons and Riverside over the Des Plaines River would seem an obvious point of friction between the two communities. Both villages were responsible for upkeep of the bridge, which became impassable in late 1912. While Riverside residents who wanted an elite enclave might have been willing to watch the connection to Lyons taverns and picnic groves erode away, this did not happen. Instead, residents of both villages worked to rebuild the bridge and eagerly anticipated its completion in October 1913 (fig. 7.16). A local account noted that the area had "scenery which is not equaled anywhere around Chicago," and the bridge would bring more tourists to the area.[18]

The Riverside Brookfield High School stands as another symbol of the close connection between Riverside and another of its neighbors. Brookfield, like Riverside, was a commuter suburb, but composed of more modest homes and lots west across the Des Plaines River. In 1909, a high school district was created by the residents of Riverside and Brookfield. While classes were initially held in the Riverside Village Hall, the communities built the current high school in 1918 in Brookfield. Cooperation between neighbors made the high school possible.[19]

These stories of interaction are often lost because local history focuses tightly on one community. While interactions—both positive and negative—between adjoining communities along the Des Plaines or the North Shore were frequent in the years before the first

7.12 Canoes and rowboats dotted the Des Plaines River on summer days. This is a 1908 image of boating on the Des Plaines River north of Riverside at Forest Park. Boat concessions on both the Riverside and Lyons banks of the Des Plaines River offered rentals to local residents and metropolitan visitors. (Chicago Historical Society, DN-0006816)

7.13 From the 1870s, Lyons was home to picnic groves, taverns, and other entertainments. By the early twentieth century, the Cream City Amusement Park was among the largest enterprises in the town (seen here in 1908). The park closed and was sold to the Cook County Forest Preserve District in the 1920s. (Chicago Historical Society, DN-0006805)

7.14 Directly across the river from Riverside, Lyons businessman George Hoffman ran his family's brewery and picnic grove along the scenic river which had also drawn Riverside residents. He built a tower to attract customers (seen here under construction in 1908). While Olmsted and Vaux may have sought to design a retreat which insulated Riverside residents from urban life, on any summer Sunday the noise and crowds across the river regularly disturbed the elite enclave. (Chicago Historical Society, DN-0006804)

World War, they have not become a part of our historical memory. But these interactions are repeated over and over again across the metropolitan area and over time. No community operated in a vacuum, despite the insular way in which most local history is presented.

More generally, a close look at virtually any area within Chicagoland would produce tales of interactions, conflicts, and cooperation. Temperance, zoning, incorporation, and annexation have all been employed as a response to interactions between groups. We cannot tell these local stories in isolation—they are grandly interrelated. This is the essence of a metropolitan area—a region where layers upon layers of relationships between individuals, institutions, businesses, and communities have been shaped and reshaped by larger social, economic, political, and cultural forces.

Differential Development: Naperville and Douglas

Although many suburbs and neighborhoods began in the second half of the nineteenth century as farm centers, industrial towns, institutional/recreational centers, or commuter suburbs, most changed differentially in the face of wider economic, social, and political forces. Some communities had more resources and advantages with which to respond, while others had distinct disadvantages. Neighbors mattered: relationships with neighboring communities often muted or heightened wider regional trends, leading to differential growth and development.

The region was not a level playing field: location in the region, access to transportation, neighbors, and natural resources all affected the ways a community would grow and change. In addition, some communities had more (or fewer) options because of the class (and/or race) of residents or their neighbors.

We can see this differential development by comparing virtually any two settlements in Chicagoland.

7.15 The Hoffman Tower still stands today, decades after the picnic grove closed down at 3910 Barry Point Road. Now operated as the Hoffman Tower Museum by the Lyons Historic District, the tower houses exhibits on the history of Lyons. (Joseph C. Bigott)

7.16 While Riverside and Lyons residents disagreed on many issues both communities supported the construction and maintenance of a bridge linking their communities (seen here in 1908). They were metropolitan neighbors, very different, but inevitably shaped by each other. (Chicago Historical Society, DN-0006795)

Consider two places which stand in sharp relief in the metropolitan area today, but whose nineteenth-century origins and early history warrant comparison: Naperville and Douglas. Naperville and Douglas are each actually a group of neighborhoods or development efforts which are bound together: in Naperville by being part of the same city, and in Douglas by having a semiofficial designation as a community area since the 1920s.

Naperville today is a city of more than 128,000 residents about twenty-eight miles directly west of downtown Chicago along Interstate 88. It is a predominantly white, upper-middle-class city, one of a growing group of places both in the United States and globally which have been identified by terms like "edge cities" or "technoburbs."[20] These suburban areas, in which there are more jobs than housing, are characterized physically by substantial office and commercial space, highway access, chain stores, and interchangeable subdivisions. Naperville, in recent decades, has captured a disproportionate share of the region's affluent residents, jobs, and amenities.

Douglas, three miles directly south of downtown Chicago along Lake Michigan, stands in sharp contrast to Naperville. Douglas has slightly more than 30,000 residents, predominantly African Americans, and a high poverty rate. Its unofficial boundaries run from 26th Street to 35th Street (named Pershing Road on the western side of the area) and from the lake west to the railroad tracks just east of the Dan Ryan Expressway. It is considerably smaller than Naperville in both size and population. Since the 1980s, parts of Douglas have been identified nationally as home to a group which some researchers have called "the truly disadvantaged," or an "underclass."[21] For nearly fifty years, the Stateway Gardens project of the Chicago Housing Authority provided more than 1,600 housing units in Douglas to some of the poorest residents in the metropolitan area. Beginning in 2001, the CHA demolished these high-rises and is in the process of building a new mixed-income community called Park Boulevard.

Douglas is a place that has changed in response to the same wider regional forces that have affected Naperville. The end results are quite different. But laying the histories of these two localities alongside one another offers us a view that looks beyond the stark comparisons of black and white, city and suburb, advantaged and disadvantaged, to the regional history that they both share.

Naperville in the Nineteenth Century

Naperville's early development preceded the railroad—perhaps surprisingly, given its distance from Chicago's center. In the 1830s, Naperville emerged as a small farm center with mills, stores, and a tavern. Its early growth rested on its location at the intersection of the west branch of the DuPage River and roads in and out of Chicago. Joe Naper platted the first subdivision in 1842, after he had successfully lobbied for Naperville to be named the county

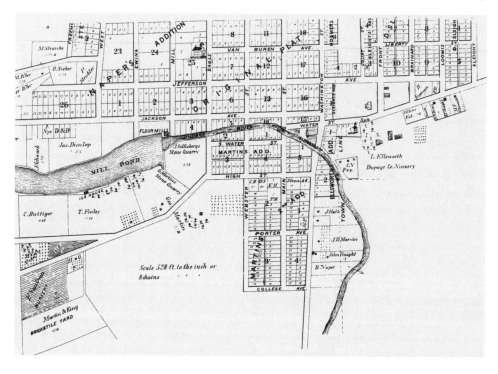

7.17 (a) The first subdivision of Naperville was made by Joe Naper in 1842 along the west branch of the DuPage River, near the established route from Chicago west to the Fox River at what would become Aurora. **(b)** (opposite) With the arrival of the railroad twenty years later, subdivisions would move northward toward the train station. Naperville's downtown, however, has remained along the river to the present. (*1874 Atlas of DuPage County*)

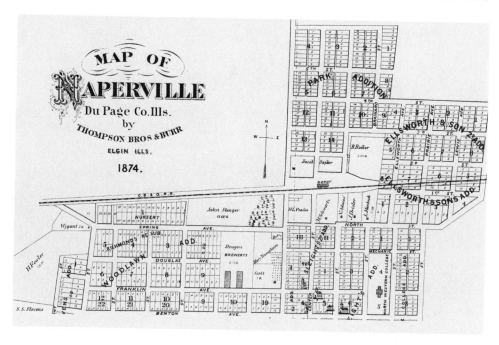

seat of the newly formed DuPage County (fig. 7.17). Today this first subdivision forms Naperville's downtown, complete with Starbucks and Eddie Bauer.

Originally located within Naper's first subdivision, the recently reconstructed Pre-Emption House stands as a reminder of this early era when Naperville was a river town with road connections to surrounding communities (fig. 7.18). In 1834, George Laird built the original two-and-a-half story frame structure with the largest rooms in the community. The Pre-Emption House housed travelers, business meetings, and local events, much as the Sauganash Hotel did at Chicago's center (and not wholly unlike its current use a visitors' center for Naper Settlement).[22]

The Pre-Emption House is important to Naperville's local history, but it also has a place in metropolitan history, as it was just one of dozens of taverns located along roads in and out of Chicago. In the 1830s and 1840s, before the arrival of the railroad, the Chicago metropolitan area was dotted with these structures, which served as hotels, taprooms, and meeting places. More generally Naperville's early history is linked to at least fifteen other communities across the metropolitan area, including Chicago, Elgin, St. Charles, Geneva, Batavia, Aurora, Joliet, Lockport, Blue Island, and Thornton. All were platted as river towns before 1850. Like Naperville, each was settled in the 1830s and 1840s; these towns share common landscape features, despite their often disparate stories since 1850.

The arrival of the railroad in 1848 began to reshape the logic of settlement in the met-

7.18 The Pre-Emption House (1834) was the first hotel and tavern west of Chicago. During its early years, the building served as a county courthouse, tavern, and market-place. It was demolished in 1946, but was reconstructed by the Naper Settlement in the late 1990s. The reconstructed building, at 523 S. Webster, serves as a visitors' center for the settlement, which is operated through the Naperville Park District. (Joseph C. Bigott)

ropolitan area. Soon towns that had Naperville's early advantages languished if they were bypassed by the railroad. Naperville's story is instructive. At first residents of Naperville did not see the need for the railroad—they had excellent road connections to other towns in the metropolitan area. The first railroad went miles north of Naperville and helped boom new towns like Wheaton.

During the 1850s Naperville stagnated. Once the county seat, it lost that plum to the railroad town of Wheaton. Business and residents gravitated toward the railroad. In an area in which only a few railroad lines would ever be built, Naperville might have stood as a testa-ment to ill-advised conservatism. Instead, the many rail lines in and out of Chicago provided Naperville with a second chance. In 1864, Naperville became a railroad town, as a compet-ing rail line established a track that ran parallel to the original line (just a few miles to the south) through the area west of Chicago.

Naperville joined the ranks of other railroad towns like Norwood Park, Winnetka, Whea-ton, Riverside, Hyde Park, and Austin. Unlike settlements founded around rail transporta-tion, such as Wheaton, Naperville's downtown was not located immediately adjacent to the train station. Instead, Naperville's core settlement remains along the river, with new sub-divisions radiating out from this center. Naperville businessmen were able to provide new services to area farmers, including stockyards.

In 1870, North Central College relocated to Naperville from Plainfield (fig. 7.19). Local landowner Delcar Sleight platted a residential subdivision just south of the train station around land he donated to the College. Area merchants and business owners, as well as college faculty and staff, were joined by Naperville's first commuters in creating the area that today comprises a designated historic district.

Naperville was also home to two major industrial employers: the Kroehler furniture factory, and the George Martin quarry. Many of the employees were German immigrants sought out because of their stonecutting or woodworking skills. At the end of the nineteenth century, many workers lived near employers on the near west side of Naperville.

To the north of the railroad, the furniture factory began operation in the 1880s in a five-story structure adjacent to the rail station (fig. 7.20). By 1915, Kroehler Manufacturing Company was the largest maker of upholstered furniture in the United States. It was also the largest employer in Naperville until the plant closed in 1978.[23]

In 1900, Naperville was a small community of about 3,000 people. It had a business center catering to area farmers and local residents. The largest employer was the furniture factory, while the local college and quarry also offered jobs enough to sustain a stable population. The stone and furniture was shipped into Chicago, while students were drawn to the town from the region and beyond. Only a very small number of residents regularly commuted to jobs in Chicago.

Like their urban counterparts, the Naperville workers lived in small cottages or rented rooms in larger houses. Different from urban cottages, however, most of these were on wider lots, and the longer side of the building faced the street. Their frame and sim-

7.19 The Evangelical Association, a group of German Protestants, built Old Main for North Central College when it moved from Plainfield to Naperville in 1870. The five-story limestone building was designed by John M. Van Osdel and initially comprised all classrooms, an auditorium for public lectures, administrative offices, and even student housing. The building, at 30 N. Brainard, now anchors both the college campus and the surrounding historic residential district. (Joseph C. Bigott)

7.20 The Kroehler Manufacturing Company produced furniture from the 1880s through 1978. Via the Chicago, Burlington, and Quincy Railroad, raw materials and finished products made their way quickly between Naperville and Chicago. When the furniture factory closed, the building was converted to retail and office space (renamed Fifth Avenue Station). (Joseph C. Bigott)

ple brick styles were quite similar to those found in Chicago neighborhoods. Groceries and taverns were nearby.

The quarries were closed by the Great Depression, and Kroehler closed its furniture manufacturing plant in the late 1970s. By the 1980s, teardowns were common, however, as rather than suffer a decline, Naperville grew with new industries and businesses. The old frame worker cottages were replaced with large homes for new white-collar Napervillians, who in turn replaced their earlier counterparts.[24]

Douglas in the Nineteenth Century

Douglas, like many parts of the metropolitan area, did not have a single, simple start. During the 1850s, John B. Sherman and Stephen A. Douglas envisioned very different usages for the area. Douglas purchased property along Lake Michigan between 31st and 35th streets in 1852, just as the Illinois Central was laid out alongside it. He built a suburban cottage, Oakenwald, for himself and laid out two of the region's first suburban subdivisions: Groveland and Woodland Parks (fig. 7.21). Area Baptists constructed the first University of Chicago just west of Groveland Park on land donated by Douglas (fig. 7.22). The university opened in 1860, and many faculty lived in the adjoining subdivision. The familiar linkage of residential suburb and college town, later seen in Lake Forest, Evanston, Wheaton, Elmhurst, and Naperville, seemed to set the area on a firm beginning.[25]

Another story, however, was unfolding just to the north. In 1856, Sherman purchased property at 29th and Cottage Grove that included Myrick's Tavern. He opened a stockyards there, near the intersection of two important highways from the south: Vincennes and Cottage Grove avenues.

Stockyards and elite retreats are not the best neighbors. Added to this, during the Civil War, Camp Douglas was sited just south of Groveland and Woodland Parks (fig. 7.23). Here hundreds of Confederate prisoners were held during the war, and a veteran's home was built here just after the war for survivors. Both the camp and the home spurred development of housing for institutional workers.

Stockyards, a prisoner of war camp, and a suburban college retreat competed for the fu-

7.21 Stephen A. Douglas built this cottage, Oakenwald, on his extensive real estate holdings on the South Side after he moved to Chicago in 1847. Initially far beyond city settlement, the area built up rapidly in the late nineteenth century alongside the Illinois Central Railroad. Just to the east of Oakenwald, at 34 E. 35th Street, a monument to Douglas was built which still stands. The Douglas cottage was torn down in 1907. (Chicago Historical Society, DN-005331)

ture for just a short time. In 1865, Sherman joined other meatpackers in creating the Union Stock Yards a couple of miles west and closed down his lakefront operation. The Confederate prison closed down at the end of the war. Seemingly Douglas's vision would prevail, but a disastrous fire and financial difficulties led to the closure of the University of Chicago in 1886. While Groveland Park has survived to the present, it did not serve as the nucleus for future development that Douglas had envisioned.

Instead, other developments shaped growth in the area. To the west, the Union Stock Yards and several rail lines offered employment opportunities first to European immigrants and then African American migrants. Inexpensive worker housing developed along streets like Federal Street (fig. 7.24). To the east, streetcars provided quick transportation to the Loop and elegant houses and apartments developed at the end of the nineteenth century for middle-class downtown workers.

Affluent residents built handsome graystone and brick houses (fig. 7.25). Jewish and Catholic residents joined Protestant counterparts in building churches, synagogues, and community institutions. Among the religious structures constructed in the late nineteenth century were the First Baptist Church—built while the first (and Baptist-affiliated) University of Chicago was still open in the area—and the Kehilath Anshe Ma'ariv (KAM) Synagogue (fig. 7.26). Michael Reese and Mercy hospitals on the north end of the area provided jobs, access to health care, and a substantial institutional presence in the area. Larger apartment buildings, including the Mecca, were built in advance of the 1893 World's Columbian Exposition to take advantage of the large number of sojourners on the South Side. By 1900, Douglas had reached "residential maturity."[26]

7.22 Just to the north of Oakenwald, Douglas donated land for the first University of Chicago. The university, sponsored by the Baptist Church, operated between 1860 and 1886. This view of the university building on Cottage Grove between 33rd and 34th streets, shows a six-story limestone structure. The building was damaged by a fire in 1886 and torn down. (Chicago Historical Society, ICHi-01517)

Douglas and Naperville Compared for the Nineteenth Century

During the nineteenth century, Naperville and Douglas responded to a similar set of social, political, and economic trends, but developed in very distinctive ways. Both were developed by individuals who saw real estate speculation possibilities. Yet neither community developed as their initial subdividers envisioned: Naperville did not grow as a river town; Douglas never grew beyond a small commuter enclave. Naperville lost the county seat that Joe Naper felt would assure its growth, and the first University of Chicago burned to the ground, changing Douglas's development trajectory.

7.23 Just to the south of Oakenwald, Camp Douglas served as a prisoner of war camp during the Civil War. Barracks such as these stood around a several acre encampment. These buildings, later destroyed, are seen here in 1864 on 37th Street and Lake Park. (Chicago Historical Society, DN 0086695)

7.24 (opposite, top) Philip D. Armour, a scion of the meatpacking family, funded the construction of a manual training school designed by Patton & Fisher between 1891 and 1893 along the west end of Douglas at 3300 S. Federal. The four-story masonry construction took up most of a city block. In this 1909 image, a fire at Armour Institute is being extinguished. Today, the Armour Institute stands along the east side of the Dan Ryan Expressway and is part of the Illinois Institute of Technology. (Chicago Historical Society, DN-0007561)

Douglas grew very quickly in the closing fifteen years of the nineteenth century. In that time, it went from part of the suburban Village of Hyde Park to a neighborhood in the City of Chicago and was largely built up by 1900. In contrast, Naperville remained an independent small city of several thousand residents, primarily of Yankee or German stock. In Douglas, Irish and Jews joined Yankees and a small group of African Americans. In both communities, though, a wide range of housing was constructed: from lodging houses for the most modest incomes to large graystones and Victorians for wealthy residents.

What is distinctive about Naperville and Douglas is that each enjoys a unique combination of landscape features. Naperville shares a great deal with water towns like Lockport, industrial towns like Pullman, and service centers such as Deerfield. Although Douglas's start was similar to that of Lake Forest or Elmhurst, where a college anchored early development, Douglas's physical development was shaped by different forces, and as a result, Douglas does not look like either of those towns. While Naperville's or Douglas's stories can be examined narrowly, a broader comparative approach helps us to see larger Chicagoland patterns, and also to understand how individuals, events, and public policy shaped these areas in particular ways.

Together Naperville and Douglas provide us with examples of some of the key layers to Chicago's metropolitan history in the railroad era. Before 1848, river and crossroads towns served area farms. The arrival of the railroad after 1848 had a dramatic effect on settlement patterns in the metropolitan area. Farm towns along the railroad emerged to compete with older crossroads towns; industry located along rail lines in and out of the city center; and commuter enclaves developed for moneyed downtown workers. Cars and the expressway system once again reordered the landscape—industrial, residential, and commercial space settled into areas which were convenient to new transportation systems in areas that had often remained farmland into the twentieth century.

Douglas and Naperville in the Twentieth Century

African Americans began moving into Douglas in the early twentieth century. Because of housing discrimination, they had little choice about where to live and they generally paid more for what was available. Because black stockyards workers were excluded from neighborhoods around the stockyards, they often moved to Douglas.

In Douglas, African Americans did not build a new neighborhood from scratch, but worked with an inherited landscape. This is clearly seen in the shifting control of churches and synagogues. In 1917, the Olivet Baptist Church, the largest black congregation in the city, purchased the First Baptist Church on the southeast corner of 31st and King Drive, for their

7.25 Along several of the streets in the eastern part of Douglas (especially S. Michigan, Calumet Avenue, and Martin Luther King, Jr., Drive (Grand Boulevard), large mansions for wealthy Chicagoans were constructed in the late nineteenth century. Seen here is a 1917 image of the home of J. Ogden Armour, president of Armour & Company, at 3724 S. Michigan Avenue. (Chicago Historical Society, DN-0067674)

own use. Similarly, the KAM congregation sold their synagogue on the southeast corner of 33rd and Indiana to the Pilgrim Baptist Church, an African American congregation. By the 1920s, there were approximately 20,000 in the congregation. The exterior of the building still includes a Hebrew inscription over the entrance, coupled with crosses on the front door (fig. 7.27).

A substantial business district developed along 35th Street at State Street by the 1920s (fig. 7.28). The armory for the Eighth Regiment Infantry (made up of African American National Guard members) was built at 35th Street and S. Forest Avenue (fig. 7.29). Banks, retail stores, and other businesses were joined by many nightclubs. Massive physical changes took place in this area again beginning in the 1940s. Douglas's urban renewal was shaped by the South Side Planning Board, with heavy leadership from Michael Reese Hospital and the Illinois Institute of Technology. IIT began a substantial land clearance project in order to build a new campus. Federal urban renewal projects leveled worker housing along the western part of the area. The Chicago Housing Authority's Stateway Gardens Project included more than 1,600 units along the western edge of the area (fig. 7.30), which was soon bounded by the new Dan Ryan Expressway. The privately owned Lake Meadows and Prairie Shores housing developments together provided over 3,200 units aimed at middle-class residents.[27]

7.26 (top) Kehilath Anshe Ma'ariv Synagogue (Congregation of the Men of the West) was constructed in 1890–91 by Adler & Sullivan for the growing Jewish community at 3301 S. Indiana in Douglas. (Chicago Historical Society, ICHi-21603)

7.27 (bottom) Since 1922, the building at 3301 S. Indiana constructed for the KAM Congregation has been home to Pilgrim Baptist Church. The transition from Jewish synagogue to Baptist Church reflected the population change taking place in Douglas, as African Americans moved into the neighborhood. (Leslie Schwartz)

At the beginning of the twenty-first century, Douglas was a diverse area with a wide range of housing types. Many of the public housing high-rises in the Stateway Gardens development had been demolished, making way for mixed-income development. Private investment has brought new and renovated housing to the east, but not much in the old Stateway Gardens corridor.

The twentieth century brought very different development for Na-

7.28 By the 1910s, 35th Street had developed as a thriving business district for a growing African American population. This is a view of the corner of 35th and S. State during the 1919 race riots. In the background are a Walgreen Drugs and many other small retail shops. (Chicago Historical Society, DN-0071297)

perville. Little changed until the 1960s, when the interstate highway opened up considerable new development. Agricultural trade declined as residential subdivisions replaced farm fields. Several companies, including Amoco Chemical and Bell Laboratories, located research facilities in Naperville in the 1960s. Naperville joined yet another set of metropolitan communities, including Deerfield, Northbrook, Schaumburg, Rolling Meadows, and Harvard, that boomed in the postindustrial service economy.

The Kroehler furniture plant closed in 1978 and after several false starts was transformed into a multiuse complex. Unlike many of its industrial cohorts, however, as industry declined, Naperville boomed. High-tech industry and research facilities dramatically expanded job opportunities, while subdivision growth expanded the city's population to more than 120,000.

One hundred years after Douglas became part of the contiguous settlement out from downtown Chicago, Naperville became part of it as well. Into the twenty-first century, Naperville continues to annex territory and build up more acreage primarily at the southern edge of the "edge city." In contrast, Douglas was built up by 1900, and densities increased as older housing was broken into smaller units for arriving populations. Land clearance reduced the number of housing units available at various times in the second half of the twentieth century, right down to the destruction of the Stateway Gardens public housing towers along the community area's western border. In the last two decades, new housing and rehabilitation of remaining nineteenth-century structures have fueled development in Douglas.

Naperville residents benefited from the economic, political, and transportation developments in the second half of the twentieth century, including the FHA and VA-insured loan programs which eased investment for residential subdivisions, the interstate system, and the expansion of a postindustrial economy. These same programs discriminated against Douglas's African American residents through reductions in public transit, redlining, and deindustrialization. Much of Douglas was leveled by urban renewal in the 1950s, replaced by a new campus for the Illinois Institute of Technology, public housing, and empty fields. In contrast, Naperville neither sought nor was forced to accept public housing. Instead, zoning in Naperville encouraged developers to construct expensive single-family houses.

In twentieth-century Douglas, African Americans inherited a landscape which they made their own by midcentury. They then witnessed the leveling of much of this inherited landscape in the name of slum clearance. Many twentieth-century Naperville farmers inherited their land from family members. As residential subdivisions overcame farms, Naperville farmers lost their inherited landscape. In contrast to Douglas residents, however, Naperville farmers who owned land profited by this transformation.

All of this has led to very different landscapes and populations in Naperville and Douglas at the start of the twenty-first century. Naperville is one of the most homogeneous places in the region today: its population is overwhelmingly white; its housing is primarily single-family and owner-occupied; and its residents are affluent. In contrast, Douglas has one of the highest poverty rates in Chicagoland; most of its housing is multifamily and rental. Naperville has more jobs than people, Douglas has far more residents than jobs.

Examining these two places alongside one another highlights the dramatic inequality and differences that exist in the metropolitan area today. Douglas and Naperville highlight the shifting value of political consolidation and independence. In the nineteenth century, Douglas's annexation to Chicago brought growth and development. In the twentieth century, Naperville annexed territory into itself and remained independent as it developed rapidly. Because of this independence, as well as differences in the race and class of their populations, public policy has affected these communities in very different ways.

Naperville and Douglas show the differential effect of broader trends on individual histories. Both communities evolved in the same metropolitan area, facing many of the same trends. Both are products of metropolitan-wide changes as well as local stories. Their stories show that any given locality within the metropolitan area has been influenced and changed by wider patterns and by the policies adopted at vari-

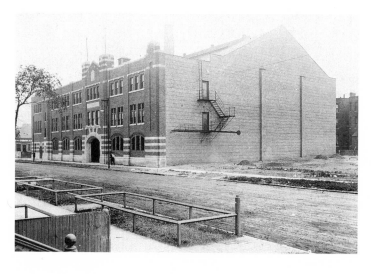

7.29 Among the new buildings constructed as African Americans moved into Douglas in the 1910s was the armory for the Eighth Regiment Infantry at 35th Street and S. Forest Avenue. African American National Guard members made up this regiment. Today, the building houses a charter school affiliated with the U.S. military. (Chicago Historical Society, DN-0064686)

7.30 This 1959 image shows one part of the transformation of Douglas which came in the mid-twentieth century as urban renewal leveled blocks of the neighborhood. The Illinois Institute of Technology, several private middle-income residential developments, and public housing were all built on slum clearance land. In this image of S. Dearborn looking north to 39th Street, the newly constructed Stateway Gardens looms over nineteenth-century housing soon to be leveled. (Chicago Historical Society, Clarence W. Hines, ICHi-23483)

ous levels of government. By returning to the history of any given local area armed with a metropolitan lens, we can see how wider patterns influenced the story.

Most places in Chicagoland have changed their primary functions over time, as they have grappled with economic and transportation changes. One result has been dramatic changes in how settlements fit into the metropolitan order. Naperville, begun as a farm center, has become an edge city. Douglas, begun as an elite enclave, became a dense neighborhood with a wide range of housing by 1900, was subject to intense urban renewal in the 1950s, and has emerged again in the late twentieth century as the site of private residential development.

What Douglas and Naperville look like today is a result of a complex layering of public policy, functions, and interactions within Chicagoland. At the same time that communities interacted and grew, they changed in response to wider economic, social, and political forces. These places were also shaped by the decisions of the people who have been their residents and by groups outside their bounds. Their histories have been shaped by competition and cooperation with their neighbors and with communities in distant parts of Chicagoland, as well as by wider national trends.

8

The Legacy of the Railroad Era in Chicagoland

Downtown skyscrapers are important regional landmarks of the railroad age. They remind us that the spectacular is certainly a central part of urban regions. Cities are all about pushing the limits of who we are so that we can accomplish extraordinary things—like building skyscrapers. Cities are a physical manifestation of our attempts to move beyond subsistence to a more complex and hopefully grander existence.

But the complexity of metropolitan regions also comes from the repetition of common patterns in hundreds of neighborhoods and suburbs. Metropolitan regions are both spectacular *and* mundane; they are important because they hold one-of-a-kind buildings, sites, and opportunities *and* because they offer hundreds of similar places and opportunities to eager residents. These common landscapes are also important regional landmarks, to be set alongside downtown skyscrapers.

Many of Chicagoland's common landscapes are tied to the railroad. Chicago's meteoric rise has long been associated with railroads. One nineteenth-century writer went so far as to describe Chicago as "the child of Railroads."[1] When Carl Sandburg defined Chicago in his 1916 iconic poem of the same name, railroads were central to the city's identity. Chicago was the "Player with Railroads and the Nation's Freight Handler."[2] But in the twenty-first century, Chicago appears to have moved far beyond the influence of the railroad. Expressways and airports seemingly have pushed the railroad into the distant past.

But the past is not distant. Instead, the railroad legacy is fundamental to understanding the contemporary landscape of Chicagoland. Chicagoans continue to live in places defined by the railroad. Many of the commuter stations, old factories, worker housing, and rural churches of the railroad era have not disappeared. They have been become component parts of edge cities, urban neighborhoods, and other new developments.

The historic sites in this region are like pieces of a jigsaw puzzle. They may be interesting, beautiful, and compelling as individual pieces, but they have much more meaning when taken together. When put together, patterns emerge and the general contours of a region can be found. These sites can show what is distinctive about the region, in comparison to a national or international picture. Architectural historians, geographers, preservationists, and historians have all written of late about the "politics of place" or about the "politics of place construction," or "the power of place."[3] Networks of places have more power to elicit memories and responses than single historical places.[4]

Preservation of Regional Landmarks: Downtown and Beyond

The division between the spectacular and the common that so defines metropolitan areas is also seen in differing approaches to historic preservation taken in Chicagoland (and elsewhere). On the one hand are preservation groups that focus on buildings that have national significance (the architecturally spectacular). Architectural historians and national preservation groups generally focus on downtown buildings with only a few excursions into the surrounding neighborhoods and suburbs, often following the residential work of prominent architects. Local community groups and historical societies are more apt to preserve more common buildings and sites found beyond downtown. Often these buildings are not architecturally distinctive. Their significance to the history of the region rests in their typicality.

Serious preservation efforts in Chicagoland date to the second half of the twentieth century and initially focused on downtown buildings designed by prominent architects.[5] Preservation campaigns were often led by local architects and their students, who recognized the significance of downtown buildings before the general public did. One of the first campaigns, in 1960, focused on preservation of Adler & Sullivan's Garrick Theatre. While the building was torn down, it led to the creation of key regional preservation groups and the Commission on Chicago Architectural Landmarks.[6]

In the more than forty years since, preservationists have worked actively across the region, but with a strong focus on the architect-designed commercial buildings of the central business district. The Landmarks Preservation Council of Illinois and the Chicago Architecture Foundation have evolved as the key preservation organizations in the region, identifying structures worthy of preservation almost exclusively on the basis of their architectural significance or uniqueness. While many buildings, including the Chicago Stock Exchange, have been torn down, others like the Auditorium Building and the Rookery still stand.[7]

Far from downtown and fights to save buildings designed by famous architects, a different strain of preservationism emerged in neighborhoods threatened by federal programs for urban renewal, highway construction, and public housing. On Chicago's Near North Side, residents in the Old Town Triangle, just north and west of the immediate path of urban renewal, organized to stave off redevelopment which they saw as neighborhood destruction. While few of their structures had architectural significance, residents wanted to preserve their neighborhood, composed of an eclectic mix of working-class housing and businesses on narrow lots. Other efforts took place on the city's Near West and South sides.[8]

Not all neighborhood groups were organized in response to the threat of total destruction. In many neighborhoods and suburbs across the region, residents organized to preserve a single building. Often, these efforts have been led by local historical societies. The buildings saved seldom have significant architectural or historical significance beyond their own neighborhoods or suburbs. However, they do embody in some way or another important aspects of the history or character of these local places.

The preservation of historic buildings is part of the core mission of many local historical societies. The largest wave of foundations of Chicagoland historical societies dates to the 1960s and 1970s.[9] The centennial of the Civil War (1961–1965), the sesquicentennial of Illinois (1968), and preparations for the bicentennial of the Declaration of Independence (1976) were important to raising interest in local history. As well, large-scale suburbanization swelled populations in many older communities, with development threatening nineteenth-century structures.

Many suburban historical societies obtained support from local government in the form of land and building purchase, as well as annual appropriations for upkeep and staff. Some historical museums are components of park districts, as in Lisle and Waukegan, or receive substantial support from them, as in Chicago. Some have purchased and maintained buildings solely through private donations (Hinsdale), but many other sites have been purchased by local governments and operate with a substantial subsidy (Naperville, Arlington Heights).[10] Local historical societies and local governments are the foot soldiers of a movement to preserve the common landscapes of the region.[11]

Some parts of Chicagoland's past are more popular to preserve than others. Local historical societies can and want to preserve what is often perceived as a simpler rural or suburban landscape—for instance, farmhouses and small remnants of farms themselves, one-room schoolhouses, old churches, and houses which are central to commuter stories.[12]

It has been difficult to preserve complicated, large industrial structures and sites, and the preservation of these sites has lagged behind efforts to preserve historic houses and more pristine landscapes.[13] Some of the properties are too vast, others too valuable to be maintained by small, not-for-profit local groups. Still others require millions of dollars to clean away pollution left from decades of degradation, placing them beyond the means of most local historical societies. Interpretation of historic industrial sites also raises questions about past working conditions and labor strife that cannot be simply answered. The Union

Stockyards Gate remains as a lonely reminder of a once vast complex, conveying little sense of the historic processes and confrontations which took place around it.

Local preservation groups have been active on behalf of only a few historical industrial sites in Chicagoland, among the most noteworthy the Joliet Iron Works, one of the earliest iron and steel manufacturing plants in the region, dating back to the 1870s. The Will County Forest Preserve has taken the lead in preserving what is left of the works through purchase of the property. While only the shells of buildings remain, a guided tour explains the industrial processes which once took place at the site. Because the site is part of the Illinois and Michigan Canal National Historic Corridor, it is interpreted as part of a transportation and industrial region.

Little has been done to preserve other steel production sites. Consider the former South Works of U.S. Steel, running from 79th to 91st streets along Lake Michigan on Chicago's Southeast Side. Taking advantage of a site at the mouth of the Calumet River and at the intersection of several rail lines, the North Chicago Rolling Mill Company built the South Works in 1880. Residential areas grew up around the South Works initially as suburban areas and then as city neighborhoods. The works were purchased by the U.S. Steel Corporation in 1901, as Poles, Mexicans, and African Americans joined earlier German and Irish workers. Employing as many as 13,000 into the 1970s, production at the South Works plummeted in the 1980s. In 1992, U.S. Steel closed the South Works.

Acres and acres of furnaces, rolling mills, and more stood for more than a hundred years; today very little of the South Works still stands on this brownfield site. Hoping to attract new industry, the city leveled most of the industrial buildings.[14] Redevelopment plans have included an airport and the summer Olympics. While spurring economic redevelopment is paramount, this place also specifically represents the history of heavy industrial development and subsequent deindustrialization. Nonetheless, the question of preserving even a part of the South Works has played only a very minor role in redevelopment discussions.[15]

The stalled efforts to open the Pullman Car Works as a historic site become even more important in the context of industrial sites like the South Works, which have been leveled in recent decades. After the closure of the Pullman Car Works in 1981, the Historic Pullman Foundation organized to preserve as much of this industrial legacy as possible. Preservation of the car works, especially the Administration Building, was beyond the resources of this private group. Intent on founding a transportation and/or industrial museum in the old car works, the foundation and other volunteers eventually persuaded the State of Illinois to purchase the property.

Preservation at Pullman has barely moved forward since the State of Illinois purchased the property in 1991. Although restoration work is underway at the Hotel Florence, a fire destroyed much of the Administration Building. This is particularly unfortunate given the overall paucity of industrial preservation across Chicagoland.

Market Preservation

While local groups and preservationists have played an important role in saving and maintaining historic regional structures, most nineteenth-century buildings that remain are here because they continue to serve in the market. They stand not because of the active efforts of preservationists, but because of their continued usefulness or adaptability to new uses.[16] Downtown skyscrapers such as the Monadnock or the Rookery remain as office space more than a hundred years after their construction. Similarly some houses, churches, and schools have been in steady use for more than a hundred years. Old Main in Naperville was built in 1870 for use by North Central College. More than 130 years later, the building still functions as a college building.

Preservation is done by private investment, which finds profit in adaptive reuse. While some of the decisions to retain parts or all of old plants are made for aesthetic or historical reasons, buildings are generally preserved because it makes good economic sense. The reuse and rehabilitation of old structures can sometimes be cheaper than new construction, and distinctive landmarks become a premium for new tenants.

Housing comprises the vast majority of nineteenth-century structures still standing in the metropolitan area. Most are still used as dwelling units. Infrastructure connections such as running water, sewers, electricity, gas, and phone lines have been added to many houses, pointing up the changing requirements of urban life. But the basic size of houses, lots, and rooms have remained stable enough to keep housing usable.

This is not true of factories, and so industrial sites are often the most changed. Built during the wave of heavy industrialization in the nineteenth and early twentieth centuries and shuttered in the closing decades of the last century, factories have either been adapted to new uses, destroyed, or abandoned. Interestingly, many of the former factories have been converted to housing units. They stand because they are adaptable to current needs.[17] Adaptive reuse provides a very different kind of preservation than that pursued by historical societies and conservation groups. This is market preservation.

The preservation of Chicagoland's railroad landscape, then, emerges from at least three very different motivations. Preservation groups have championed threatened buildings and sites with a national (or international) architectural or historic significance. Local historical societies have worked to save structures that have importance in their communities, often with little interest in their significance beyond their boundaries. Finally, many buildings and sites remain in active use, with preservation of secondary importance to their market value.

Interpretation of Historic Sites

The interpretation of these structures varies from virtually none to detailed investigations of the uses and users of a site. For the most part, sites that are still in current use (or reuse) have little immediate interpretation. While their past is of interest, it is not central to their contemporary value, nor are there many visitors. In contrast, most buildings preserved by historical societies, government agencies, or architectural groups have both explicit and implicit interpretations.

Local historians—supported by local funds and societies—often emphasize independence, self-reliance, and isolation from the wider region in their interpretations. Preservation often emphasizes women's work, because of the disproportionate number of domestic spaces. At the same time, there is a very real class bias in preservation. There is very little, if any, industrial worker housing preserved outside the market; almost all formally preserved housing comes from the middle or upper-middle class.[18]

Local historical societies and government agencies generally recount the basic history of the site's usage and integrate the story into that of the local area. Everyday life is carefully examined, providing us with a rich comparison between the past and the present, a real testament to public interest in social history. However, interpretation often celebrates the unique story which unfolds within a locale, with little sense of the broader historical context.

The Railroad and Chicagoland

The railroad provides a useful organizing tool for regional history in Chicagoland. Chicago was only a very small town when the railroad began its transformation. The millions of people drawn to Chicago during the late nineteenth and early twentieth centuries did not all come by railroad (though many of them did), but they all came to a city whose landscape and lifeblood had been formed by the railroad economy. Houses, factories, commercial structures, and institutions that Chicagoans built to serve this quickly growing population are all artifacts of the railroad era.

Key features of the railroad landscape included a dense downtown area characterized by skyscrapers and large railroad stations. Beyond downtown, development took place almost exclusively around rail stations, leaving areas beyond them undeveloped into the twentieth century (and beyond). The sharp distinction between areas along the railroad and those at a distance from a rail line mattered both within the limits of the City of Chicago and outside those boundaries.

Twentieth- and twenty-first-century development has been layered onto this historical landscape. Sometimes Chicagoans have used buildings and sites in ways very similar to their nineteenth-century purposes; at other times they have renovated and reorganized their use of the historic structures; and in still other cases, they have leveled the nineteenth-century landscape to make way for something completely new. In each case, however, later groups inherited a physical legacy and have shaped (and been shaped) by it.

Spinelike Development of the Railroad Age

Development during the railroad age was characterized by a star pattern of rail lines in and out of downtown. The region in the nineteenth century (and by extension to the present) came to have two parts: settlements that hugged the rail lines and settlements in the areas between them. Places near rail stations with regular train service into Chicago were often closer in time to the city center than inner city neighborhoods. Residents of Evanston, Morgan Park, or Riverside at the beginning of the twentieth century could arrive downtown in little more than half an hour. Farmers in Chesterton, Lisle, and Harvard could get their milk and garden produce to Chicago's market on a daily basis. Furniture from Naperville, wallpaper from Joliet, and watches from Elgin could be shipped to Chicago (and beyond) with as great an ease as products manufactured in the city center.

Arguably, what constituted Chicagoland in the railroad age was not a contiguous geographic region, but lines of railroad stops in and out of the city center which had regular daily trains (but not necessarily commuter runs). In areas beyond easy reach of rail stations, though, intensive development languished. Farmers were less able to serve the urban market; the distance from raw materials and consumers precluded the building of factories; idyllic spots were not worth developing as recreational sites; and commuters had no hope of reaching Chicago, even in a day's time, from many places between rail lines. These areas awaited the arrival of streetcars or automobiles to bring them into the easy reach of metropolitan markets. Not until the twentieth century would infilling result in a contiguous built-up region spreading out from the city center. By then, the railroads had already defined the basic contours of the region.

The brick bungalow, so distinctive a Chicagoland housing type, marks the end of the railroad era. A product of this infilling process in the first half of the twentieth century, the bungalow became the mainstay of wholly new neighborhoods and suburbs, made possible by the extension of streetcars and the increasing use of automobiles. Bungalows provided a marked improvement in housing Chicagoland's middle classes: brick, instead of frame, construction and modern kitchens and bathrooms. They were made possible through the quantity production of fixtures and fittings, providing comfort at a relatively modest cost. By the 1920s, the bungalow belt (not so much a belt as a set of places both inside the city and in suburban areas) consisted of new homogeneous neighborhoods of single-family houses and two-flats.[19]

Neighborhoods of bungalow construction are a ready marker of areas beyond the reach of nineteenth-century Chicagoland, even though they might have only been four or five miles from the Loop. Portage Park, Berwyn, West Rogers Park, and Marquette Park are all Chicago neighborhoods that developed in the early twentieth century, filling in the older railroad landscape. These bungalow neighborhoods were in areas too far from a rail station for intensive development until the advent of mass transportation and the car.

Commuters to Downtown and Beyond

Most residents of nineteenth-century Chicagoland lived close to where they worked, just the opposite of the situation today. Farmers worked in adjacent fields, industrial workers in nearby factories, and service workers near recreational or institutional centers. Only affluent male residents of residential suburbs were regular commuters along the region's many rail lines. They developed commuter suburbs around rail stations which provided ready transportation to mainly white-collar and professional jobs in the city center. But these were the minority of settlements in Chicagoland during the railroad age.

The commuter rail suburbs which developed around train depots across the region in the late nineteenth century remain among the most durable legacies of the railroad era. Riverside, Lake Forest, Kenilworth, Hinsdale, and Wilmette remain elite residential suburbs, while Norwood Park, Morgan Park, and Rogers Park are among the formerly independent suburbs which are now part of Chicago. All retain characteristics from their earliest foundation: train stations with regular commuter runs into and out of the city center; single-family houses on large lots; churches and schools.[20]

But these suburbs have changed. White-collar work is now found across the region, not just downtown. Commuters from these suburbs not only take the train, but hop in their cars to travel across the region to new job sites. Women have joined men as commuters, changing the tenor of everyday life in these suburbs. Market Square in Lake Forest points to the effect of automobiles. Located adjacent to the rail station, this shopping district was designed with easy parking. In addition, many of these commuter suburbs have actively courted commercial and retail development, bringing white-collar work within their boundaries.

Farms to Sprawl

The physical expansion of metropolitan areas in the late twentieth century is often described as "sprawl," or "mass suburbia," to distinguish it from the suburban patterns of the railroad era.[21] In most descriptions of sprawl, subdivisions replace farm fields, creating a line of urban development that is clearly distinguished from agriculture. Because of the spinelike development of the railroad age, however, this "line" has not been continuous. As a later step in the infilling between rail lines begun in the bungalow era, even this process is shaped by the spatial dynamics of the railroad age.

Descriptions of sprawl often situate farms beyond a metropolitan area. Farms seemingly have no place in the region. This is, however, a narrow, static, and ahistorical approach to metropolitan development. First, the relationship between agriculture, railroads, and metropolitan dairy and vegetable markets during the railroad era compels a broad understanding of the metropolitan region that includes farms and farm centers. Second, the process by which sprawl replaces farms involves changes in transportation and real estate markets that establish dynamic urban-rural relationships of a metropolitan nature.

Food did not come from across the country or across the globe. Regional farmers raised vegetables, fruits, and flowers and produced milk, eggs, and other dairy products for sale across Chicagoland. They also raised the hay and oats needed for the thousands and thousands of horses used by streetcar lines, business deliveries, and private owners. Regional farmers were in large measure responsible for providing food to millions of metropolitan residents.

These farmers established more than ninety towns in the region, first at crossroads and then at rail stops. The basic logic of town location, as well as the siting of local government and institutions, reflects agricultural not urban origins—but all within a metropolitan system.

Sprawl is typically described as a first incursion of a metropolitan area into a formerly isolated rural district. But in Chicagoland, sprawl is physically linked to farms and farm centers, because the form of sprawl is shaped by the contours of nineteenth-century farm fields, landholdings, roads, and commercial centers.[22] The region's agricultural past lives on through these sites and institutions, shaping Chicagoland's recent history in a distinctive way. Long after the last fields have been redeveloped, Chicagoans live with the real estate patterns (the farm fields), commercial centers, roads, schools, churches, and local governments developed by farmers in the nineteenth century.

Industrialization and Deindustrialization

Chicago's startling rise in the nineteenth century certainly rested on a rich agricultural hinterland, but industrialization was key to the dramatic expansion in the region's economy. Industry early sought and developed suburban locations along regional rail lines. Excellent water and rail transportation drew some of the largest employers in nineteenth-century Chicagoland to suburban areas. Thousands of industrial jobs lay beyond the city borders by the 1880s, including the stockyards in Lake Township, the steel mills at Joliet and South Chicago, and railroad car works at Pullman, Aurora, and West Chicago. The suburban locus of industrial work in the railroad age is clouded because so many of these sites are now neighborhoods within the City of Chicago.

The suburban location of industrialization is also obscured by the destruction of factories and work sites in Chicago in the second half of the twentieth century. Thousands of these factory jobs were lost as some of the region's largest employers, including the stockyards and many of the steel mills, shuttered their doors. In 1947, factory employment within the city reached its peak at 668,000 jobs. By 1982, the number of factory jobs in the city had declined 59 percent to 277,000. More than 100,000 more jobs were lost beyond the Chicago city limits during that period.[23]

The effect on Chicagoland was profound. Across the region large industrial sites disappeared in the final third of the twentieth century as industrial production shifted out of the region, and often out of the United States entirely. Factories, warehouses, and processing facilities that once consumed acres of regional land seemingly evaporated.

Deindustrialization has eliminated thousands of jobs at both large and small factories. But the housing stock and community institutions remain, perhaps the most important legacy of the industrial era for the current Chicago metropolitan landscape. Especially on the South Side and in the south suburbs, neighborhoods of worker housing continue to function long after the departure of the behemoth plants.

The very largest industrial plants, employing thousands of workers at sites adjacent to one or more railroads, fostered the development of large worker suburbs. Workers built communities of cottages, two-flats, stores, saloons, churches, schools, and other institutions within walking distance of these suburban work sites. Most workers had ready access to jobs by living adjacent to factories and stockyards. While these places were among the most polluted sites in the nineteenth-century landscape, immigrant workers had few options. The high cost of commuting prevented workers from living beyond the shadow of industry. The exception was the small group of African Americans employed in manufacturing in the Chicago area before 1917.[24] They often lived at some distance from work sites, because residents of neighborhoods adjacent to factories refused to accept them as neighbors.

Over the course of the twentieth century, infilling and further urban growth have knit these once isolated industrial suburbs into the fabric of metropolitan development. Most are now city neighborhoods, not independent suburbs. Their histories remind us that work is not recently arrived in suburban areas.[25]

Development of the North Side in the nineteenth century contrasted with that of the South Side. Perhaps most significant is that while there were many industrial sites on the North Side, none matched the scale of South Side enterprises. Smaller factories offered different options in jobs, employers, and work settings. Some factories were set alongside residential areas, but many others were on the same streets as housing and small businesses. Workers went in different directions for work. With deindustrialization, some of these smaller factories (like their larger South Side counterparts) have been torn down to be replaced by residential or commercial structures. However, many of these smaller factories have been converted to residential or commercial use, maintaining a far more variegated streetscape than in the largest South Side worker neighborhoods.[26]

Gentrification of Worker Housing

In some neighborhoods and suburban settlements where factories have been shuttered, redevelopment has led to gentrification. Gentrification is most prevalent in former worker neighborhoods in which factories and other work sites helped create an eclectic streetscape. The urban cottages, flats, churches, grocery stores, and saloons were joined by factories which were on street scale.

The integration of factories and processing plants into the fabric of neighborhood streets meant that residents could not escape the odors and smoke from these factories during the years that they operated. They lived with the noxious (and sometimes toxic) by-products of tanneries and breweries because these neighborhood factories offered options in jobs, employers, and work settings.

It was not until these neighborhoods lost their factories that they became appealing to anyone except workers tied to these areas by jobs. The North Side neighborhoods of Bucktown, Wrigleyville, and Old Town all began as worker neighborhoods with small factories. As the factories closed down in the second half of the twentieth century, the neighborhoods languished for a time. But then some Chicagoans chose to live in loft conversions of the former Best Brewery, Western Wheel Works, Montgomery Ward's warehouses, and other old industrial sites, attracted by their interesting facades, unique spaces, and links to the past.

Such sites were also part of interesting streetscapes, which became even more varied with gentrification. New, more affluent residents began to move into the neighborhoods. Some of the abandoned factories were torn down to make way for expensive townhouses and condominiums. With the conversion of small groceries, saloons, and other small businesses, the neighborhood became more solidly residential as real estate values soared.

Worker Neighborhoods without Work

Gentrification is bringing a radical change in the class composition of some formerly worker neighborhoods. In other neighborhoods and suburbs, workers remained in housing even after plants closed and jobs disappeared. In order to survive, these workers increasingly became commuters, sometimes traveling great distances to get to jobs.

African Americans were among the earliest workers who commuted to jobs in Chicagoland. Racial discrimination kept newly arriving African Americans in the early twentieth century from taking up the jobs in large industries. And because discrimination often kept them from living close to work sites, they commuted to small factories and service sector jobs across the region. As bars to employment in the stockyards and steel mills fell, African Americans were still not welcomed in the surrounding white neighborhoods.

White workers followed African Americans as commuters. With twentieth-century deindustrialization, factories and plants shut down, but housing remained. Workers who continued to live in these old industrial neighborhoods necessarily commuted to work, or commuted further than had their counterparts in the early twentieth century. Horsecars, cable cars, streetcars, and the elevated provided more affordable public transportation and access to areas outside the downtown district. By the late twentieth century, residents of old worker neighborhoods regularly drove automobiles to jobs across the metropolitan area.

Into the Twenty-First Century

Most discussions of metropolitan areas in the United States assume a set of simplistic binary characteristics distinguishing a central city from its surrounding suburbs. Cities are heterogeneous; suburbs are homogeneous. Cities are characterized by multifamily units; suburbs by single-family houses. Cities are old; suburbs are new. These generalizations do pertain to many parts of cities and suburbs, but too frequently they mask crucial differences among suburbs and similarities between city neighborhoods and suburbs.

If we step back from the political distinction between city and suburb and instead focus on generational development of settlements across the region, the distinction between city and suburb, while real, becomes only one of a series of salient characteristics for any place in the region. In particular, the Chicago settlements that began during the railroad era share a logic and development patterns which cross city and suburban lines.

Common sites and structures are found in many neighborhoods and suburbs in Chicagoland. The repetition of building types and forms is the basis for this common landscape. Chicagoland can in a very real sense be represented by the Wright Schoolhouse, the Stockyards Gate, the Riverside Train Station, the McHenry County Court House, and the Des Plaines Camp Meeting. They stand for the basic settlement types which defined Chicagoland during the railroad age and which continue to shape the region down to the present.[27]

A regional interpretation is particularly important in the early twenty-first century. Metropolitan planning agencies ask Chicagoland residents to think beyond their neighborhood or suburbs in order to address critical issues related to housing, employment, transportation, and the environment. In some ways, this is not difficult, since these residents live and work and play across Chicagoland. They are not confined by suburban or city boundaries. But residents experience only their own patterns, they do not necessarily have a wider view. Knowledge of this shared regional history can provide a base from which to negotiate seemingly intractable regional challenges. Reconstructing the past of Chicagoland provides the base for a future.

Appendix: Regional Tours and Selected Sites

One of the great pleasures of being an urban historian is the way that it has enriched what I see around me as I roam the region. This is how *Chicagoland* began, and so it seems fitting to end back on the road. I've divided this appendix into two parts: suggested tours (one near the core and five radiating in different directions from the city center), and a list of sites sorted by settlement origins. Both show that across the region, common kinds of sites can be found springing from agricultural, industrial, recreational/institutional, and commuter settlements in the railroad age.

The tours begin straight west, exploring the interplay between historical sites before and after the arrival of the railroad. The southwest tour, along the historic canal corridor, contrasts settlements that grew around industries with those founded by commuters. The south tour includes some of the largest industrial sites in the region, drawn by natural resources, abundant transportation, and ready access to a large labor market. Moving northward along Lake Michigan, the north tour acknowledges the privilege of the commuter suburbs founded along the shoreline, but also shows the range of neighbors that elite commuter suburbs interacted with. The northwest tour illustrates the dominance of agriculture that was replaced by rapid suburban development in the late twentieth century. The final tour returns to the central city and explores not the spectacular skyscrapers and world-class architecture of the Loop, but structures which are examples of common regional types. Use these tours as a base for actually getting out to sites or to virtually tour the region.

West Tour

Roosevelt Road (SR 38) and North Avenue (SR 64) were early roads heading straight west out of Chicago, while Lake Street and Ogden Avenue headed west but angled north and south respectively. The first railroad line in Chicago was built west from downtown by the Galena and Chicago Union Railroad Company (known for most of its history as the west line of the Chicago and North Western Railway) beginning in 1848. A second line (the Chicago, Burlington, and Quincy Railroad) made its way west during the Civil War in the 1860s. These four roads and two railroads fostered an east-west orientation between communities along the routes.

It is here, to the west of Chicago, that the juxtaposition of a railroad and prerailroad landscape is seen most easily. Places near rail stops on the two west lines were drawn into a tight orbit with Chicago (and each other) over the course of the nineteenth and early twentieth centuries. At the same time, in the large swathes of territory between the railroads, older settlements languished but did not disappear from the landscape. The most recent wave of suburbanization in the late twentieth century has transformed many of these areas, but historical societies have successfully saved a sampling of older sites.

Austin and Oak Park were among the first railroad stops out from the city center, and became early sites for commuter settlement. The **AUSTIN TOWN HALL** (W1) on Lake Street at Central Avenue, while a twentieth-century building, is a reminder of Austin's roots as an independent commuter suburb in the nineteenth century (annexed to Chicago in 1889). The Austin Historic District to the south is noted for its ornate Victorian frame single-family houses. Traveling west on Lake Street into Oak Park, historic districts are to the north and south, filled with houses built when this residential commuter suburb boomed, between the 1870s and 1920s. The **FRANK LLOYD WRIGHT HOME AND STUDIO** (W2), north of Lake Street on Forest at Chicago Avenue, is among around sixty other buildings constructed in an early modern style.

Heading south across Oak Park and then west along Roosevelt Road (State Route 38), we drive through the many cemeteries found in Forest Park, including the Jewish Waldheim (1870), Concordia (1872), German Waldheim (1873), Forest Home (1876), and Woodlawn (1912) cemeteries. These cemeteries were founded in the late nineteenth century when funeral trains reached the area on either side of the Des Plaines River. Around these cemeteries developed picnic groves, restaurants, and early amusement parks.

Continuing west along Roosevelt, crossing from Cook into DuPage County, turn south on York Road past 31st Street. On the west side of York Road at the Salt Creek stands the **GRAUE MILL** (W3). Completed in 1852 by the German American Graue family, this four-story brick structure with a large water wheel takes us back before the dominance of steam power and the railroad. Three generations of Graues ground grain at this site, which served

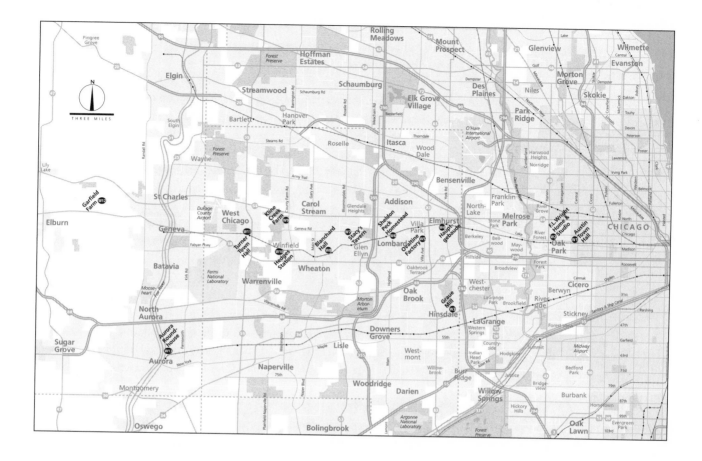

WEST TOUR

W1. Austin Town Hall (1929) | 5610 West Lake Street, Chicago

W2. Frank Lloyd Wright Home and Studio (1889) | 951 Chicago Avenue, Oak Park

W3. Graue Mill (1852) | York Road at Spring Road, Oak Brook

W4. Hauptgebaude (1879) (Elmhurst College) | 190 Prospect Street, Elmhurst

W5. Ovaltine Factory (1917) | 1 Ovaltine Court, Villa Park

W6. Sheldon Peck Homestead (1837) | 355 East Parkside, Lombard

W7. Stacy's Tavern (1846) | 557 Geneva Road, Glen Ellyn

W8. Blanchard Hall (1853) (Wheaton College) | 501 College Avenue, Wheaton

W9. Kline Creek Farm (1890s) | County Farm Road, north of Geneva Road, Winfield

W10. Hedges Station (1849) | 0N555 Winfield Road, Winfield

W11. Turner Town Hall (1884) | 132 West Main Street, West Chicago

W12. Garfield Farm (1846) | 2N016 Garfield Road, LaFox

W13. Aurora Roundhouse (1855) | 205 North Broadway, Aurora

farmers for miles around. In the middle of the nineteenth century, dozens of mills ground grain and milled lumber. Most disappeared as farmers shifted from grain to dairy, and lumber was shipped around the region along the rail lines.

Returning northward along York Road we pass through the post-1945 suburban development around Oak Brook: toll roads, shopping centers, corporate headquarters, and residential subdivisions. Further north, Elmhurst evidences older patterns, with a nineteenth-century residential core around its rail station and Elmhurst College, with **HAUPTGEBAUDE** (W4) (the Old Main structure on the college grounds). Turning west on St. Charles Road, take Ardmore north into Villa Park. Villa Park first developed along the railroad and then the interurban line running to Aurora in the early twentieth century. The old **OVALTINE FACTORY** (W5), adjacent to the train, was built at the end of World War I and operated until the 1970s. Three stories high, with the spare brick construction of the modern style, the factory includes terra cotta trim in white and deep blue. In the first years of the twenty-first century, the structure was converted to townhouses and condominiums.

Returning to St. Charles Road, just past Main Street in Lombard on the south side of the train tracks stands the **SHELDON PECK HOMESTEAD** (W6). The Peck family arrived in this region from upstate New York in the mid-1830s, years before the arrival of the railroad. St. Charles Road connected them to other farmers and Chicago. They built this modest, one-and-a-half-story frame house in 1837, which family members occupied until 1996. It served as a center for a busy farmstead, the first school in the area, and as a studio for Sheldon Peck, who was a portrait painter.

Just a few miles further west along St. Charles Road, **STACY'S TAVERN** (W7) was a near neighbor to the Peck family during their early years. At the intersection of St. Charles and Geneva Road, the Stacy family purpose-built this frame, two-story tavern in 1846, after finding farmers and other travelers often knocking on their farmhouse door for accommodations. Taverns such as this dotted Chicagoland before the railroad, when it took more than a day to travel to the outer reaches of the region. Travelers could shelter their horses, catch a drink in the taproom (or tea in the ladies' parlor), eat a meal in the adjacent dining room, and share upstairs bedrooms. Today a part of Glen Ellyn, this site lost its purpose as travelers switched to the nearby rail lines.

Following Geneva Road from Stacy's Tavern, take Main Street south into downtown Wheaton. Unlike Stacy's Tavern or the Peck Homestead, Wheaton's development came with the railroad. Warren Wheaton offered land to the Galena and Chicago Union Railroad when company officers were plotting its route in the late 1840s. He got a rail station in exchange, which fostered an initial burst of town development. Wheaton also donated land to a school which became Wheaton College in 1860. **BLANCHARD HALL** (W8), whose central part was constructed in 1853, is the oldest structure on the Wheaton College campus. The town of Wheaton developed between the rail station and the college.

Continuing west along Roosevelt Road (just south of downtown Wheaton), and turning north on County Farm Road, we come to **KLINE CREEK FARM** (W9), which preserves a farmstead of the 1890s, including a house, outbuildings, and small fields as a living history museum. The Kline family raised hay to sell to urban horse owners. They were among a large number of Chicagoland farm families who raised horses (as well as hay and oats) needed in the city, particularly for the extensive horsecar system. Returning to Roosevelt Road, north on Winfield Road is the next stop on the Galena and Chicago Union Railroad from Wheaton. The **HEDGES STATION** (W10) (now moved south of the railroad on the east side of Winfield Road) is the oldest extant rail station in Illinois. The Winfield Historical Society is working to preserve this structure, which served this small rural community from 1849 into the twentieth century, when suburbanization overtook older patterns. Farmers such as the Kline family would have brought their hay, dairy, and fresh produce to this station for shipment into Chicago.

Continuing north along Main Street, turn west on Geneva Road into West Chicago. In a town originally named Turner, the railroad built yards and a repair shop here in the mid-nineteenth century. They also hoped to attract factories to this town, which developed in a pattern quite distinct from its agricultural and commuter neighbors. In the closing decades of the twentieth century, the railroad sold off its landholdings, turning industrial land into parkland. The **TURNER TOWN HALL** (W11) stands as a reminder of West Chicago's nineteenth-century roots.

Return to Geneva Road and travel west until the road merges with Roosevelt Road (SR 38). Continue west on Roosevelt Road through Geneva and over the Fox River. The westernmost site is the **GARFIELD FARM** (W12), north of Route 38 between Geneva and Elburn in LaFox. The Garfield family owned this farm from 1841 until 1977. In the early years, the Garfield home served as a tavern, providing accommodations to travelers, as well as meeting space for area farmers. The two-story structure was built with brick made by the Garfield family on-site. Today, the Campton Historic Agricultural Lands, a not-for-profit that controls the land on which the farm sits, is actively seeking to preserve the surrounding farmland in the face of suburban encroachment.

Returning east on Roosevelt Road (SR 38), travel south on Broadway (SR 31) into Aurora. Aurora was founded in the 1830s along the Fox River. The arrival of the railroad in 1855 led to the construction of the **AURORA ROUNDHOUSE** (W13) on Broadway north of New York Avenue. The complex currently includes the Aurora Transportation Center and the adjacent Walter Payton Restaurant. The massive limestone structure accommodated forty stalls for building and repairing locomotives. Aurora supported many more industries and attracted workers, managers, and factory owners to its thriving economy in the late nineteenth and early twentieth centuries.

West out from Chicago, nineteenth-century structures show the multiple kinds of settlements which emerged both before and after the arrival of the railroad. Instead of an undifferentiated rural landscape before the hypersuburbanization of the close of the last century, this tour has shown the very clear development paths which were laid in the nineteenth century.

Southwest Tour

Development to the southwest of Chicago was dominated by a transportation corridor which connected Lake Michigan with the Mississippi River system. Before 1848, this connection was made overland and through the Chicago Portage. After 1848, the Illinois and Michigan Canal linked the South Branch of the Chicago River with the Illinois River. By 1854, the original canal was joined by a railroad line. At the opening of the twentieth century, the Sanitary and Ship Canal reinvigorated water travel along the corridor, and the construction of the Stevenson Expressway in the early 1960s provided another form of transportation in this old corridor.

Transportation in and out of Chicago also followed a shallower corridor to the north of the canals. The Southwest Plank Road (now Ogden Avenue, Route 34) paralleled the canal to the Des Plaines River, but then continued westward as the canal corridor headed southward. Our tour will follow the more westerly route out from the city center and then return into the city along the more southerly route.

We might expect that settlement in this corridor would be oriented toward trade and industry, and to a large degree that is the case. Interestingly, residential commuter suburbs, farms, and recreational sites also took advantage of the geography southwest of downtown Chicago to create a diverse mixture of settlements in the nineteenth and early twentieth centuries.

The **UNION STOCK YARDS GATE** (SW1) (1879), off Halsted at Exchange Avenue, is a reminder that the Stock Yards District operated here from 1865 until 1971. Large districts devoted to industrial enterprises also located at West Chicago, Harvey, South Chicago, Lawndale, Cicero, Hammond, Chicago Heights, Waukegan, and Joliet. Very little remains of these districts, which have been redeveloped with light industry and warehouses or stand empty once again.

While the stockyards have disappeared, the neighborhoods which surrounded them remain. The housing, parks, businesses, and churches now serve residents who work across the region. In Back of the Yards, **ST. JOSEPH ROMAN CATHOLIC CHURCH** (SW2) is one of three churches between 4600 and 5000 South Hermitage founded by Roman Catholic immigrants from Bohemia, Lithuania, and Poland. Polish immigrants organized St. Joseph in 1886. Architect Joseph Molitor designed the present church, completed in 1914.

This tour continues by traveling north to 47th Street and west to Cicero. Near Cermak Road stand remnants of the once extensive **HAWTHORNE WORKS** (SW3) of Western Electric.

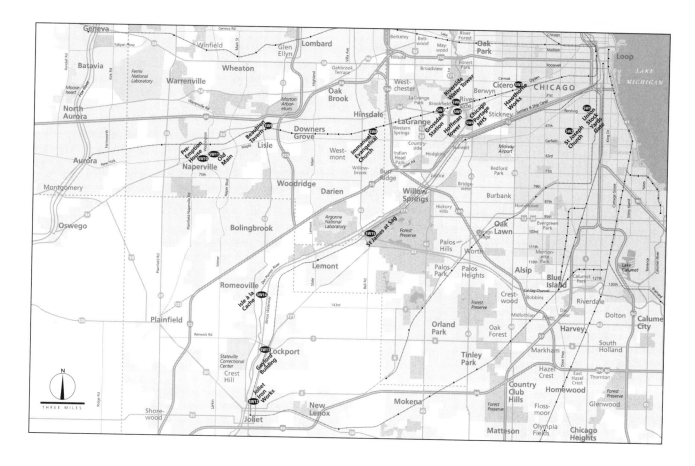

SOUTHWEST TOUR

SW1. **Union Stock Yards Gate (1879)** | 850 West Exchange Avenue, Chicago

SW2. **St. Joseph Roman Catholic Church (1914)** | 1729 West 48th Street, Chicago

SW3. **Hawthorne Works (1903)** | Cermak Road, Ogden and Cicero Avenues, Cicero

SW4. **Chicago Portage National Historic Site** | 4700 South Harlem Avenue, Lyons

SW5. **Hoffman Tower (1908)** | 3910 Barry Point Road, Lyons

SW6. **Riverside Water Tower (1871)** | 10 Pine Street, Riverside

SW7. **Grossdale Train Station (1889)** | 8820 Brookfield Avenue, Brookfield

SW8. **Immanuel Evangelical Church (1900)** | 302 South Grant Street, Hinsdale

SW9. **Beaubien Tavern (1830s)** | 921 School Street, Lisle

SW10. **Pre-Emption House (1834)** | 523 South Webster, Naperville

SW11. **Old Main, North Central College (1871)** | 30 North Brainard, Naperville

SW12. **Joliet Iron Works (1869)** | Collins Street off Columbia, Joliet

SW13. **Gaylord Building (1838)** | 200 West 8th Street, Lockport

SW14. **Isle à la Cache** | 501 East 135th Street, Romeoville

SW15. **St. James at Sag Roman Catholic Church (1852)** | Archer Avenue near 106th Street, Lemont

Relocated from the near west side in 1903, the five and six story red brick buildings have distinctive terra cotta trim visible behind the strip malls on the east side of Cicero.

West on Ogden Avenue (U.S. 34), and then south on Harlem Avenue (SR 43) in the Portage Woods to the west (Forest Preserve District of Cook County), stands a monument to this earlier era: the **CHICAGO PORTAGE NATIONAL HISTORIC SITE** (SW4). The historic site was established in 1952, and the large steel sculpture at the site was later installed to commemorate the three hundredth anniversary of the 1673 trip by Father Jacques Marquette and Louis Joliet through the region. The sculpture shows the two Frenchmen with an unidentified Indian (who quite probably was leading the two strangers as well as providing the physical labor exemplified in this sculpture). The Des Plaines River is just to the west of this site, and footpaths leading off from the site give a glimmer of what the landscape might have looked like three hundred years ago.

Returning north along Harlem and then west on Ogden Avenue, we cross the Des Plaines River and drive through more forest preserve lands. Since the mid-nineteenth century, beer gardens and picnic groves have dotted these woods, close to Ogden and Archer avenues, as well as at the start of Joliet and Plainfield roads that angle out further southwest. On the left, the Cream City Amusement Park front gate stood in the first decades of the twentieth century. North a short block off Ogden Avenue at Barry Point Road is the **HOFFMAN TOWER** (SW5). George Hoffman's family had a beer garden and brewery here for decades before he built this tower in 1908 as a further attraction. Visitors could rent boats, climb the tower, or enjoy the view.

Just across the bridge north from Hoffman's operation is Riverside, established in 1869 as an elite residential enclave. Following the curvilinear streets northward (on a path designed by the landscape architect Frederick Law Olmsted), we pass large, single-family houses on spacious lots built primarily between the 1870s and the 1920s. The families who built these residences enjoyed the scenic beauty of the site, but also shared it with visitors to entertainment venues like George Hoffman's across the river. The plan of Riverside centers on a rail station, which provided ready commuter access. Across the tracks is the **RIVERSIDE WATER TOWER** (SW6), which made it possible for Riverside families to have indoor plumbing long before many of their neighbors.

Returning south to Ogden Avenue, which runs roughly parallel to the Chicago, Burlington, and Quincy Railroad, head west to Maple Street. North on Maple Street, beyond the tracks is the **GROSSDALE TRAIN STATION** (SW7)—which was the original name of this commuter suburb founded by S. E. Gross in 1889. With smaller lots and fewer amenities than Riverside, Grossdale attracted a less affluent population as it grew along the railroad. The original train station has been moved across the street from the railroad and serves the Brookfield Historical Society.

Ogden Avenue (U.S. 34) continues to skirt a string of railroad suburbs that emerged during the 1860s and 1870s: La Grange, Western Springs, and then Hinsdale, whose train station is south of Ogden Avenue at York Road. The original plat of Hinsdale was commissioned in 1864, just after the railroad came through this area. Several additions to this original plat left nineteenth-century Hinsdale with a wide range of lot sizes—to accommodate large mansions or modest worker cottages. Growth in Hinsdale was slow and steady, and skilled German workers were kept busy building houses for decades. Many lived in modest houses in the original Hinsdale subdivision and supported the construction of the **IMMANUEL EVANGELICAL CHURCH** (SW8) (1900) on Grant Street a few blocks southwest of the train station.

West along Ogden Avenue (U.S. 34) through Downers Grove (which has its historical society in a restored nineteenth-century house off Main Street) and into Lisle, is the original site of the **BEAUBIEN TAVERN** (SW9) (on the north side of Ogden just east of Karns Road). The tavern was dragged east on Ogden to Park Street and south on Park to a site adjacent to the Lisle Train Station (just east of SR 53) in the late 1980s. Restoration over the 1990s confirmed that the structure dates to the early 1830s and served as a tavern both before and after Mark Beaubien, Jr., bought the property in 1843. As with other taverns in the region, it lost out to the railroad by the 1860s. Perhaps nowhere is this point made more strongly in the landscape than at Lisle, where the Beaubien Tavern now stands across the street from the Lisle Depot Museum, which served area farmers as a shipment point beginning in the 1870s.

Traveling south to Maple Avenue, drive west a few miles to Naperville (Maple Avenue becomes Chicago Avenue in Naperville). Naperville began as a settlement along the west branch of the DuPage River in 1831. It is a town which grew first because of its proximity to the plank road (now Ogden Avenue) and to the west branch of the DuPage River. In 1834, George Laird constructed the **PRE-EMPTION HOUSE** (SW10), a replica of which stands as the visitors' center of Naper Settlement just south of Chicago Avenue at Main Street. Other nineteenth-century buildings have been dragged onto the settlement grounds from around Naperville, including the Murray house built in the 1840s. Together they comprise the largest collection of preserved nineteenth-century structures in the region.

In the 1830s and 1840s, Naperville grew as the DuPage County seat along a key route (Ogden Avenue) out from Chicago. Unlike northern neighbor Warren Wheaton, Naperville residents failed to understand that the railroad would change the logic of regional development. But Naperville got a second chance, and its own rail stop, when the Chicago, Burlington, and Quincy Railroad came through the area in the early 1860s. Returning east on Chicago Avenue and then north on Brainard, we come to North Central College, which moved to Naperville from Plainfield in 1871 because of the new rail connection. With the support of local German Evangelicals, architect John M. Van Osdel designed a large limestone building for the college in 1871, **OLD MAIN** (SW11). Nearby quarries, breweries, and a furniture factory also provided local employment into the mid-twentieth century.

The next stop moves the tour south into the Canal Corridor. Take Chicago (Maple) east to SR 53 and then south through Romeoville and past Stateville Prison. Travel east on Bridge Street across the waterways and then north on Collins Street.

On the north side of Joliet on Collins Street off Columbia, in sight of the Old State Prison, are the remains of the **JOLIET IRON WORKS** (SW12). Visitors can walk an interpretive path maintained by the Forest Preserve District of Will County, which weaves through the remains of the steel operations which closed in 1980.

Following SR 171 northward we come to Lockport, which was designated as the headquarters for construction of the Illinois and Michigan Canal. The canal commissioners' house (1836) just north of SR 7, is a low, white frame structure just off Archer Avenue. Just behind the canal commissioners' headquarters on 8th Avenue stands the **GAYLORD BUILDING** (SW13), a substantial limestone structure completed in 1838 as a storehouse for the canal. Today, the building includes an exhibit on the evolution of Lockport and surrounding towns. Just outside the front entrance to the Gaylord Building, we can see what remains of the Illinois and Michigan Canal, which operated from 1848 until traffic all but ceased in 1914. Up the hill are several churches which date back to the era of canal construction.

North along SR 171 (now Archer Avenue) and west on 135th Street in Romeoville is **ISLE À LA CACHE** (SW14), an island museum dedicated to the French fur trade and operated by the Forest Preserve District of Will County. Continuing to the northeast along Archer Avenue (and 106th Street), we see **ST. JAMES AT SAG ROMAN CATHOLIC CHURCH** (SW15), which sits on a high bluff. The small limestone church and cemetery was built by Irish canal workers and contractors in 1852. Around it in the Cook County Forest Preserves are sloughs and wetlands which have remained undeveloped.

Traveling southwest along the canal corridor, we have seen examples of every basic kind of settlement in nineteenth-century Chicagoland: farm, industrial, recreational, and commuter. The complexity of nineteenth-century settlement is clear, even though much of this landscape was radically transformed by the hypersuburbanization of the late twentieth century.

South Tour

Lake Michigan and railroads are central to understanding development south of downtown Chicago. Waterways and harbors have been created, straightened, reversed, and dredged to improve the transportation advantages of particular sites. Multiple rail lines crisscrossed this portion of the region by the early twentieth century.

Stephen Douglas was one of the very first to grasp the importance of the railroad to development south from Chicago. He purchased land along the proposed path of the Illinois Central Railroad, established a residence there in the early 1850s, donated land for the first University of Chicago in 1860, and surveyed two residential subdivisions. His house was

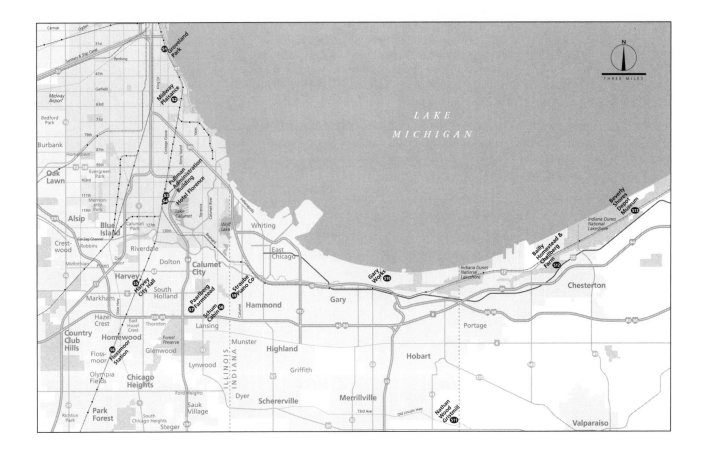

SOUTH TOUR

S1. Groveland Park (1855) | 3335 South Cottage Grove Avenue, Chicago

S2. Midway Plaisance (1870s) | Between 59th and 60th streets, Stony Island and Cottage Grove avenues

S3. Pullman Administration Building (1880) | Northeast corner of 111th Street and Cottage Grove Avenue, Chicago

S4. Hotel Florence (1881) | 11111 South Forestville Avenue, Chicago

S5. Harvey City Hall (1890s) | 154 East 154th Street, Harvey

S6. Flossmoor Station (1906) | 1035 Sterling Avenue, Flossmoor

S7. Paarlberg Farmstead (1870) | 172nd Place and Paxton Avenue, South Holland

S8. Thomas Agge Schrum Heritage Cabin (1836) | 760 Wentworth Avenue, Calumet City

S9. Straube Piano Company (1904) | 252 Wildwood Road, Hammond

S10. Gary Works (1906) | Broadway and West 2nd Place, Gary

S11. Nathan Wood Gristmill (1876) | 9410 Old Lincoln Highway, Hobart

S12. Bailly Homestead (1822) and Chellberg Farm (1884) | Mineral Spring Road between U.S. 12 and U.S. 20, Chesterton

S13. Beverly Shores Depot Museum (1929) | 525 Broadway, Beverly Shores

torn down and the university burned, but the Illinois Central still runs through the South Side, and one of his subdivisions is still visible at 3300 S. Cottage Grove. **GROVELAND PARK** (S1) consists of a center square park surrounded by residential lots, with a small guardhouse at the entrance to the private park. After the Civil War, wealthy Chicagoans like Joy Morton lived in large new houses in this area. Today only some of the residences remain, just to the north of the Stephen Douglas monument.

What began with Douglas's investment evolved into the African American community of Bronzeville by the early twentieth century. South on King Drive, which was developed as part of the boulevard system after 1869, are large residences once home to prominent black Chicagoans, including Ida B. Wells-Barnett (3624 S. King Drive). At 51st Street, King Drive becomes the western edge of Washington Park. At 60th Street, the **MIDWAY PLAISANCE** (S2), links Washington Park to Jackson Park. Frederick Law Olmsted and Calvert Vaux did the initial landscape designs for the South Parks. By 1892, both the University of Chicago and the World's Columbian Exposition were under construction alongside and on the Midway Plaisance. The Ferris wheel and other attractions at the 1893 fair stood on the Midway, which later served as the front yard for the University of Chicago.

Further south from the Midway along Stony Island, is an area where several rail lines converged by the mid-nineteenth century. Settlements in the railroad age skirted low-lying marshes and sought out transportation advantages. Early iron and steel production also took advantage of harbor and rail connections (such as the former South Works of U.S. Steel in the South Chicago neighborhood just north of the mouth of the Calumet Harbor). Some of the largest industrial enterprises in the region located in this area. The bridges over the Calumet River (including the Skyway) provide a marvelous vantage point to take in the substantial industrial region that surrounded the Lake Calumet Harbor.

At 95th Street, go west to Cottage Grove. At 111th Street and Cottage Grove, George Pullman created an industrial town between 1880 and 1884. Near both the Illinois Central Railroad and the Lake Calumet Harbor, Pullman built both a plant to manufacture and repair his sleeping cars and a town for industrial workers on low-lying land that had little value for farmers. To the north, Dutch farmers raised crops and built homes in the Roseland community along Michigan Avenue.

Only a small part of the **PULLMAN ADMINISTRATION BUILDING** (S3) still stands on the northeast corner of 111th and Cottage Grove. Across the street the **HOTEL FLORENCE** (S4) serves as an entrance into a neighborhood which contains many of the features designed by S. S. Beman in the 1880s. The red brick of townhouses contrasts with the green stone of the one church built by Pullman, in a misguided effort at fostering interdenominational mingling.

From Pullman travel west on 115th Street and then south on Halsted (SR 1) to 154th Street and west to Harvey. South along the Illinois Central Railroad, beginning in 1889, the Harvey

Land Association built a waterworks, a sewerage system, and electric works as an incentive for industry (and residents) to locate in this temperance town. In order to maintain these systems, the residents and owners of industries in Harvey incorporated as a city in 1891. The **HARVEY CITY HALL** (S5), on 154th Street in downtown Harvey, which for many years housed the Thornton Township Historical Society, was the first seat of local government.

South on Wood Boulevard and South Park the combination of meandering streams (here Butterfield Creek) and a rail stop on the Illinois Central out from downtown Chicago led to a very different kind of development: golf courses. The **FLOSSMOOR STATION** (S6), which now houses a local restaurant, was built in 1906 by the railroad to accommodate members of the country clubs developing around the station. Golfers came in the summer months for weekends and longer getaways from the more hectic pace of the central city. By the 1920s, this recreational area was becoming a residential commuter suburb, as club members took to commuting to Chicago to their jobs instead of commuting to Flossmoor for their golf.

From the Flossmoor Train Station head north and east to South Holland, a very different nineteenth-century landscape: a farm center on the Little Calumet River founded by Dutch farmers in the 1840s. Truck farming continued in the area into the late twentieth century, but the nineteenth-century rural landscape is preserved at the **PAARLBERG FARMSTEAD** (S7) just north of the Kingery Expressway and east of SR 83 at 172nd Place and Paxton. The Paarlberg family came from the Netherlands in 1846. Peter and Cornelia Paarlberg established this farmstead in 1870, making additions to the house in the 1890s.

Travel east from the Paarlberg Farmstead on Bernice Road to 760 Wentworth Road in Calumet City, where the **THOMAS AGGE SCHRUM HERITAGE CABIN** (S8) draws visitors back to the 1830s. The lower portion of the cabin dates to the early 1830s, while the upper section was built in the 1860s. The Schrum family emigrated from Hamburg, Germany, in 1860 and lived in the cabin. Members of the Schrum family donated the cabin to the Calumet City Historical Society, which dismantled and rebuilt it along the banks of the Little Calumet River west of Burnham Avenue where it stands today.

East from Calumet City, our south tour moves into Indiana. The Calumet River system links sites in Illinois and Indiana despite the political divide. Hammond, with access to the Grand Calumet River (and Indiana Harbor through a short canal) as well as rail lines, grew in the second half of the nineteenth century as an industrial center with a bustling business district. A substantial stockyard and many smaller factories fueled economic growth well into the twentieth century. The **STRAUBE PIANO COMPANY** (S9), off Hohman, still stands as an example of the many factories that underlay the economies of Hammond and other industrial towns in the Calumet Region.

Northeast of Hammond, the planned industrial city of Gary is now nearly a hundred years old. The U.S. Steel Company chose an undeveloped site on Lake Michigan for a large steel production center in 1906. The **GARY WORKS** (S10), still in operation today, stand north of the Indiana Toll Road (I-90) at Broadway (SR 53). South of the rail lines (and now the interstate highway), the city of Gary developed quickly. U.S. Steel laid out a town in a gridiron plan and built some housing, but most residential development was done by private speculators and builders.

South of Gary off Old Lincoln Highway (and just east of I-65) stands the **NATHAN WOOD GRISTMILL** (S11). A gristmill and sawmill were built here in 1838. Nathan Wood purchased the mills in the 1850s and constructed the extant brick gristmill in 1876. It is now operated as a museum and part of the Deep River Valley County Park.

Traveling northward takes us to the Indiana Dunes National Lakeshore, operated by the National Park Service. The **BAILLY HOMESTEAD** and **CHELLBERG FARM** (S12) are both located east of Route 49 in Chesterton, Indiana. The Bailly Homestead is located on a bluff above the Little Calumet River near the old Michigan City Road. The National Park Service has rebuilt several of the log buildings that comprised the trading post of Joseph and Marie Bailly after their arrival in 1822. The site also includes the frame Bailly House built in the 1830s during the transition from Indian to American settlement.

The Chellberg family began farming in this area in the 1860s. With the arrival of the railroad in the late nineteenth century, the family switched from grains to dairy production. The farmstead contains an 1880s farmhouse, outbuildings, and garden plots and pastures.

East along Lake Michigan, Beverly Shores was one of the last railroad towns founded in Chicagoland. Frederick H. Bartlett Company purchased 3,600 acres of lakeshore west of Michigan City in 1927. The town was sited between Lake Michigan and the Chicago, South Shore and South Bend Railroad (today the region's only surviving electric interurban line). The developers constructed the **BEVERLY SHORES STATION** (S13) to transport visitors and residents back and forth into Chicago. The site was envisioned as a recreational haven, with gardens, a golf course, and a hotel. Today this resort community is surrounded by the Indiana Dunes National Lakeshore.

This tour south from downtown Chicago shows the great importance of industry in the development of the region. However, it also shows that even in areas of heavy industrialization, agricultural, recreational, and residential sites are still part of the mix.

North Tour

This northward trip is oriented around the prerailroad routes (such as Milwaukee and Ridge avenues) that angled out from the city center like a fan in every direction, as well as the Chicago and North Western Railway, which first began running north near the Lake Michigan shoreline in the early 1850s. While much of this area is considered the "North Shore," conjuring up visions of elite commuter suburbs, there were in fact a wide range of settlements, including old farm centers, recreational communities, and institutional towns. Drinking

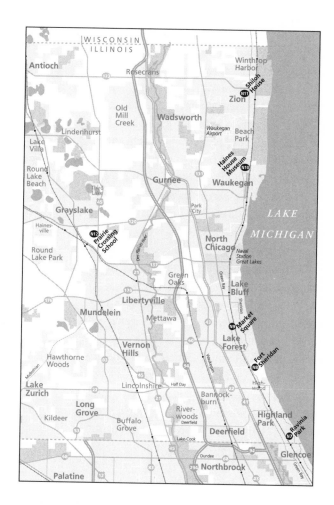

NORTH TOUR

N1. Best Brewery (1880s) | 1317 West Fletcher Street, Chicago

N2. The Grove (1856) | 1421 Milwaukee Avenue, Glenview

N3. University Hall (1869) | 1897 Sheridan Road, Evanston

N4. Willard House (1865) | 1730 Chicago Avenue, Evanston

N5. Gross Point Village Hall (1896) | 609 Ridge Road, Wilmette

N6. Kenilworth Train Station (1890) | 400 Richmond Road, Kenilworth

N7. Ravinia Park (1904) | 418 Sheridan Road, Highland Park

N8. Fort Sheridan (1887) | East of Sheridan Road at the northern end of Highland Park

N9. Market Square (1916) | Western Avenue north of Deerpath Road, Lake Forest

N10. Haines House (1843) | 1917 North Sheridan, Waukegan

N11. Shiloh House (1901–1902) | 1300 Shiloh Boulevard, Zion

N12. Prairie Crossing Charter School (1857) | 1571 Jones Point Road, Grayslake

versus temperance, farming versus gardening, and private versus public recreation were among the battles waged by area residents into the twentieth century.

The Best Brewing Company purchased an existing brewery at 1317 Fletcher Avenue (near Belmont and Southport) in 1891. The **BEST BREWERY** (N1) expanded two years later to include machine, brew, mill, boiler, and engine houses. The brewery, which abutted a railroad spur line to the east, stood on a block which was otherwise residential. After the brewery shut down in 1961, the buildings were eventually renovated as housing units.

The second stop is the oldest site on this tour, and moves us beyond the City of Chicago. Traveling northwest along Milwaukee Avenue in present-day Glenview, along one of the oldest roads in Chicagoland, is **THE GROVE** (1856) (N2). John Kennicott and his family lived in this Gothic Revival house set between the Milwaukee Road and the Des Plaines River. The Kennicotts chose this area, as did many other farmers, because of ready road and water access, as well as a nearby stand of trees, which suggested fertile land and provided building materials and fuel. Across the Chicago area in the nineteenth century, farmsteads with houses such as these were built with ready access to roads and markets.

Traveling eastward from the Grove along Golf Avenue (south of the Grove) to Sheridan Road (Golf becomes Emerson in Evanston), we come to the south end of Northwestern University. **UNIVERSITY HALL** (1869) (N3), located east of Sheridan Road, just south of where Emerson Street would lie if it continued, was built of local limestone in a Gothic style. Northwestern University began operations in Evanston in 1854 shortly after the arrival of the railroad and under its state charter, outlawed the sale of liquor in a four-mile radius from University Hall. This was of little concern to its Evanston neighbors, who embraced temperance from its founding in 1855. Just blocks south from University Hall (south on Sheridan to Chicago Avenue) is the **WILLARD HOUSE** (N4), home for more than forty years to Frances Willard, who served as dean of women at Northwestern and, as founder of the Woman's Christian Temperance Union, devoted much of her life's work to temperance. Willard called her home the Rest Cottage, which remains in the hands of the WCTU.

Return to Emerson and travel west to Green Bay Road and north to Lake Street. To the northwest, is the farm crossroads that was known as Gross Point (after a road angling into the area from the southwest). Away from the lake and railroad, the settlement catered to German farmers who came into the area in the late 1830s and early 1840s. These farmers supported St. Joseph Roman Catholic Church and Cemetery (1843), as well as stores and saloons.

In response to the temperance crusades of Evanstonians and Northwestern University students and faculty, residents organized as a village and built the **GROSS POINT VILLAGE HALL** (1896) (N5). The village government remained independent until national prohibition shuttered their saloons and led to the absorption of Gross Point into its eastern neighbor, Wilmette. Wilmette, like Evanston, was an early proponent of temperance and prohibition.

Follow Lake Street east back to Green Bay Road and north to Kenilworth. One of the most affluent communities in the United States, Kenilworth was founded in 1890, after a flag stop on the North Western Railway was established. Catering to affluent Chicagoans seeking to escape the travails of urban life (what travails there were for the wealthy living on Prairie Avenue in 1890), new residents built expansive houses on large lots along the curvilinear streets of the first subdivisions, which centered on the **KENILWORTH TRAIN STATION** (1890) (N6). Well into the twentieth century, their ornamental gardens and lawns contrasted with the truck farms and greenhouses of Gross Point residents just to the south.

For many years there was an unincorporated tract fronting Lake Michigan between Wilmette and Kenilworth. Although Wilmette and Kenilworth prohibited nonresident access to their beaches, the beaches in "No-Man's Land" were open to paying customers, and restaurants and saloons sold liquor to visitors from near and far. Wilmette annexed this land after Prohibition and eliminated public beach access by allowing the sale of the lakefront property to private developers.

North from Kenilworth, the elite commuter rail suburbs of Winnetka, Glencoe, and Highland Park also developed. Continue north on Green Bay Road to Lake Cook Road and east to Sheridan Road. North on Sheridan Road between Glencoe and Highland Park, A. C. Frost developed an amusement park adjacent to both a stop on the Chicago and North Western Railway and the Chicago, North Shore, and Milwaukee Railway. Opened in 1904, **RAVINIA PARK** (N7) has offered outdoor music and amusements for more than one hundred years. Residents of adjoining residential suburbs steered the park away from an open amusement area with beer garden and concerts to a semiprivate venue for classical music. In particular, residents wanted to keep the venue unattractive to the thousands of soldiers stationed just to the north at Fort Sheridan.

FORT SHERIDAN (1887) (N8), off Sheridan Road at the northern end of Highland Park, was established at the behest of Chicagoland elites, unnerved by the labor and social unrest of the 1870s and 1880s (especially the 1886 Haymarket bombing). They successfully lobbied the U.S. government for the establishment of a military base between Highland Park and Lake Forest on bluffs high above Lake Michigan. Fort Sheridan served as a military post until 1993. Today the military base has been turned over to private development, with some acreage left in the hands of the Lake County Forest Preserve District. Holabird & Roche designed the many yellow-brick buildings placed on a landscape design by Ossian Simonds. Among the most striking buildings are the former infantry barracks and watchtower.

Continue north on Sheridan Road into Lake Forest. For many years, Lake Forest was an uneasy northern neighbor to Fort Sheridan (until the transient military officers, enlisted men, and families were replaced by affluent residents who could afford the luxury houses, townhomes, and condominiums which emerged from the shuttered military base). Lake Forest was an early North Shore suburb, developed around a rail stop and Lake Forest College in the 1850s. **MARKET SQUARE** (1916) (N9), one of the oldest planned shopping centers in the United States, was built adjacent to the train station along Green Bay Road. While public squares are familiar across much of the country, rail stations centered most settlements founded in Chicago. Market Square was purpose-built next to the train station long after the establishment of the town, as much for shoppers in automobiles as railroad commuters.

The juxtaposition of insular elite suburbs with communities built around more open recreational uses continues to the north of Lake Forest, as we return to Sheridan Road and go northward. Lake Bluff was initially developed as a site for Methodist summer camp meetings. Frances Willard and other members of the Woman's Christian Temperance Union journeyed here for conventions and conferences until the facility was shuttered in 1898. North from Lake Bluff, nineteenth-century settlement turned from commuter and recreational uses to commerce and industry.

Waukegan's settlement predates the railroad. In fact, its harbor was used by the French and then designated as a port of entry by the federal government in 1846. By the 1880s, factories manufacturing goods that ranged from envelopes to sausage jammed the area between the harbor and the railroad. Today, few of the factories remain, and the lowlands near the harbor are being redeveloped for recreational uses. Just to the north of downtown Waukegan, Louise de Koven Bowen donated a seventy-two-acre site between Sheridan Road and Lake Michigan for the Joseph T. Bowen Country Club, a summer camp for boys from the Hull House neighborhood. The house, built in 1843, had for many years served as the summer home of John C. Haines and family. The camp included what is now the **HAINES HOUSE** (N10), and brought young men from the Near West Side to this Far North site well into the twentieth century. Today the property is operated by the Waukegan Historical Society.

Continuing north on Sheridan Road from Waukegan, we come to Zion. Zion was the brainchild of John Alexander Dowie, a self-proclaimed faith healer from Scotland, who purchased land to found a town for members of his Christian Catholic Apostolic Church in 1899. Dowie intended for members of his church to work at factories which were planned for the town. Dowie established a grand plan for Zion, including wide boulevards and ample space for a large church, hotel, and religious encampments. Dowie built the **SHILOH HOUSE** (N11) as his residence (now the Zion Historical Society, west of Sheridan on Shiloh Boulevard).

A final stop turns the tour westward along Rosecrans Road and then south on U.S. 45 to just beyond Belvidere Road (SR 120) in Grayslake. There the Prairie Crossing development includes both a historic one-room schoolhouse and a barn. The **PRAIRIE CROSSING CHARTER SCHOOL** (N12) functioned as the Wright School between 1857 and 1957. Today it serves as part of the new community's magnet school. Farmers dominated this landscape just a few miles west of Lake Michigan and its North Shore suburbs.

Across the north, then, we have seen sites related to farming, commuters, institutions, industry, and recreation. While the elite commuter suburbs dominated, they negotiated with competing (and often neighboring) uses for much of their histories. Temperance and various leisure-time activities were issues which divided residents, evidencing fissures along class, ethnic, and religious lines.

Northwest Tour

Traveling northwest out from downtown Chicago today, most traverse the Kennedy Expressway and Northwest Tollway. In the mid-nineteenth century, roads such as Irving Park, Talcott, and Northwest Highway and the northwest line of the Chicago and North Western Railway connected communities to each other and downtown. The historical dominance of agriculture is seen through the preservation of farmsteads and one-room schoolhouses, now through the prism of heavy suburbanization. But even in the nineteenth century, factories, commuters, and recreational users vied with farmers for space in this metropolitan corridor.

One of the oldest extant houses in the region (and the oldest structure in the City of Chicago), is located off Talcott Road just east of Harlem (and just north of the Kennedy Expressway). Located on a small rise, the southern wing of the **NOBLE-SEYMOUR-CRIPPEN HOUSE** (NW1) was built in 1833 with long windows opening onto a veranda. The Noble family were emigrants from England and early supporters of Methodism in this region. Methodists from across the region came to worship at the Noble House, as it was an early stop on the region's first Methodist circuit.

After the railroad opened a station about a half mile north of the homestead in the 1860s, a group of speculators platted a curvilinear commuter suburb, and the Seymour family put an Italianate addition onto the original Noble homestead. The homestead had become a suburban residence (which became a part of Chicago after annexation in 1893), showing how farmsteads even in the nineteenth century fell to more intensive uses as the railroad encouraged commuter settlement.

Following Talcott northwest to W. Algonquin Road, the **DES PLAINES METHODIST CAMP GROUND** (NW2) is located between a former flag stop on the northwest line of the North Western Railway and the Des Plaines River. Beginning in the 1860s, the camp, modeled on a Chautauqua experience, drew Methodist congregations and families from across the region for a day, a week, or a summer season to escape the city, take classes, and participate in special lecture series and musical events. By the beginning of the twentieth century, they had built cottages, which they returned to season after season. At the center of the camp ground today is the Waldorf Tabernacle, built in 1903 and still used for lectures and musical events. The camp ground is no longer a railroad stop; today's visitors come by car or bus.

Suburban towns like Norwood Park, Park Ridge, Des Plaines, Mount Prospect, Arling-

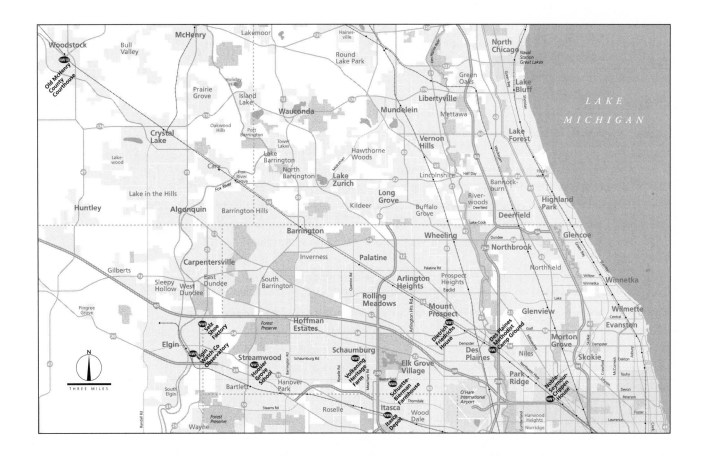

NORTHWEST TOUR

NW1. Noble-Seymour-Crippen House (1833) | 5924 North Newark Avenue, Chicago

NW2. Des Plaines Methodist Camp Ground (1860) | 1250 Campground Road, Des Plaines

NW3. Dietrich Friedrichs House (1906) | 101 South Maple Street, Mt. Prospect

NW4. Schuette-Bierman Farmhouse (1860s) | 499 Biesterfield Road, Elk Grove Village

NW5. Volkening Heritage Farm (1880s) | 1111 East Schaumberg Road, Schaumberg

NW6. Itasca Historical Depot (1873) | 101 North Catalpa Avenue, Itasca

NW7. Hoosier Grove School | 700 West Irving Park Road, Streamwood

NW8. Selz Shoe Factory (1891) | Northeast corner of Congden and Dundee Roads, Elgin

NW9. Elgin Watch Company Observatory (1910) | 312 Watch Street, Elgin

NW10. Old McHenry County Courthouse (1857) | 101 North Johnson Street, Woodstock

ton Heights, and Barrington all grew dramatically after 1945, but they trace their histories back to small settlements around rail stops in the nineteenth century. Near the downtown core in each of these towns are found houses which date back to the late nineteenth and early twentieth centuries that were residences for early commuters, local businessmen, and retired farmers. North on River Road into Des Plaines is Northwest Highway (U.S. 14). Traveling northwest on U.S. 14 to Mount Prospect Road brings us to downtown Mount Prospect. On Maple Street, the **DIETRICH FRIEDRICHS HOUSE** (NW3), built in 1906, serves as another clear example of historical single-family residences near the train station. It is home to the Mount Prospect Historical Society.

Farmsteads were located across the northwest corridor out from downtown Chicago by 1900. These farms were located between the rail lines, where land values would not sky-rocket until the arrival of improved highways in the mid-twentieth century. Traveling south on SR 83 to Biesterfield Road, we come to Elk Grove. A post-1945 suburb which grew with O'Hare Airport just to the east, Elk Grove nevertheless maintains a farmstead from the 1860s, the **SCHUETTE-BIERMAN FARMHOUSE** (NW4). The site preserves evidence of the German farmers who lived in this area long before Elk Grove Village came to be. A few miles north and west on Schaumburg Road, we come to a similar site, the **VOLKENING HERITAGE FARM** (NW5). This farmstead, a part of Spring Valley Nature Preserve, is an 1880s German farmstead, including a house and outbuildings. Schaumburg, a small farm crossroads until the 1950s, is now better known for Woodfield Mall than its agricultural past. But the German farmers of the preceding century, raising crops for themselves and for the market, also saw themselves as part of a commercial region.

To the south of these farms, the **ITASCA HISTORICAL DEPOT** (NW6) is maintained by the Itasca Historical Society as it would have been used by area farmers. The depot was built in 1873 soon after the Chicago and Pacific Railroad (later the Chicago, Milwaukee, and St. Paul) established a line through the area. Farmers quickly turned to dairying, taking advantage of the regular rail service.

The agricultural heritage of the region continues to be celebrated moving northwest along Irving Park Road (SR 19) into Streamwood, another post-1945 suburb. Hoosier Grove Park is located on the north side of Irving Park Road. There stands the **HOOSIER GROVE SCHOOL** (NW7), a modest white frame structure constructed in 1904 by German American farmers. Area children attended the school until 1954, when suburbanization transformed their educational needs. The building operates as a museum, like dozens of other one-room schoolhouses across Chicagoland. Farmhouses, farmsteads, schools, churches, and depots now punctuate the suburban subdivisions which came to dominate this area in the closing decades of the twentieth century.

While farming predominated in this part of the region in the nineteenth century, as we move west toward the Fox River, factories and other industrial sites were more common.

Many were small enterprises in close proximity to farm fields. Continuing west on SR 19 and north on Route 25 takes the tour to the outskirts of Elgin, where a small factory typical of many which once dotted this landscape still stands on Shoe Factory Road. The **SELZ SHOE FACTORY** (NW8) employed men and women into the twentieth century. The three-story brick building has many large windows designed to capture as much natural light as possible. Today the building has been rehabbed into residential space.

Larger factory sites often have not survived long beyond their closure. Returning south on SR 25, the Elgin National Watch Company began operation along the Fox River, south of downtown Elgin, in the mid-nineteenth century. Employing thousands of workers into the mid-twentieth century, the plant encompassed whole blocks along the river. Within a year of its 1965 shuttering, the plant was leveled. All that remains today is a corner of the fence which once circled the operation which now stands just south of the Lady Elgin Casino. However, just to the east of the former plant site, the **ELGIN WATCH COMPANY OBSERVATORY** (NW9) still stands and is used by local school groups.

Crossing the Fox River, take State Road 31 northward to U.S. 14 west into Woodstock for the final stop on the northwest tour: Woodstock, a town which has served farmers, small factories, and government workers from its founding in the 1840s. The Woodstock town square includes the **OLD MCHENRY COUNTY COURTHOUSE** (NW10), designed by John M. Van Osdel in local limestone in 1857. For generations, this building served county farmers and businessmen. It is one of the few surviving public buildings in the region dating back before the Civil War. The Woodstock Opera House also stands on this square, built in the 1890s and restored a century later.

On this northwest tour, there is considerable evidence of the heavy suburbanization of the second half of the twentieth century. New developments have grown on former farm fields. Still, farmers were not alone in the nineteenth century, just as suburbanites in the twenty-first century share this landscape with varied uses which have developed over time.

Central Area Tour

Chicagoland began with a look at the distinctive landscape of the city center. Skyscrapers like the **MONADNOCK BUILDING** (1891) (C1) and large rail terminals like the **DEARBORN STREET STATION** (1885) (C2) distinguished the Loop from other places in the region. But the central city also offers examples of the common structures found across Chicagoland from the nineteenth and early twentieth centuries. Into the mid-nineteenth century, the central city served both as a unique and powerful regional core and as part of the common landscapes found across the region. Indeed, there remain a few structures representative of common regional landscapes.

South from downtown at 18th Street, in the Prairie Avenue Historic District, are the

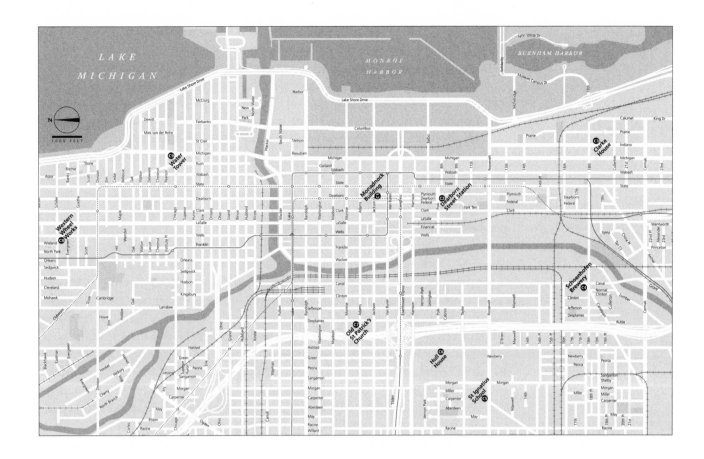

CENTRAL AREA TOUR

C1. Monadnock Building (1889–1893) | 53 West Jackson Boulevard, Chicago

C2. Dearborn Street Station (1885) | 47 West Polk Street, Chicago

C3. Henry and Caroline Clarke House (1836) | 1855 South Indiana Avenue, Chicago

C4. Schoenhofen Brewery (1903) | 18th Street at Canalport Avenue, Chicago

C5. St. Ignatius College Prep School (1867–69) | 1076 West Roosevelt Road, Chicago

C6. Hull House (1856) | 800 South Halsted Street, Chicago

C7. Old St. Patrick's Church (1852) | 700 West Adams Street, Chicago

C8. Western Wheel Works (1889–1891) | 1350 North Wells Street, Chicago

C9. Water Tower (1869) | North Michigan Avenue at Chicago Avenue

Glessner House (1887) and the **HENRY AND CAROLINE CLARKE HOUSE** (1836) (C3). The Clarke House was moved several times before landing at its current location (although its initial location was not distant). The Greek Revival style is clearly visible, with colonnades, windows that open onto the front veranda, and a central hall plan. Henry Clarke made his fortune in an early hardware business, but it was his widow, Caroline Clarke, who lived in the house for decades. The Clarke House is among a group of houses standing from the 1830s and early 1840s that includes the Noble-Crippen-Seymour House (1833; NW1) in the Norwood Park neighborhood; the Murray house (1842) on the Naper Settlement Grounds; the Bailly Homestead (early 1830s; S12) in Chesterton, Indiana; the Canal Commissioners' House (1836) in Lockport; and the Peck Homestead (1837; W6) in Lombard. All were built with ready access to area roads by the generation of new settlers who poured into this region at the end of Native American settlement.

Early industries in Chicagoland processed the farm produce from a rich agricultural hinterland. Mills and breweries were among the earliest enterprises in Chicagoland.

The **PETER SCHOENHOFEN BREWING COMPANY** (1903) (C4) at 18th and Canalport Avenue was established at this site in Pilsen in 1886. Peter Schoenhofen was among a group of brewers in Chicago who transformed production methods. By 1900, there were sixty breweries in Chicago that together produced over 100 million gallons of beer a year. The Schoenhofen brewery building withstood prohibition and competition from national brands, and is still used for bottling beverages (but no longer beer). Breweries, pickle and cheese factories, and stockyards dotted Chicagoland by the mid-nineteenth century; the Schoenhofen Brewery was typical in this region, although many enterprises were located not in the city center, but along the new rail lines which converged there.

Institutions anchored new neighborhoods and suburbs. Schools, churches, and courthouses spread out across the region along the same rail lines as industries. For instance, **ST. IGNATIUS COLLEGE PREP** (1867–1869) (C5), founded as St. Ignatius College, shares much with other college buildings across the region, including Hauptgebaude (1879; W4), Elmhurst College; Old Main (1871; SW11), North Central College, Naperville; University Hall (1869; N3), Northwestern University, Evanston; and Blanchard Hall (1853; W8), Wheaton College. However, at walking distance from downtown rail stations, St. Ignatius did not provide a retreat from the congestion of the city as did remote locations along the railroad lines.

Other new settlement types came to dominate the landscape with the arrival of the railroad. Charles J. Hull, a successful businessman, chose to build his house walking distance from downtown. The **HULL HOUSE** (1856) (C6) was quickly overrun by dense growth out from the city center. Other affluent Chicagoans began to congregate around railroad stations, building houses at a distance from the city center. The Willard House (1865; N4) in Evanston; the Haines House (1843; N10) in Waukegan; and the the Grove (1856; N2) in Glenview are all residences built in the same era as Hull House but near to outlying stations.

OLD ST. PATRICK'S ROMAN CATHOLIC CHURCH (1852) (C7) first served the largely unskilled Irish immigrants who worked on the docks along the South Branch of the Chicago River, on railroad construction, and in new industries. The church served as an anchor in the burgeoning immigrant neighborhood to the west of downtown. As the canal and railroad drew industry out from the city center, new settlements developed at some distance. For instance, St. James at Sag (1852; SW14) in Lemont, Immanuel Evangelical Church (1900; SW8) in Hinsdale, and St. Patrick's Roman Catholic Church in Lockport served immigrant workers along the new transportation lines out from the city center.

By the late nineteenth century, industry in Chicago had expanded well beyond food processing. Clothing, shoes, furniture, and a myriad of other products were manufactured in small and large plants across the metropolitan area. While whole districts were dedicated to industry, neighborhoods and suburbs also evolved which integrated factories and other enterprises into already established residential and commercial areas. The **WESTERN WHEEL WORKS** (1889–1891) (C8) manufactured bicycles in its first decade of existence. The very latest production methods were employed, but the company failed. For much of the twentieth century, a shoe factory operated from this space. In the late twentieth century, manufacturing was abandoned and the space was renovated as a residential/commercial development known as Cobbler Square. Across the metropolitan area stand similar structures, most near to rail lines, which have been converted to residential or commercial use: the Selze Shoe Factory (1891; NW8) (now housing) in Elgin; 5th Avenue Station (former Kroehler Furniture Company) in Naperville; the former Ovaltine Factory (1917; W5) (now housing) in Villa Park; and the Straube Piano Factory (1904; S9) in Hammond.

One of the most recognizable historic landmarks in Chicago, the **WATER TOWER** (1869) (C9) on N. Michigan Avenue, was built of a local limestone found in contemporaneous government buildings, colleges, and churches across the region. Over the course of the late nineteenth and early twentieth centuries, water towers also appeared in villages and cities in many parts of Chicagoland, from Winnetka to Riverside (SW6) to Pullman. Thus through its age, architectural style, and building material, the Water Tower connects us to regional patterns. Although the tower stands for many Chicagoans (and visitors) as a monument to the 1871 fire, which it survived, the building also tells other stories. Like the Monadnock Building, the Water Tower reminds us of the dense development of the nineteenth-century core in Chicago, including the amazing water system (with a tunnel one mile out into Lake Michigan) already under construction by midcentury to protect the valuable property of the city core. It also stands as a monument to the hubris of Chicagoans who thought that such a water system could save their city from a disastrous fire.

The Sum of the Tours

In any direction out from downtown Chicago, we can see examples of the four basic kinds of settlements founded in Chicagoland during the railroad age. Extant sites help us to understand the railroad landscape, even when twentieth-century settlement has radically transformed the look of the region. However, the mix and interaction of these original settlements, as well as later developments, mean that there is great diversity across the region. To understand Chicagoland, it helps to develop a basic understanding of these variations across the region, even while acknowledging their common building blocks.

Selected Sites

PRERAILROAD LANDSCAPE

S12   Bailly Homestead (1822)
       Mineral Spring Road between U.S. 12 and U.S. 20
       Chesterton, IN
       Indiana Dunes National Lakeshore
       National Park Service
       www.nps.gov

SW9   Beaubien Tavern (1830s)
       1825 Short Street, Lisle
       Lisle Station Park
       630-964-3410 (www.lisleparkdistrict.org)

SW4   Chicago Portage
       Harlem Avenue, two blocks north of Stevenson Expressway (I-55), Lyons
       Cook County Forest Preserve
       Portage Woods, Cook County Forest Preserve
       www.chicagoportage.org

C3   Clarke House Museum (1836)
       1855 S. Indiana Avenue, Chicago
       Chicago Architecture Foundation
       312-745-0077 (www.clarkehouse@interaccess.com)

W12   Garfield Farm Museum (1846)
2N016 Garfield Road, LaFox
Campton Historic Agricultural Lands
630-584-8485 (www.garfieldfarm.org)

SW13   Gaylord Building (1837)
200 W. 8th Street, Lockport
Canal Corridor Association
815-588-1100 (www.canalcor.org)

W3   Graue Mill and Museum (1852)
3800 S. York Road, Oak Brook
DuPage County Forest Preserve District
630-655-2090 (www.grauemill.org)

N2   The Grove (1856)
1421 Milwaukee Avenue, Glenview
Grove Heritage Association
847-299-6096

C6   Hull House (1856)
800 S. Halsted Street, Chicago
University of Illinois at Chicago
www.uic.edu/jaddams

SW14   Isle à la Cache Museum
501 E. 135th Street, Romeoville
815-886-1467 (www.fpdwc.org/isle2.cfm)

NW1   Noble-Seymour-Crippen House (1833)
5924 N. Newark Avenue, Chicago
Norwood Park Historical Society
773-631-4633

C7   Old St. Patrick's Church (1852)
700 W. Adams, Chicago
Archdiocese of Chicago
630-852-7269 (www.olstpats.org)

W5   Sheldon Peck Homestead (1837)
        355 E. Parkside, Lombard
        Lombard Historical Society
        630-629-1885 (www.villageoflombard.org)

SW10   Pre-Emption House (reconstructed, original 1834)
        523 S. Webster, Naperville
        Naper Settlement
        630-420-6010 (www.napersettlement.org)

S8   Thomas Agge Schrum Heritage Cabin (1836)
        760 Wentworth Avenue, Calumet City
        Calumet City Historical Society
        708-832-9390 (www.lakenetnwi.net/org/cchs)

C5   St. Ignatius College Prep School (1867–1869)
        1076 W. Roosevelt Road, Chicago
        www.ignatius.org

W7   Stacy's Tavern (1846)
        557 Geneva Road, Glen Ellyn
        Glen Ellyn Historical Society
        630-858-8696 (www.glen-ellyn/historical)

S11   Nathan Wood Gristmill (1876)
        9410 Old Lincoln Highway, Hobart, IN
        Deep River County Park
        219 947-1958

AGRICULTURAL LANDSCAPE

S12   Chellberg Farm (1884)
        Mineral Spring Road between U.S. 12 and U.S. 20
        Chesterton, IN
        Indiana Dunes National Lakeshore
        National Park Service
        www.nps.gov

N5   Gross Point Village Hall (1896)
        609 Ridge Road, Wilmette
        Wilmette Historical Society
        847-653-7666 (www.wilmettehistory.org)

W10   Hedges Station (1849)
        0N555 Winfield Road, Winfield
        Winfield Historical Society
        630-653-1489

NW6   Hoosier Grove Schoolhouse Museum (1904)
        700 W. Irving Park Road, Streamwood
        Streamwood Park District
        630-372-7284 (www.streamwoodparkdistrict.org)

NW7   Itasca Historical Depot (1873)
        101 N. Catalpa Avenue, Itasca
        Itasca Historical Society
        847-773-3363

W9   Kline Creek Farm (1890s)
        County Farm Road, north of Geneva Road, Winfield
        Forest Preserve District of DuPage County
        630-876-5901 (www/dupageforest.com)

NW10   McHenry County Courthouse (1857)
        101 N. Johnson Street
        Woodstock, IL 60098-0044

S7   Paarlberg Farmstead (1870)
        172nd Place and Paxton Avenue, South Holland
        South Holland Historical Society
        708-596-2722 (www.southholland.org)

N12   Prairie Crossing Charter School (1857)
        1571 Jones Point Road, Grayslake
        847-543-9722 (www.prairiecrossing.com)

SW14   St. James at Sag Roman Catholic Church (1852)
       Archer Avenue and 106th Street, Lemont
       St. James at Sag Bridge Parish

NW4   Schuette-Bierman Farmhouse Museum (1860s)
       Elk Grove Historical Society
       499 Biesterfield Road, Elk Grove Village
       www.parks.elkgrove.org

NW5   Volkening Heritage Farm (1880)
       1111 E. Schaumburg Road, Schaumburg
       Schaumburg Park District
       847-985-9692

INDUSTRIAL LANDSCAPE

W13   Aurora Roundhouse (1855)
       Walter Peyton Roundhouse Restaurant
       205 N. Broadway, Aurora

N1   Best Brewery (1880s)
       1317 W. Fletcher Street, Chicago

C9   Western Wheel Works (1889-91)
       1350 N. Wells, Chicago

NW9   Elgin National Watch Company Observatory (1910)
       312 Watch Street, Elgin
       www.elginhistory.org

S10   Gary Works, U.S. Steel (1906)
       Broadway and W. 2nd Place, Gary, IN

S5   Harvey City Hall (after 1891)
       154 E. 154th Street, Harvey
       Thornton Township Historical Society

SW3   Hawthorne Works of Western Electric (1903)
        (site now includes Hawthorne Works Shopping Center)
        4621 S. Cicero, Cicero
        (Cermak Road, Ogden and Cicero Avenues)

S4   Hotel Florence (1881)
        11111 S. Forrestville Avenue, Chicago
        Historic Pullman Foundation
        773-785-8181 (www.pullmanil.org)

SW12   Joliet Iron Works Historic Site (1869)
        Collins Street off Columbia Street, Joliet
        Forest Preserve District of Will County
        815-727-8700 (www.fpdwc.org/ironworks.cfm)

W4   Ovaltine Factory (1917)
        1 Ovaltine Court, Villa Park
        www.vphistoricalsociety.com

S3   Pullman Administration Building (1880)
        11100 S. Forestville Avenue, Chicago
        Historic Pullman Foundation
        773-785-8181 (www.pullmanil.org)

SW2   St. Joseph Roman Catholic Church (1914)
        1729 W. 48th Street, Chicago

C4   Schoenhofen Brewery (1903)
        Canalport Avenue and Eighteenth Street, Chicago

NW8   Selz Shoe Factory (1891)
        Northeast corner Congdon and Dundee Roads, Elgin
        http:/elginpostcards.tripod.com

N11   Shiloh House (1901–1902)
        1300 Shiloh Boulevard, Zion
        Zion Historical Society
        847-746-3806

S9 Straube Piano Company (1904)
    252 Wildwood Road, Hammond
    www.hammondindiana.com

W11 Turner Town Hall (1884)
    132 Main Street, West Chicago
    West Chicago City Museum
    www.westchicago.org

SW1 Union Stock Yards Gate (1879)
    850 W. Exchange Avenue, Chicago
    Central Manufacturing District

COMMUTER LANDSCAPE

W1 Austin Town Hall (1929)
    5610 W. Lake Street, Chicago
    Chicago Park District
    312-746-5009

S6 Flossmoor Train Station (1906)
    1035 Sterling Avenue, Flossmoor
    Flossmoor Station Brewing Company
    www.flossmoorstation.com

NW3 Dietrich Friedrichs House (1906)
    101 S. Maple Street, Mount Prospect
    Mount Prospect Historical Society
    847-392-8995 (MPHIST@aol.com)

SW7 Grossdale Train Station (1889)
    8820½ Brookfield Avenue, Brookfield
    Brookfield Historical Society

S1 Groveland Park Cottage (1855)
    601 E. Groveland Park Avenue, Chicago

SW8   Immanuel Evangelical Church (1900)
       302 S. Grant Street, Hinsdale
       Hinsdale Historical Society
       630-789-2600

N6   Kenilworth Train Station (1890)
       400 Richmond Road, Kenilworth
       847-251-1267 (www.kenilworthhistory.org)

N9   Market Square (1916)
       Western Avenue north of Deerpath Road, Lake Forest

SW6   Riverside Water Tower (1871)
       Longcommon and Pine Roads, Riverside
       Riverside Historical and Community Museum
       708-442-0711 (www.riverside-illinois.com)

N4   Frances Willard House (1865)
       1730 Chicago Avenue, Evanston
       847-328-7500 (www.wctu.org/house.html)

W2   Frank Lloyd Wright Home and Studio (1889)
       951 Chicago Avenue, Oak Park
       708-848-1976 (www.wrightplus.org)

RECREATIONAL/INSTITUTIONAL LANDSCAPE

S13   Beverly Shores Station (1929)
       525 Broadway Street, Beverly Shores, IN

W8   Blanchard Hall (1853)
       501 College Avenue
       Wheaton College, Wheaton
       www.wheaton.edu

NW2   Des Plaines Methodist Camp Ground (1860)
       1250 Campground Road, Des Plaines

N8   Fort Sheridan (1887)
        Old Elm and Sheridan Road, Highland Park
        www.fortsheridan.com/history

N10   Haines House (1843)
        1917 N. Sheridan Road, Waukegan
        Waukegan Historical Society
        847-336-1859 (www.waukeganparks.org)

W4   Hauptgebaude (Old Main) (1879)
        190 Prospect Street, Elmhurst
        Elmhurst College
        www.elmhurst.edu

SW5   Hoffman Tower Museum (1908)
        3910 Barry Point Road, Lyons
        Lyons Historic Commission
        708-447-8886

SW11   Old Main (1871)
        30 N. Brainard, Naperville
        North Central College
        www.noctrl.edu

N7   Ravinia Park (1904)
        200 Ravinia Park Road, Highland Park
        Ravinia Festival
        www.ravinia.org

N3   University Hall (1869)
        1897 Sheridan Road, Evanston
        Northwestern University
        www.library.northwestern.edu/history/univhall.html

Notes

Acknowledgments

1. Harold M. Mayer and Richard C. Wade, *Chicago: Growth of a Metropolis* (Chicago, 1969), ix.

Chapter 1

1. David Lowe, *Lost Chicago* (Boston, 1975), 56–57; and Alice Sinkevitch, ed., *AIA Guide to Chicago* (New York, 1993), 144–49.

2. So much of importance, so much of lasting value is represented in this small area. Historians have been drawn to tell these important stories—of politics and corporations, of architecture and high culture—that make Chicago "the city of the century." For instance, Donald L. Miller, *City of the Century: The Epic of Chicago and the Making of America* (New York, 1996).

3. The Monadnock's clean lines were much admired in the twentieth century. Interestingly, contemporary Chicagoans were less impressed with its clean lines, finding in its spareness a lack of style. This point is made by Robert Bruegmann, *The Architects and the City: Holabird & Roche of Chicago, 1880–1918* (Chicago, 1997), especially 117–20. See also Sinkevitch, especially Perry Duis, "The Shaping of Chicago," 3–24.

4. This phenomenon was not limited to Chicago. See Robert M. Fogelson, *Downtown: Its Rise and Fall, 1880–1950* (New Haven, 2001); and Alison Isenberg, *Downtown America: A History of the Place and the People Who Made It* (Chicago, 2004). Geographer David Harvey has interpreted this and other urban landscapes as "a built environment to function as the collective means of production for capital." "On Countering the Marxian Myth—Chicago-Style," in *Spaces of Capital: Towards a Critical Geography* (New York, 2001), 80.

5. Everett C. Chamberlin, *Chicago and Its Suburbs* (Chicago, 1874), 108.

6. William Cronon, *Nature's Metropolis: Chicago and the Great West* (New York, 1991), traces this important relationship between farmers and the railroad.

7. Daniel H. Burnham and Edward H. Bennett, *Plan of Chicago* (Chicago, 1909), 61–68.

8. From 1856 until 1974, railroad engines were built and/or repaired here. In 1872, more than 2,000 people were employed in the repair and construction of engines and railcars. Jim and Wynette Edwards, *Aurora: A Diverse People Build Their City* (Charleston, SC, 1998), 30.

9. The shop operations closed down in 1974. After a long period of disuse, the roundhouse was converted into a restaurant by a consortium which included Walter Payton, with help from the City of Aurora.

10. Historical societies have also preserved dozens of train stations in farm centers, institutional towns and recreational sites across Chicagoland—ready for further exploration and study. Some historians have followed these historical societies outward from the city center, studying especially residential commuter suburbs. More recently, a group of historians and geographers has documented the industrial towns that joined commuter suburbs along metropolitan rail lines by 1900. For the best summary discussion of the state of research on American suburbs, see the special issue "North American Cities and Suburbs," edited by Richard Harris, *Journal of Urban History* 27, no. 3 (March 2001).

11. In a recent article University of Alabama at Birmingham historian Ray Mohl calls for urban historians to think regionally. He argues that urban historians in the United States have not focused on the linkages between city and region. Mohl contrasts this with Canadian urban history, where regionalism is considered in imaginative ways. Raymond A. Mohl, "City and Region: The Missing Dimension in U.S. Urban History," *Journal of Urban History* 25, no. 1 (November 1998): 3–21.

12. This systematic view was facilitated by my work as coeditor of the *Encyclopedia of Chicago* (Chicago, 2004). My encyclopedia coeditors, Janice L. Reiff and James R. Grossman, and I defined the Chicago metropolitan area as Cook, DuPage, Lake, McHenry, and parts of Will and Kane counties in Illinois and Lake and Porter counties in Indiana. (Two additional places in Grundy County have been included: Morris and Diamond.) The encyclopedia includes entries on every suburb and city neighborhood in the region. Based on these encyclopedia entries (and further research), I examined more than 260 neighborhoods and suburbs, tracing the origins of 233 of these places to the nineteenth and early twentieth centuries. These neighborhoods and suburbs were founded either before or during the railroad age. The youngest place included is Beverly Shores, Indiana, founded in 1927 along the Chicago, South Shore, and South Bend Railroad.

13. My work on Chicagoland makes possible a response to Mary Corbin Sies's 2001 article, in which she called for a "systematic, empirically derived and comprehensive morphology of types of North American settlements," to better understand metropolitan areas. See Sies, "North American Suburbs, 1880–1950: Cultural and Social Reconsiderations," *Journal of Urban History* 27, no. 3 (March 2001): 313–47.

14. Roderick D. McKenzie, a member of the Chicago school of sociology and coauthor of *The City* (Chicago, 1925), championed an ecological approach to studying cities. In one of the essays in that volume, "The Ecological Approach to the Study of the Human Community," McKenzie identified four types of communities: primary service towns, commercial communities, industrial towns, and a final category "lacking in a specific economic base." McKenzie described the primary service towns as "the agricultural town, the fishing, mining, or lumber community which serves as the first step in the distributive process of the outgoing basic commodity and as the last stage in the distributive process of the product finished for consumption" (66–67). This description closely matches that used here for farm centers found in nineteenth-century Chicagoland.

15. The major exception has been the work of William Cronon, who has skillfully shown that agricultural hinterlands are vital parts of metropolitan areas like Chicago. William Cronon, *Nature's Metropolis: Chicago and the Great West* (New York, 1991). More generally, I have modeled my work most closely on that which Henry C. Binford did for suburban Boston in *The First Suburbs: Residential Communities on the Boston Periphery, 1815–1860* (Chicago, 1985).

16. Michael H. Ebner has taken a wide lens to the suburbs which emerged along Chicago's North Shore. He explores the wide range of housing, jobs, and leisure activities found along the railroad line north from the city center, setting these suburbs within a metropolitan context, in *Creating Chicago's North Shore: A Suburban History* (Chicago, 1988).

Two other areas in the region have a substantial number of nineteenth-century commuter suburbs—along the two lines running west out of the city. While each of these commuter suburbs was surrounded by farms and other neighbors, these rail lines provided a common experience. Riverside is along the southern route through DuPage County on the Chicago, Burlington, and Quincy Railroad. It shares this line with other commuter suburbs: Downers Grove, Clarendon Hills, Hinsdale, Western Springs, LaGrange, Brookfield. To the north, Austin, Oak Park, River Forest, Elmhurst, Lombard, and Glen Ellyn are along the Chicago and North Western Railroad.

Neither of these lines of commuter suburbs hold the cache of the North Shore. Neither has a special name for their group of commuter suburbs. Perhaps sharing lakeshore helped to define the North Shore as a subset of the region. Or perhaps the western suburbs felt more overwhelmed by the farmers who surrounded them.

While they do not abut each other and are not neighbors, the commuters who used the rail lines in and out of the city share cars with riders from these other suburbs. Commuters in Hinsdale, for instance, were well aware of developments around the train stations in Western Springs, LaGrange, Brookfield and Riverside. There was (and still is) a solidarity in sharing experiences, but also a subtle competition that often manifested itself in station upkeep and landscaping.

17. My model here is W. G. Hoskins, *The Making of the English Landscape* (London, 1955), especially 210. There, he explains that after exploring any English town, "questions begin to arise in the mind, which even the best of guide-books does not answer. Why is the town just like this, this shape, this plan, this size? Why do its streets run in this particular way . . . and so on. In short, what gives the town this particular landscape?"

18. Robert Park, Louis Wirth, and other members of the Chicago school of sociology in the 1920s and 1930s wrote at length about the composite parts of cities like Chicago, especially in *The City* (Chicago, 1925). There, Robert Park characterized a city as a "mosaic of little worlds which touch but do not interpenetrate." Although Park was writing about "the city," I think a mosaic is also an apt description for the settlement types in the wider metropolitan area. Interestingly, Park also argued that this mosaic of little worlds "makes it possible for individuals to pass quickly and easily from one moral milieu to another, and encourages the fascinating but dangerous experiment of living at the same time in several different contiguous, but otherwise widely separated, worlds" (40–41).

A mosaic, however, implies a static picture set in stone, and we know that metropolitan areas are characterized by individuals who are mobile and travel across the region, as well as by different kinds of settlements which often abut one another. These settlements may be pieces of a mosaic, but it is a changing mosaic. A kaleidoscope might be a better metaphor for thinking about the region, where suburbs or neighborhoods are in constant interaction with their neighbors.

19. Across the low-lying metropolitan area, there are many marshes and sloughs, which Rees gives a darker shade. See the following chapter for more discussion on this landscape.

20. Rees also includes the three railroads constructed or proposed by that date, but which did not yet dominate the landscape. Milo Quaife wrote extensively about the road system in his 1923 *Chicago's Highways, Old and New: From Indian Trail to Motor Road* (Chicago, 1923). Quaife identified at least five plank roads in the metropolitan area in 1852.

21. Ebner, 16–18. While water links are important, in many cases platting was spurred not so much by transportation potential as water power potential. Mills quickly emerged in most of these towns. Rees's map clearly sets off another kind of real estate: five areas reserved for individual Indians or Métis. The reservation lands are at Hickory Creek in Will County, along the Fox River in Kendall County, along the northern Des Plaines River and the North Branch of the Chicago River in Cook County, and north along Lake Michigan at what today is Wilmette. The U.S. government reserved these tracts in the late 1820s as a reward for the aid offered by these individuals to U.S. westward expansion.

22. Everett C. Chamberlin, *Chicago and Its Suburbs* (Chicago, 1874), devotes an entire section to sixty-four railroad towns (a substantial subset of railroad towns in existence in 1874). His choices were determined to some degree by the real estate agents and companies willing to place advertisements in the guidebook. But Chamberlin assures readers that he "has not in any case waived his prerogative of preventing exaggeration and securing justice to all" (8).

23. The major exception here is the very first place treated—Lake View, which has the largest essay, the most illustrations, and a number of prominent advertisements. While the suburban towns are ordered along train lines in the body of the text, Chamberlin lists them alphabetically in the table of contents.

24. Chamberlin, 456.

25. Ibid., 369.

26. Ibid., 398–99.

27. They identified industrial towns and commuter suburbs. They also noted that "On high-days and holidays the great city allures the people from the neighboring parts, and sends its own people on the water or into the country for rest and refreshment, so that there is a constant interchange of comers and goers." Burnham and Bennett, 34.

28. Ibid., 36–37.

29. Ibid., 34.

30. Ibid., 67.

31. Ibid., 93–94.

32. Charles Edward Merriam, Spencer D. Parratt, and Albert Lepawsky use the term to describe the Chicago metropolitan area in *The Government of the Metropolitan Region of Chicago* (Chicago, 1933), 37–38. Merriam uses it as well in the title of his *Scrambled Government: Who Rules What in Chicagoland?* (Chicago, 1934). "Chicagoland" was also used by newspaper columnist Harley Bradford Mitchell (The "Tatler") as the title for a collection of his columns, *Historical Fragments of Early Chicagoland* (Chicago, 1928).

33. Arguably, the structures that remain are "unrepresentative," because the history of metropolitan Chicago is one of change and destruction. David Allan Hamer, *History in Urban Places: The Historic Districts of the United States* (Columbus, 1998), 28, makes this point about historic districts in the United States, but it also can be applied to historic sites within the Chicago region.

34. Fortunately for me, while academic historians have slighted the study of areas beyond the Loop, hundreds of local historical societies have chronicled the stories of their communities and preserved buildings and sites. Taken together, this "weave of small patterns" in the nineteenth century undergirds Chicagoland today. Sam Bass Warner, Jr., *Streetcar Suburbs: The Process of Growth in Boston, 1870–1900* (Cambridge, 1962).

35. As Hoskins notes, the landscape provides much information, "if only we have the eyes to see, the records to follow up the visual evidence and the imagination to read the records aright" (29).

36. In fact, most of the history that is investigated, written, and preserved concerning the Chicago

metropolitan area is in the hands of these local societies, operated by both professional public historians and volunteers to whom history is an avocation.

In contrast, academic historians work generally only with archived materials. Historic preservation is a wholly separate field, occasionally bridged by public historians, but often operating wholly separate from academic historians. In fact, training for historic preservation is often done not through history departments, but through art, architecture, or planning schools.

37. The 1965 centennial of the end of the Civil War, the sesquicentennial of Illinois statehood in 1969, and the 1976 national bicentennial anniversary all increased interest in preserving history, particularly at a local level.

38. Landscape studies have an established place in geography, landscape architecture, material culture, and American studies. Among the most important works: John Brinckerhoff Jackson, *American Space: The Centennial Years, 1865–1876* (New York, 1972); D. W. Meinig, ed., *The Interpretation of Ordinary Landscapes: Geographical Essays* (New York, 1979); and especially John R. Stilgoe, *Common Landscape of America, 1580 to 1845* (New Haven, 1982).

Chapter 2

1. Colbee C. Benton, *A Visitor to Chicago in Indian Days: Journal to the Far-Off West* (Chicago, 1957), 79–80.

2. Benton, 83.

3. In 1904, amateur archeologist Albert Scharf described an Indian village at Half Day Road on the Des Plaines River. In his notes, Scharf describes the name as "taken from a Potawattomie [*sic*] chief, whose village was on the Des Plaines river at the mouth of Indian Creek." Albert Scharf Collection, box 1, folder 30, "Indian Trails and Villages in Lake County," typescript, Chicago Historical Society.

4. William Cronon, *Changes in the Land: Indians, Colonists, and the Ecology of New England* (New York, 1983), showed the ways in which northeastern Indians used controlled burning of the forest floor to aid in hunting.

5. Helen Tanner noted that "White folks are just a thin veneer—a couple of hundreds of years—on top of Indian people. That's the way the Indian people look at it." Helen H. Tanner as quoted in Scott Fornek, "Finding the Real Chicago Natives," *Chicago Sun-Times*, May 28, 1998.

6. There were periods of time when the area was abandoned due to war. This seems to have been the case after the Fox Wars in the early eighteenth century. For a generation or so, few inhabited this area because it was perceived as too dangerous. See Helen Hornbeck Tanner, ed., *Atlas of Great Lakes Indian History* (Norman, OK, 1987), 39–53.

7. Ed Lace, "Native Americans in the Chicago Area," in *Native Chicago*, ed. Terry Straus (Chicago, 2002), 24–25.

8. Tanner, 98–99.

9. Helen Hornbeck Tanner, "Tribal Mixtures in Chicago Area Indian Villages," in *Indians of the Chicago Area*, ed. Terry Straus (Chicago, 1989), 21.

10. "A list of chiefs of the Potawatomie tribe of Indians to whom annuities were paid by Alex. Wolcott Indian Agent Chicago, July 15, 1826," Alexander Wolcott Collection, Chicago Historical Society.

11. Milo Quaife, *Chicago's Highways Old and New: From Indian Trail to Motor Road* (Chicago, 1923), 39.

12. Henry R. Schoolcraft, *Narrative Journal of Travels through the Northwest Region of the United States* (Albany, 1821), 385.

13. William R. Keating was the traveler (no relation to the author); *Narrative of an Expedition to the Source of the St. Peter's River* (Philadelphia, 1824), 164–66.

14. Quaife has chapters on these old roads and their origins as Indian trails.

15. These portage sites are perhaps best seen on historic maps, as area residents have changed the path and direction of many area rivers. Today, virtually all of the rivers and creeks in the Chicago metropolitan area flow toward the Mississippi River. Beginning in 1848 with the Illinois and Michigan Canal, and later with the Sanitary and Ship Canal and the Cal-Sag Channel, drainage patterns were altered for both transportation and sanitation purposes. Channelization of many of the rivers and creeks in the area have transformed what used to be a muddy, marshy maze in spring and early summer. See Libby Hill, *The Chicago River: A Natural and Unnatural History* (Chicago, 2000); and David M. Solzman, *The Chicago River: An Illustrated History and Guide to the River and Its Waterways* (Chicago, 1998).

16. Bessie Louise Pierce, *History of Chicago*, vol. 1, *The Beginning of a City, 1673–1848* (Chicago, 1937), 6.

17. Native peoples had been in contact with Europeans and Africans for over two hundred years and their ways of life had been significantly altered. The melding of these worlds has been described by Richard White as a "middle ground." Richard White, *The Middle Ground: Indians, Empires, and Republics in the Great Lakes Region, 1650–1815* (New York, 1991).

18. Traders, like the Indians for generations before them, moved with the seasons. Only in the very late eighteenth century did traders begin to construct more permanent outposts in the Great Lakes region. Jacqueline Peterson, "Many Roads to Red River: Métis Genesis in the Great Lakes Region," in *The New Peoples: Being and Becoming Métis in North America*, ed. Jacqueline Peterson and Jennifer S. H. Brown (Lincoln, 1985), 37–71.

19. Jacqueline Peterson, "The Founding Fathers: The Absorption of French-Indian Chicago, 1816–1837," in *Native Chicago*, ed. Terry Straus (Chicago, 2002), 35.

20. Joseph and Marie Bailly's granddaughter remembered that groups of Indians also came to the area "for the purpose of gathering herbs, roots and barks for dyes and medicinal purposes." See Frances R. Howe, *The Story of a French Homestead in the Old Northwest* (Columbus, OH, 1907), 84; and Frank Straus, "Monee: Fur Trade, Family, and Individual Reservation," in *Native Chicago*, 118–36.

The amateur archeologist Albert Scharf interviewed area residents about a century ago, and some remembered that in the Calumet, "several Indian villages in these marshes were all located along the canoe routes or portage trails of which they form a part." See Scharf Collection, box 2. "The Indian Villages of the Calumet Marshes." typescript, Chicago Historical Society.

21. Charles Fenno Hoffman, *A Winter in the West: Letters Descriptive of Chicago and Vicinity in 1833–4* (Chicago, 1882), 11.

22. Hoffman, 12. The reconstructed buildings provide an opportunity to better visualize the fur trading operations, but must be considered with great care as they are not themselves historic structures.

23. Other traders had operations in the Chicago region. To the southwest in what became Plainfield, a French fur trader by the name of Vetal Vernnette established a squatter's claim to property along the DuPage River in 1823. Gurdon S. Hubbard came to the region in 1818 as an Indian agent for the American Fur Company. Brothers David and Bernardus (Barney) Laughton (Lawton) came to the Chicago area in the 1820s. At first they settled along the Chicago River near what is today Bridgeport at a site known as Lee's Farm. In 1828, the Laughtons moved twelve miles west of Fort Dearborn to a site along the Des Plaines River near the Chicago Portage Site.

The area fur trade is chronicled at the Isle à la Cache Museum in Romeoville. A part of the Forest Preserve

District of Will County, this island in the Des Plaines River has an interpretive museum which explores the French fur trade in this area. By legend, the island was used by a French trader in the 1600s to hide or "cache" his goods. Every June, an Island Rendezvous is held here—with reenactors playing the roles of French voyageurs and local Native Americans.

24. Some informal trading likely took place on the premises over the years that DuSable lived there, although DuSable did not serve as an official agent of any trading company. By 1800, DuSable had a considerable establishment, but he did not own any land. In that year, he sold the forty-by-twenty-two-foot wood house, one horse mill, a pair of millstones, a bake house, tools, furniture, household goods, and livestock, perhaps in anticipation of the arrival of American troops. He moved south to Spanish Louisiana and apparently never returned to Chicago.

There remain many unanswered questions about the DuSables. On Catherine DuSable's role, see Susan Sleeper-Smith, *Indian Women and French Men: Rethinking Cultural Encounter in the Western Great Lakes* (Amherst, 2001), 92–93. For two views on Jean Baptiste Point DuSable, see Pierce, 12–13; and John F. Swenson, "Jean Baptiste Point De Sable, The Founder of Modern Chicago," in *A Compendium of the Early History of Chicago: To the Year 1835 When the Indians Left*, ed. Ulrich Danckers and Jane Meredith (River Forest, IL, 2000), 388–94.

25. Peterson, 37.

26. The careful work of archeologists is helping us to see that it is not enough to simply find evidence of Indian occupation in the landscape (or in the historical record). There is a long and complicated history which cannot be seen in our landscape today. See Charles W. Markmam, *Chicago Before History: The Prehistoric Archaeology of a Modern Metropolitan Area*, Studies in Illinois Archaeology, no. 7 (Springfield, IL, 1991), 114.

27. Closely connected to Indian village sites identified by Albert F. Scharf were a number of taverns and settlements which were founded in the 1830s and early 1840s, as the native populations were forced westward and American settlers poured into the region. Because of the way in which Scharf collected and recorded information, he provides an interesting link between the Indian and the American era. Scharf interviewed members of families who moved into the area in the 1830s who lived near Indian sites he had identified. What is clear from Scharf's notes is that he found no sharp dividing line between an Indian and American occupation.

28. The Kennicott family established an extensive nursery that served all of northern Illinois. Dr. John Kennicott was not only an avid horticulturalist, but traveled across the area visiting patients as the area's first practicing physician. See A. T. Andreas, *History of Cook County* (Chicago, 1884), 868.

29. He served as a regular columnist for the *Prairie Farmer*.

30. For more on Robert Kennicott, see Joel Greenberg, *A Natural History of the Chicago Region* (Chicago, 2002), 360–61, 380–81.

31. The southern "Indian boundary line" ran through Lake Calumet to the Kankakee River. The northern boundary line ran from Howard Street, now Chicago's northern border, southwest across the Des Plaines River at Grand Avenue and beyond DuPage County.

32. Donald Miller has skillfully explored this transformation, particularly through the life of Gurdon Hubbard, who began as a fur trader but became a speculator and businessmen as Chicago grew. See *City of the Century: The Epic of Chicago and the Making of America* (New York, 1996), 48–65.

33. John R. Stilgoe, *Common Landscapes of America, 1580 to 1845* (New Haven, 1982), 99.

34. Andreas, 148.

35. The Illinois and Michigan Canal was an important part of a national system of internal improvements which was well underway by 1830. First proposed by Alexander Hamilton, when he was secretary of the treasury under George Washington in the 1790s, a network of roads, turnpikes, canals, and natural waterways increasingly bound together that part of the United States east of the Mississippi River, fostering economic, political, and cultural links between regions.

36. Andreas, 154, 158.

37. Michael P. Conzen, and Kay J. Carr, eds., *The Illinois and Michigan Canal National Heritage Corridor: A Guide to Its History and Sources* (DeKalb, IL, 1988); John M. Lamb, "Early Days on the Illinois and Michigan Canal," *Chicago History*, n.s., 3, no. 3 (Winter 1974–1975): 168–76; and Michael P. Conzen and Adam R. Daniel, eds., *Lockport Legacy: Themes in the Historical Geography of an Illinois Canal Town*, Studies on the Illinois and Michigan Canal, no. 4 (Chicago, 1990).

38. Carole Rifkind, *A Field Guide to American Architecture* (New York, 1980), 38, 180–87. Rifkind notes that Americans saw themselves as heir to Greek democracy and therefore embraced the Greek Revival style as their own.

39. Mrs. John H. Kinzie, *Wau-Bun: The 'Early Day' in the North-West* (Chicago, 1932), 214.

40. Joseph and Marie Bailly's house on the Little Calumet River told a similar tale. The long portico, with narrow columns, resonated both with the Greek Revival style of new arrivals and the older French colonial style with which the Baillys had grown up. By the 1830s, the Baillys, American by naturalization, saw the need to join the new era with a dramatic gesture.

41. Ann Durkin Keating, *Building Chicago: Suburban Developers and the Creation of a Divided Metropolis* (Urbana, 2002), 176. Information taken from Homer Hoyt, *One Hundred Years of Land Values in Chicago* (Chicago, 1933), 474, 483, 487.

42. The Clarke House is often mistakenly cited as the oldest house in Chicago, but it was built several years after the Noble House, probably for several reasons: Noble House was built well outside the center city; an addition in 1860s greatly expanded the house; and the Clarke House restoration was taken up by large Chicago preservation groups, while the Noble House was restored by a small local historical society.

43. Andreas, 235; Henry Higgins Hurlbut, *Chicago Antiquities; comprising original items and relations, letters, extracts, and notes, pertaining to early Chicago* (Chicago, 1881), 479.

44. See *Chicago Democrat*, May 1, 1839; and Stephen R. Beggs, *Early History of the West and North-West: Embracing reminiscences and incidents of settlement and growth, and sketches of the material and religious progress of the States of Ohio, Indiana, Illinois, and Missouri, with especial reference to the history of Methodism* (Cincinnati, 1868), 94, 143–44.

45. Keating, 176.

46. Caroline Palmer Clarke to Mark Clarke Walker, November 1, 1835, Chicago Historical Society.

47. John Drury, *Old Chicago Houses* (Chicago, 1941), 4–8.

48. Michael H. Ebner, *Creating Chicago's North Shore: A Suburban History* (Chicago, 1988), 16–18.

49. Andreas, 341.

Chapter 3

1. Victoria Ranney, quoted in Lisa Frieman Miner, "Historic Wright School," *Daily Herald*, November 4, 1996.

2. Other one-room schoolhouses include the Little Red Schoolhouse in Willow Springs, the Hoosier Grove Schoolhouse in Streamwood, the Little White Schoolhouse in Oswego, the Churchville Schoolhouse in Elmhurst, the Copenhagen School on the grounds of Naper Settlement, the Cass Schoolhouse in Darien, the Pioneer Sholes School in the LeRoy Oakes Forest Preserve in St. Charles, and a schoolhouse moved to Lockport by the Will County Historical Society.

3. Perhaps no historian has made us more aware of the need to follow these wagons than William Cronon. In *Nature's Metropolis: Chicago and the Great West* (New York, 1991), Cronon describes the crucial role that its regional hinterland played in Chicago's rise. Grain, stock, and lumber raised and harvested in the Midwest made its way to Chicago's growing markets. Chicago grew as a regional financial and manufacturing center to serve this rich hinterland.

4. The home remained in the hands of the Peck family until donated to the Lombard Historical Society in the 1990s. The land was purchased by the Village of Lombard. Restoration work removed stucco and rebuilt the west wing of the house, which was opened to the public in 1999.

5. Silas, Lyman, and Harvey Meacham journeyed west into what became Bloomingdale Township along the Elgin Road from Chicago in 1833. They claimed lands and pitched tents in March 1833 just east of where the Peck family would settle a few years later. After building homes and starting farms, families like the Meachams regularly traveled into Chicago to trade or find service. See C. W. Richmond, *A History of the County of DuPage, Illinois*, 1857 (republished Naperville, 1974), 135–36.

6. These preserved structures remind us that farming predominated in this region for more than a century. One of the older preserved farmhouses is the Netzley/Yender House, an 1850s structure preserved by the Lisle Park District at the Lisle Station Park. More typical is the Durant-Peterson House, part of the LeRoy Oakes Forest Preserve, just west of Randall Road in St. Charles. Originally built in 1843, the house has a large 1880s kitchen addition. The Elk Grove Farmhouse Museum on Biesterfield Road includes a museum exhibit with artifacts from 1860s German settlers.

Early twentieth-century farm families are also represented in the metropolitan area. For instance, the River Grove Historical House and Barn is an 1876 Italianate structure restored to represent life in River Grove at the turn of the twentieth century. The Mount Prospect Historical Society maintains the Dietrich Friedrichs House as a 1917 midwestern farmhouse, while the Morton Grove Historical Museum has furnished the Victorian farmhouse built by local farmer Nicholas Haupt in 1888 with items from the 1920s.

7. For instance, the Kline Creek Farm in Winfield (now part of the DuPage County Forest Preserve District) was established by Caspar Kline in 1835. The Kline family farmed the property across much of the nineteenth and twentieth centuries. As a living history center, interpretation focuses on the 1890s. See Richard A. Thompson, *DuPage Roots* (Wheaton, IL, 1985), 28.

8. Garfield Farm is operated as a private museum by a not-for-profit organization founded by the last Garfield farm owner, Elva Ruth Garfield, in 1977. Information from David Buisseret, *Historic Illinois from the Air* (Chicago, 1990), 110–11.

9. The reaper did not come into regular use until the 1850s, when local companies, including Cyrus McCormick's factory, began selling farm implements.

10. The case of the Fischer family, who settled to the east in Dunklee's Grove in what would become

Addison Township of DuPage County, provides another example. In 1834, Henry Dietrich Fischer traveled to Chicago from Hanover, Germany. Fischer worked in Chicago as hod carrier, at a sawmill in Green Bay, and as a laborer on the Illinois and Michigan Canal.

In 1836, Fischer and other family members settled on the south side of Dunklee's Grove. Fischer married a daughter of their German neighbors and they raised a large family. He helped to found the first schoolhouse in the area. Over time, the Fischers purchased more land and farmed in the area between Addison and Elmhurst well into the twentieth century.

The 1836 Fischer farmstead stands today on Addison Park District and DuPage County Forest Preserve properties, on a road known in the years before the Civil War as the Elgin Road. In 2001, the old homestead was a weather-beaten one-and-a-half story frame structure. Little or no preservation work had been done, except to save the site from development. See 1874 *Atlas and History of DuPage County, Illinois* (reprint, Wheaton, IL, 1975), 8–11, 116–17.

11. In Cook County, agricultural production shifted over the middle decades of the nineteenth century. In 1850, Cook County overall produced 238,952 bushels of wheat. By 1883, after the development of over a dozen rail lines through the county, wheat output dropped while dairy production increased. In 1850, there were 8,596 milk cows. By 1870, Cook County supported 23,063 milk cows. See A. T. Andreas, *History of Cook County* (Chicago, 1884), 344–45.

Within the Chicago metropolitan area was the northern boundary of the corn belt. Wheat was no longer a significant crop in the metropolitan area by 1924. Corn flourished particularly to the southwest of Chicago, while dairying developed in northern DuPage, Lake, and McHenry counties. Vegetable production, indicating truck farming, was focused in the farms surrounding (as well as just within) the City of Chicago. Robert H. Engle, "The Trends of Agriculture in the Chicago Region" (PhD thesis, University of Chicago, 1941), 180–86.

12. Martha Miller, *The Chellberg Family, The Chellberg Farm* (Chesterton, IN, 1982). Other preserved farmsteads in the region include Blackberry Farm in Aurora, operated by the Fox Valley Park District. Their campus includes a pioneer cabin, 1840s home, blacksmith, spinning and weaving demonstrations, a schoolhouse, a potter, a hotel, and a museum, which contains farm implements and other objects. The Volkening Heritage Farm at Spring Valley Nature Sanctuary in Schaumburg interprets a German American farm family in the 1880s—including a fully furnished farmhouse, gardens, crops, and animals.

Along with dairying, truck farming became an important part of agriculture in Chicagoland. Initially truck farming took place relatively close to the city. For instance, German farmers north of North Avenue began raising vegetables for sale in Chicago by the 1840s and 1850s. By the 1860s, German farmers had moved further north of Diversey along the Chicago River, where they leased land from long-term investors. The arrival of the Northwestern Railroad provided these farmers with ready access to Chicago markets, and farmers began to raise celery and other crops. Haying also grew in importance, due in part to the thousands and thousands of horses kept in Chicago for street railways by the 1880s.

13. The 1851 Rees Map is dotted with the names of these official taverns. Because so many of the houses were built along the roads into and out of Chicago, families in the 1830s often found themselves entertaining travelers. Over time, some the houses located at crossroads or convenient distances from Chicago evolved into more formal taverns.

14. Some of the taverns were regularly frequented by farmers bringing stock to market. Stockyards developed around a number them. For instance, Charles Cleaver purchased twenty acres along the lakeshore in 1851 along Cottage Grove. He erected a slaughterhouse near the stockyards north of his property at Myrick's Tavern.

Other taverns with stockyards included the Bull's Head Tavern to the west of the city on Madison Street, the Southern or Jackson Stock Yard on South State and the Darrow Stock Yard further south on State.

15. For more information about taverns in this region see Harry Ellsworth Cole, *Stagecoach and Tavern Tales of the Old Northwest* (Carbondale, IL, 1997); and Milo Quaife, *Chicago's Highways, Old and New: From Indian Trail to Motor Road* (Chicago, 1923).

16. Janice Perkins, "Glen Ellyn," in *DuPage Roots*, ed. Richard A. Thompson (Wheaton, IL, 1985), 158.

17. Another tavern in this area still stands at Warrenville.

18. In older metropolitan areas, these taverns became the nucleus of many urban neighborhoods and outlying towns. In Chicago, they were quickly eclipsed as the railroad transformed the metropolitan landscape.

19. Four flour (grist) mills adjoined the Chicago River in the city center: on North Canal, on North Water, on South Water, and on Lake Street at the South Branch. By 1870, there were seventeen mills in Chicago and more in the metropolitan area as a whole. See Weston A. Goodspeed and Daniel D. Healy, *History of Cook County* (Chicago, 1909), 582, 610.

One of these mills still stands directly west of downtown Chicago along the Fox River at Montgomery. Clearly visible at a distance, the Gray-Watkins Grist Mill remains the largest structure in the area, substantially more massive than the surrounding homes, stores, and taverns. The Gray-Watkins Mill was constructed of the warm cream limestone found in nearby quarries. The mill's boxy three-story facade is relieved by a front porch and lighter stone ornamentation on the four corners of the building.

Daniel S. Gray and his son-in-law, Vine A. Watkins, constructed the mill in 1853, at a time when the area was known as Graystown. The mill was then part of a thriving town which also had a store, two foundries, and a reaper manufacturer. The mill produced flour until 1922 under the brand name of Daisy and White Rose.

The Gray-Watkins Grist Mill was placed on the National Register of Historic Places in 1979 and has most recently housed a restaurant.

20. Buisseret, *Historic Illinois from the Air*, 112–13.

21. The Lisle Historical Society has preserved the 1874 train station which served as a milk stop for area farmers. In 1873, the Chicago, Milwaukee, St. Paul, and Pacific Railroad extended a line through the northeast section of DuPage County. Milk stops developed at Bensenville, Itasca, and Roselle. Mason Smith, an early farmer, platted his land around the train station, hoping that a town would emerge around his milk stop. Just to the west of the train station, E. C. Schroeder started a cheese factory, as well as a carriage and wagon shop which catered to area farmers. While the Smiths and the Schroeders may have hoped for further development at Itasca, it remained a very small settlement until the massive wave of suburbanization in the closing decades of the twentieth century. DuPage County continued to develop grow and develop at the end of the nineteenth century. During the 1880s, four more railroads came through the county: the Atchison, Topeka, and Santa Fe; Chicago Great Western; Illinois Central; and Elgin, Joliet and Eastern lines. Today the Itasca Historical Museum has developed a museum in the 1873 railroad depot which includes a doctor's waiting room, a general store, and post office.

Also in DuPage County, milk stops at Addison and Bensenville led to the development of creameries and cheese factories. Farmers across a band in southern Lake County, Indiana, sent milk, fruit, and eggs into Chicago, and received cheap lumber and building materials in return with the arrival of a rail line in 1850. St. John, Schererville, Brunswick, Klaasville, Hessville, Hanover Center, and Whiting are all communities founded by German farmers who produced milk and eggs for a Chicago market.

22. The creamery was renovated in the late twentieth century as a hotel and restaurant as Geneva evolved from a farm town to a suburban center.

23. Over time, the areas around the train stops developed certain market functions—feed and general stores, as well as churches and schools. To the south of Chicago, farmers hauled produce such as potatoes, asparagus, cabbage, onions, sugar beets, eggplants, and lima beans to the Dolton rail stop for sale in Chicago's center. Area businessmen founded packing and canning industries to take advantage of the fresh produce farmers brought to the rail stop.

24. "This old Dutch settlement claims an antiquity which dates back to 1847. In that year a body of settlers located here, and Moravian like, built their shanties, labored on industriously, improved their lands, and are to-day a prosperous and thriving community. John Kallowingeo settled here in 1847, and during the same year he was joined by Henry DeYoung, R. VanVuuren and the Gouwen and Benslip families. When in June 1850, A. Zwijenberg came to the settlement, the homes of the above-mentioned settlers were the only houses between Dolton and Thornton." Andreas, 865.

25. John Miller established a sawmill in the 1830s to the north and west of this crossroads settlement along the North Branch of the Chicago River, in what is now Morton Grove. Henry Harms built a frame house near the crossroads in 1854. A few years later he opened a hardware and provisions store in his home and eventually built a general store. He was joined by other businesses, which within a generation included two blacksmith shops, two meat markets, five stores, six saloons, one school, and three churches serving about 250 people. A schoolhouse was built south of the crossroads in 1858 and a post office was established in 1864. Andreas, 474–75.

26. Other crossroads farming communities with similar developments include Mokena, which had a German United Evangelical congregation; St. Mary's German Catholic Church; and German Lutheran Church, all founded before 1870.

27. See especially, Robert P. Swierenga, "The Little White Church, Religion in Rural America," *Agricultural History* 71, no. 4 (Fall 1997): 415–41; and "Ethnicity and American Agriculture," *Ohio History* 89 (Summer 1980): 323–44; Allan G. Bogue, *From Prairie to Corn Belt: Farming on the Illinois and Iowa Prairies in the Nineteenth Century* (Chicago, 1963); Kathleen Neils Conzen, "Immigrants in Nineteenth Century Agriculture," in *Agriculture and National Development: Views on the Nineteenth Century*, ed. Lou Ferleger (Ames, IA, 1990); Steven Hahn and Jonathan Prude, eds. *The Countryside in the Age of Capitalist Transformation: Essays on the Social History of Rural America* (Chapel Hill, 1985); Susan E. Gray, *The Yankee West: Community Life on the Michigan Frontier* (Chapel Hill, 1996); John Mack Faragher, *Sugar Creek: Life on the Illinois Prairie* (New Haven, 1986); and Susan Sessions Rugh, *Our Common Country: Family Farming, Culture, and Community in the Nineteenth-Century Midwest* (Bloomington, IN, 2001)

Chapter 4

1. Carl Sandburg, "Chicago," in *Selected Poems*, ed. George and Willene Hendrick (San Diego, 1996), 3; and Julian Street, *Abroad at Home: American Ramblings, Observations, and Adventures of Julian Street* (New York, 1914), 167.

2. Upton Sinclair, *The Jungle* (New York, 1981), 36.

3. Because of continued interest, there is now a rich body of historical work on Chicago's stockyards, their workers, and their neighborhoods. It is one of the most studied areas of any U.S. city. Among the many fine books about the area: Louise Wade, *Chicago's Pride: The Stockyards, Packingtown, and Environs in the Nineteenth*

Century (Urbana, 1987); Lizabeth Cohen, *Making a New Deal: Industrial Workers in Chicago, 1919–1939* (New York, 1990); James R. Barrett, *Work and Community in the Jungle: Chicago's Packinghouse Workers, 1880–1922* (Urbana, 1987); Robert A. Slayton, *Back of the Yards: The Making of a Local Democracy* (Chicago, 1986); Thomas J. Jablonsky, *Pride in the Jungle: Community and Everyday Life in Back of the Yards Chicago* (Baltimore, 1993); and Dominic A. Pacyga, *Polish Immigrants and Industrial Chicago: Workers on the South Side, 1880–1922* (Chicago, 2003).

4. See Alice Sinkevitch, ed., *AIA Guide to Chicago* (New York, 1993), 391.

5. Anonymous 1887 essay in The Times (London), quoted in Pierce, 233–35.

6. Ibid.

7. Meatpacking at the Union Stock Yards was in the hands of three dominant packers by 1900: Philip Armour, Gustavus Swift, and Nelson Morris. Louise Carroll Wade, "Meatpacking," *Encyclopedia of Chicago* (Chicago, 2004).

8. With World War I, African American migrants, and Mexican immigrants took up many of these same jobs. See James R. Grossman, *Land of Hope: Chicago, Black Southerners, and the Great Migration* (Chicago, 1989).

The Chicago Union Stock Yards remained home to the dominant meatpackers in the national market well into the twentieth century. However, by 1933 the use of trucks to haul livestock to market and the proliferation of chain stores with their own distribution facilities were among the factors which led smaller operations to compete successfully with the Union Stock Yard. After World War II, stunners, mechanical knives, and power saws were among the innovations which further mechanized the production process. Even as productivity rose, nearly 18,000 jobs were eliminated between 1954 and 1958. By 1960, the major packing houses at the Union Stock Yards closed their doors, affecting an estimated 30,000 workers. The Central Manufacturing District, which owned the property, closed the stockyards officially in 1971. Keith McClellan, "A History of Chicago's Industrial Development," in *Mid-Chicago Economic Development Study*, prepared by the Mayor's Committee for Economic and Cultural Development, 1966, vol. 3, pp. 39–40.

9. My understanding of this neighborhood and its structures has been profoundly shaped by the work of Dominic A. Pacyga and Ellen Skerrett, *Chicago: City of Neighborhoods: Histories and Tours* (Chicago, 1986), 450–89.

10. Sinkevitch, 394.

11. At the outset of the railroad age (1850), there were about 300 black residents in Chicago. In 1900, there were 30,000 African Americans living within the city, but this was less than 2 percent of a total population of 1.7 million. In the early twentieth century, as African Americans began to enter the region in larger numbers, they were unable to gain employment in most manufacturing and processing enterprises. Even as late as 1910, only 357 black men worked in the stockyards, while only 37 more worked in the iron and steel industry. Only 46 black women were employed in factories of any kind. See Grossman, 197–98.

12. Even with the establishment of the Union Stock Yards, meatpacking remained a late fall enterprise until the advent of refrigeration. During the slack periods, taverns served travelers and farmers selling animals for local consumption. According to McClellan, refrigeration after the Civil War made it possible to supply eastern cities from Detroit to Boston with dressed beef (13–14).

13. For instance, 25,000 of the 68,000 meatpacking workers nationwide in 1900 were in Chicago. By 1902, International Harvester Company controlled 80 percent of the world production of grain processing equipment. Wade, "Meatpacking"; and Fred Carstensen, "Agricultural Machinery Industry," *Encyclopedia of Chicago* (Chicago, 2004).

14. More than half of the total number of people working in manufacturing in Chicago by 1900 were

employed in the following industries: iron and steel, meatpacking, railroad cars, electrical equipment, clothing, and printing/publishing. As one researcher noted, "The history of manufacturing development in Chicago is mainly the history of six great industries." I would not go so far. In fact, to focus on these six to the exclusion of smaller manufacturing and other processing plants is to miss half the story. Helen Rankin Jeter, *Trends of Population in the Region of Chicago* (Chicago, 1927), 13.

15. Statistics exclude handicraft industries; McClellan, 21.

16. Wage earners comprised 15 percent of Chicago's population in 1919. This compares with 50 percent in Chicago Heights, 18 percent in Aurora, 25 percent in Elgin, and 29 percent in Joliet. See Jeter, 13, 46–51.

17. The story of the Western Wheel Works is explored by David A. Hounshell, *From the American System to Mass Production, 1800–1932: The Development of Manufacturing Technology in the United States* (Baltimore, 1984), 208–15. For a description of the building, see *Chicago: An Industrial Guide* (Chicago, 1991), 38.

18. The reuse of much of the original physical plant of St. Michael's Roman Catholic Church is along the same lines as Cobbler Square. The old high school and convent have become condominiums, while new townhouses crowd the old church grounds.

19. Most of the works were dismantled after 1932. Production finally ceased altogether in 1979.

20. Worker housing quickly followed the 1869 establishment of the Joliet Iron Works. An 1873 engraving shows the small frame cottages behind the ironworks. The engraving also emphasizes the fact that the ironworks and worker housing were to the north of the built-up area of Joliet on previously undeveloped land. See Mark A. Kolodny, "The Industrialization of Joliet: Steel and Its Dependencies, 1870–1920," in *Time and Place in Joliet*, ed. Michael P. Conzen, Studies on the Illinois and Michigan Canal Corridor, no. 2 (Chicago, 1988), 37–43. See especially the image on p. 41.

21. The site of the Joliet Iron Works has been preserved under the jurisdiction of the Will County Forest Preserve District, which has developed an interpretive trail along the remains of the manufacturing operation.

22. These industrial subdivisions are clear forebears of the post–World War II tract residential developments, perhaps even more than the individually built homes of romantic railroad suburbs. See Kenneth T. Jackson, *Crabgrass Frontier: The Suburbanization of the United States* (New York, 1985). Taylor's quote is from his *Satellite Cities: A Study of Industrial Suburbs* (New York, 1915), 7.

23. Joseph C. Bigott highlights the importance of available materials and methods in home building in *From Cottage to Bungalow: Houses and the Working Class in Metropolitan Chicago, 1869–1929* (Chicago, 2001).

24. Bigott, 19–53.

25. Perry R. Duis, *Challenging Chicago: Coping with Everyday Life, 1837–1920* (Urbana, 1998), 72–73.

26. While most of these cottages and flats are frame, builders occasionally used brick construction. This was especially true in the late 1870s and 1880s in the central district of Chicago where wood construction was prohibited because of fire. See Christine M. Rosen, *Limits of Power: Great Fires and the Process of City Growth in America* (New York, 1986).

27. Information specific to worker housing in Back of the Yards provides some detail. Back of the Yards is officially a part of Community Area 61, known as New City, which has been carefully studied, especially during a 1939 land-use study of all the community areas in the City of Chicago. In 1939, over one-third of the units in New City did not have a private bath or toilet. Not even a third of the residential structures were single-family. Instead, most people lived in houses built for two, three, or four families. There was a little more than one room for every person in an occupied residential unit. On one block (Hermitage Avenue, just south of Davis Square Park), there were 184 housing units on forty-two lots, making an average of more than four

housing units per lot. The median number of rooms in New City was 4.8 rooms, while the median number of persons in occupied units was 4.1. In 1939, almost 32 percent of the units in Back of the Yards were occupied by owners. Landlords were neighbors—often very close ones. The look of the street was in a real sense then controlled by people living on the street. Chicago Land Use Survey, *Housing in Chicago Communities* (Chicago: 1940), 8.

28. Robert Slayton has done a wonderful job of drawing this ethnic world in his study *Back of the Yards*. Perry Duis discusses the role of saloons in Back of the Yards in *Challenging Chicago*, 204–5.

29. Some, like Gary, Indiana, were wildly successful. Until 1906, this area at the southern end of Lake Michigan was an unused swampland, held by the Union Stock Yards for possible future use. Within three years, the United States Steel Company had constructed a plant covering about a square mile which could employ 14,000 men. U.S. Steel sponsored harbor improvements and supported the development of a town, which quickly had all the accoutrements of an industrial town, with houses, sidewalks, sewers, water and gas lines, an electric system, banks, hotels, newspapers, schools, and churches. See Taylor, *Satellite Cities*, 165–93.

30. Waukegan, Gary, and Michigan City are also sometimes included in the group of places known as satellite cities.

31. Andrew Wiese, *Places of Their Own: African American Suburbanization in the Twentieth Century* (Chicago, 2004). See especially pp. 19–25.

32. The Historic Pullman Foundation successfully lobbied for national landmark status for the area, making it the only Chicagoland industrial neighborhood with this designation. The State of Illinois now owns the Pullman Administration Building and the Florence Hotel, and there are preliminary plans to transform at least part of the space into a railroad museum.

33. The Administration Building served as a front door to an industrial plant which stretched for blocks to the east and north. In these shops, Pullman workers produced rail cars at the rate of more than two a day. Most of these buildings have long been torn down. What remains is now owned by the State of Illinois. However, plans to convert the structure into a transportation museum have faltered.

34. George Pullman made this comment to the U.S. Strike Commission, following the 1894 strike. United States Strike Commission, *Report on the Chicago Strike of June–July 1894* (Washington, 1895), 529.

35. Harold M. Mayer and Richard C. Wade, *Chicago: Growth of a Metropolis* (Chicago, 1969), 186.

36. Timothy R. Mahoney, *River Towns in the Great West: The Structure of Provincial Urbanization in the American Midwest, 1820–1870* (New York, 1990).

37. McClellan, 6–7.

38. Joliet, Elgin, and Aurora grew dramatically between 1870 and 1890. Joliet grew from 7,263 to 23,264; Elgin from 5,396 to 17,680; and Aurora from 11,162 to 19,688. See Jim and Wynette Edwards, *Aurora: A Diverse People Build Their City* (Charleston, SC, 1998), 26–30; Tara L. Goodwin, "The Aging of the Built Environment: Residential Trends and Neighborhood Revitalization Efforts on Joliet's East Side," in Conzen, 133–46; and Katarzyna C. Szydagis, "The Emerging Social Geography of Joliet before 1940," in Conzen, 59–66.

39. The total number of wage earners in iron and steel, meatpacking, clothing, printing, railroad cars and electrical goods in 1919 was 206,590 in the City of Chicago. This comprised just over 51 percent of the 403,942 wage earners in all of manufacturing (Jeter, 13). Philip Scranton, *Endless Novelty: Special Production and American Industrialization, 1865–1925* (Princeton, 1997), makes this important point about not ignoring the smaller industries, which in many places comprised even more of the industrial economy than they did in Chicago. Writing of Chicago, Scranton noted, "Yet even as connections solidified among agriculture,

extractive, the railroads and Chicago's bulk-processing sectors, a second set of firms making specialty goods drew on readily available raw materials, growing urban markets, and the city's omnidimensional rail network." See 164–65.

40. This area falls between two official community areas, comprising the southwest section of North Center (Community Area 5), north of Diversey west to the North Branch, and the northwest section of Lincoln Park (Community Area 7), just to the south along the river, with Lake View (Community Area 6) to the east.

41. Beyond St. Alphonsus, seven or eight smaller churches—some Roman Catholic initially serving other ethnic Catholics, Lutheran churches serving non-Catholic Germans, and various other Protestant denominations—were built by the mid-twentieth century. None was on the scale of St. Alphonsus.

42. The 1939 land use survey of the area illustrates this diversity. There were blocks in which every residential unit had private toilets and baths. But there were also blocks where nearly half the units lacked private toilets and baths. Owner occupancy ranged from 3 percent on some blocks to over 50 percent on others. Rents ranged from $16 to over $40 per month. Chicago Land Use Survey, *Land Use in Chicago*, vol. 2 (Chicago, 1943), 118–19.

43. *Chicago: An Industrial Guide*, 32.

44. Sinkevitch, 208.

45. Gregory D. Squires, Larry Bennett, Kathleen McCourt, and Philip Nyden, *Chicago: Race, Class, and the Response to Urban Decline* (Philadelphia, 1987), 28.

46. John Nolen, a landscape architect and city planner, wrote in 1915 about factory workers and housing. He estimated that factory workers who were able to earn between $750 and $1,200 a year might be able to afford a home valued between $2,000 and $3,000. Nolen argued that living near a work site provided not only a saving in time, but also about $30 a year in carfare. Nolen argued that this was a savings which could help bring families closer to home ownership. See John Nolen, "Factory and Home," in Taylor, 317–21.

African Americans seem to have had easier access to housing convenient to industries in the largest outlying industrial towns than in Chicago neighborhoods—not because these towns and cities were less segregated racially, but because of the smaller distances to be traveled. Still, the smaller scale and range of industries seemingly afforded African Americans more opportunities. Comprising less than 10 percent of the population in Joliet, Elgin, Evanston, Aurora, Gary, and Waukegan in 1930, African Americans found work in industry. In contrast to their counterparts on Chicago's South Side, these workers could live closer to work.

Chapter 5

1. Olmsted, Vaux & Co., "Riverside, Illinois: A Planned Community near Chicago," in *Civilizing American Cities: A Selection of Frederick Law Olmsted's Writings on City Landscape*, ed. S. B. Sutton (Cambridge, 1971), 295. See also Kenneth T. Jackson, *Crabgrass Frontier: The Suburbanization of the United States* (New York, 1985); Robert Fishman, *Bourgeois Utopias: The Rise and Fall of Suburbia* (New York, 1987); and Dolores Hayden, *Building Suburbia: Green Fields and Urban Growth, 1820–2000* (New York, 2003).

2. Donald Miller, *City of the Century: The Epic of Chicago and the Making of America* (New York, 1996), 286–88; Jackson, 80–81; and Harold M. Mayer and Richard C. Wade, *Chicago: Growth of a Metropolis* (Chicago, 1969), 183–85.

3. A smaller generation of commuter settlements was founded between 1890 and 1894 (a period that

included the 1893 World's Fair). Golf courses became an important draw for these communities. Some, like Flossmoor, were founded as a result of adjacent golf courses (see chapter 6).

4. Some early efforts at elite enclaves were walking or riding distance from downtown. Union Park was established in 1853, with walks, drives, and a small zoo. Wealthy Chicagoans bought lots and built homes around the park. Carter Harrison II, later mayor of Chicago, grew up in this area in the late 1860s, as did Bertha Honoré Palmer. The area did not remain remote for long, as railroad and horsecar lines soon brought the area into a closer orbit of the city center. Richard Sennett, *Families Against the City: Middle Class Homes of Industrial Chicago, 1872–1890* (Cambridge, 1970), explores the development of the area around Union Park.

The nearby suburban retreat of Charles J. Hull is now best remembered in relation to Jane Addams and Ellen Gates Starr, who encountered the home in 1889 when it was an anachronism in a densely settled urban neighborhood. Hull built his home on what is now Halsted Street in 1856, at a time when this was well beyond the built-up city.

5. John R. Stilgoe has described the local rail station "as a portal opening not only on the borderland community around it but on the railroad trains speeding to and from the city." Stilgoe, *Borderland: Origins of the American Suburb, 1820–1939* (New Haven, 1988), 208. Michael H. Ebner discusses the importance of the railroad in *Creating Chicago's North Shore: A Suburban History* (Chicago 1988), see especially 52.

6. Cole, quoted in Stilgoe, 208–9. See also Ebner, 64–68. Twelve miles north of Kenilworth, Lake Forest residents have commuted from the same station for over a century. Since 1898, Hinsdale commuters have journeyed sixteen miles eastward from this substantial brick depot to downtown Chicago. At about the same time, developer Samuel E. Gross constructed an elaborate Queen Anne station at Grossdale (now Brookfield), thirteen miles southwest of downtown Chicago. Gross used the station, along with picnics and brass bands, as a marketing tool to sell lots in his subdivision to visitors. The original station has been moved by the Brookfield Historical Society across the railroad tracks after a modern station was constructed for present-day commuters. See Mary Green Kircher, ed., *Brookfield, Illinois: A History* (Brookfield, 1994), 4.

While many of the historic train stations date back to the nineteenth century, twentieth-century stations include those along the electric interurbans. In the 1920s, Samuel Insull upgraded the interurban line to Beverly Shores on the Indiana shoreline of Lake Michigan thirty-six miles from downtown Chicago. The small station sports a blue sign with "Beverly Shores" in pink neon, making it one of the most distinctive depots in the metropolitan area.

7. Douglas purchased a seventy-acre site on the lakeshore between 31st and 35th Streets. Douglas built a home, described by an 1848 visitor as "his cottage in the suburbs of the southern division of the city." John Lewis Peyton, *Over the Alleghenies and Across the Prairies* (London, 1869), 340.

8. Douglas also donated a ten-acre site to the Baptist Church, which built the first University of Chicago there in 1860. The university did spur some residential development, but it closed in 1886. During the Civil War, the nearby Camp Douglas did not encourage a vision of idyllic suburban living. Dominic A. Pacyga and Ellen Skerrett, *Chicago: City of Neighborhoods* (Chicago, 1986), 310–11.

9. Jean Block, *Hyde Park Houses* (Chicago, 1978), 3.

10. The 1857 Hotchkiss map of Lake Forest indicates that the designer did not wholly remove the development from the grid. Underlying the curvilinear street were individual lots which conformed as much as possible to the grid. See Ebner, 27–28.

11. H. W. S Cleveland was a landscape architect who came to Chicago to work on the South Parks system in the 1860s. The Highland Park Building Company hired Cleveland and his partner William M. R. French

to design a romantic suburb twenty-five miles north along the lakeshore in 1869. Cleveland understood the role which the railroad played in opening the opportunity to carefully chose and plan outlying suburban settlements. See Ebner, 36–37.

12. Mendius quote from Kircher, 50. Norwood Park was planned with a great circle at its center in 1869 by Lemuel P. Swift. Now on the Far Northwest Side of the City of Chicago, the plat quickly reveals to anyone going through the area that they have entered into a distinctive place, a place which Chicagoans most often associate with suburbs, not the city.

13. This approach continued into the twentieth century. Again, providing leisure activities brought real estate sales. Samuel Insull invested "in upgrades and advertising to encourage commuters and vacationers" to ride his interurban line to Beverly Shores. In 1927, Frederick H. Bartlett purchased 3,600 acres of land, and in the next decade his son built a school, a championship golf course, a botanical garden, a riding academy, and a Florentine Revival hotel. Robert Bartlett also relocated a colonial village from the Century of Progress World's Fair to Beverly Shores, as well as players from the Goodman Theatre. Elizabeth Patterson, "Beverly Shores," *Encyclopedia of Chicago* (Chicago, 2004).

14. See Block, 4–8. In the 1870s and 1880s, numerous suburban developers built hotels to attract vacationers and potential land purchasers. After planning a subdivision at Norwood Park, now on the Far Northwest Side of Chicago, developers built a hotel and an artificial lake along a stop of the Chicago and North Western Railway. Marilyn Elizabeth Perry notes that the developers "hoped that the area would attract Chicagoans seeking a resort atmosphere. Although the hotel attracted residents for entertainment purposes, it never drew enough customers to be a success." Marilyn Elizabeth Perry, "Norwood Park," *Encyclopedia of Chicago* (Chicago, 2004). In western Glen Ellyn, a hotel was built along Lake Ellyn to draw visitors and potential residents. Other hotels founded in this era include the Highland House and Lake Forest Hotel.

15. Residents of Hyde Park, one of Chicago's first commuter suburbs south along Lake Michigan, built suburban villas as well as workingmen's cottages. Just blocks from the Museum of Science and Industry are a couple of the Italianate homes built by Hyde Park commuters before the 1871 fire. The real estate broker William Hoyt built the substantial Italianate brick house at 5704 Dorchester in 1869. He commuted to his office in downtown Chicago. While Hoyt's house is typical of upper-middle-class suburban housing, a short walk north to 5474 Dorchester brings us to a cottage built in the same era. Workers employed in building Hyde Park houses and maintaining commuters' property lived in cottages such as these, which were built across the metropolitan area in the second half of the nineteenth century. Hyde Park, while designed as a suburban retreat, also needed a ready labor supply to build and maintain residences. See Block, 13–15; and Joseph C. Bigott, *From Cottage to Bungalow: Houses and the Working Class in Metropolitan Chicago, 1869–1929* (Chicago, 2001).

16. Everett Chamberlin, *Chicago and Its Suburbs* (Chicago, 1874), 418–20. Downers Grove too grew as a suburban settlement with the arrival of the Chicago, Burlington, and Quincy Railroad in the 1860s. While settled as early as 1834 by Pierce Downer, J. Blodgett, Judge Blanchard, and their families, it was not the site of anything beyond agricultural development until the arrival of the railroad. Then a Chicago development company composed of H. G. Powers, L. L. Greenleaf, A. C. Ducat, and others proposed to create a commuter suburb in a parklike setting. By 1874, there were ninety residences and at least twenty-five businessmen commuting to Chicago who "find it advantageous to reside there, and who consider that the pleasures there secured are sufficient to liquidate the expenses incurred through railroad fares, etc." Other improvements by mid-1870s included three general stores, a meat market, coal and lumber yard, drug store, school, four churches and a hotel (Chamberlin, 422).

17. Hinsdale Historical Society, *Hinsdale Historical Society Bike Tour*, pamphlet (Hinsdale, 2001). "Hinsdale the Beautiful," *Campbell's Illustrated Journal* 6, no. 5 (November 1897; reprinted 1984, Hinsdale Historical Society).

18. After World War I, bungalows were the predominate style in the metropolitan area. Ranches and Cape Cods were among the most popular styles in the second half of the twentieth century. In the last few decades, much larger homes have replaced the more modest homes in many commuter suburbs, especially those with larger lot sizes.

The current debate on teardowns in Hinsdale and other suburban communities has an interesting relationship to this connection between house value and the size of the lot. Most of the homes that have been torn down in Hinsdale have been small vis à vis their lot size. Many of the smaller homes on larger lots were built in the twentieth century, as families were willing to spend more money on land and less on their homes.

19. For instance, the Frank Lloyd Wright Home and Studio in Oak Park is perhaps the most famous house museum in the metropolitan area. It is not, however, preserved by the local historical society. Instead, its preservation has been the result of efforts by those interested in architectural history, not Oak Park history.

20. In Des Plaines, a local bank eyed the land under an older house for a parking lot. The bank bought the land and offered to give the house to whoever would move it off the needed lot. The Des Plaines Historical Society, with the help of the village and park district, moved the building in 1978. The house was originally built by Benjamin F. Kinder family in 1906–07. It is a substantial brick Queen Anne, reminiscent of styles fashionable almost a generation before. It was also a more substantial house than most in Des Plaines.

21. Margaret Marsh argues that the suburban ideal was a male ideal—developed from the 1840s to the 1870s, the suburban ideal emphasized "the political importance of retaining some elements of agrarianism in order to preserve America's republican heritage, the need to be close to nature, and the necessity of respite for careworn husbands." At the same time, Marsh argues that middle-class women pursued a domestic ideal, more "concerned with the house itself, and its ability to create a moral environment, than they were with moving the house from the city." Margaret Marsh, *Suburban Lives* (Newark, 1990), 18.

22. At present, there is no museum interpreting a suburban house from the second half of the twentieth century. There are plans for a 1950s tract home in Hoffman Estates, and the model home from Levitt Brothers' last development in Buffalo Grove was used by the Buffalo Grove Historical Society for their exhibit space until recently. What is represented covers the railroad era—from the 1860s to the 1920s.

23. Quotation is taken from a flyer published by the Hinsdale Historical Society which was available to visitors in the summer of 2001. The historical society has transformed the basement into archive, exhibit, and meeting space, while the first and second floors have been restored to the 1870s.

24. See Ann Durkin Keating, *Building Chicago: Suburban Developers and the Creation of a Divided Metropolis* (Urbana, 2002 [reprint]).

25. Franz Schulze and Kevin Harrington, *Chicago's Famous Buildings* (Chicago, 1993), 270.

26. Ebner, 66–67.

27. In addition to country clubs, women and men organized clubs that provided social, cultural, and religious outlets within each suburb. While often they gathered in church or synagogue meeting rooms, in some communities clubs built separate structures. Perhaps the most distinctive is the Winnetka Community House, which was opened in 1911 near the downtown district. The Community House served as a headquarters for local clubs, for cultural and recreational activities. See Ebner, 217–20.

Chapter 6

1. North along Lake Michigan after 1875, the Lake Bluff Camp Meeting Association established a site. The primarily Methodist participants could journey from Chicago for a day on the railroad, stay at a hotel constructed on the property, and rent tents or cottages in subsequent seasons. The Lake Bluff site sponsored many temperance events; Frances Willard frequently lectured here in the 1880s.

2. Reverend John Orrington Foster, D.D., "The First DesPlaines Camp Meeting, DesPlaines, IL, August 1860." Foster wrote this account on a 1918 visit to Evanston at the request of Samuel Gardiner Ayers, the librarian of Garrett Biblical Institute, where the original manuscript remains. Accessed February 11, 2003, from the *Chicago District Camp Ground Association* Web site (http://cdcga.org).

3. Ellen Malmquist Allen, "1905 and Following," Collection of Recollections, United Methodist Camp Grounds, Des Plaines, Illinois, 125th Anniversary, edited by Evelyn C. Andersen and Patricia H. Sprinkle, typescript, 3–5, Des Plaines, IL.

4. In a real sense, workers' visions, and their children's, of the metropolitan area were defined more by leisure activities than were the visions of their more affluent neighbors. This is a point made by Thomas J. Jablonsky, *Pride in the Jungle: Community and Everyday Life in Back of the Yards Chicago* (Baltimore, 1993).

5. Perhaps George Pullman understood this, as he designed an industrial town where workers would have little reason to leave—and widen their horizons beyond his paternalism. Pullman provided a wide range of recreational activities for his workers, including boating, swimming, and fishing. Elsewhere, these were amenities for which many workers left their neighborhoods and moved across the metropolitan area. By providing them, Pullman discouraged his workers from leaving his company town. Pullman attempted to control three key areas of life—work, housing, and leisure. However, metropolitan residents then and now want as many choices—in work, in housing, in leisure activities—as their incomes can provide. Pullman town stands again as an anomaly to wider metropolitan patterns. See Wilma J. Pesavento, "Sport and Recreation in the Pullman Experiment, 1880–1900," *Journal of Sport History* 9, no. 2 (Summer 1982): 44.

6. Without question, the downtown area served as the central institutional and recreational site in Chicagoland. Landscape architect John Nolen noted in 1915 that in outlying industrial districts "there should be some convenient and inexpensive means of transportation that will give the workman and his family an opportunity to mingle in the life of the city and to draw upon, occasionally at least, the best in music, art, and drama, common only to big cities." John Nolen, "Factory and Home," in Graham Romeyn Taylor, *Satellite Cities* (New York, 1915), 319. By 1900, vaudeville houses, dime museums, traveling shows, and concerts drew workers and their families into the downtown district. Special events such as those staged at the Interstate Exposition Hall in the early 1880s drew visitors from across the metropolitan area.

7. The interrelationship of outlying institutional development and real estate investment is explored by Robin Bachin, *Building the South Side: Urban Space and Civic Culture in Chicago, 1890–1919* (Chicago, 2004).

8. Perry Duis, *Challenging Chicago: Coping with Everyday Life, 1837–1920* (Urbana, 1998), 211.

9. "Fourth of July Picnics," *Naperville Clarion*, July 10, 1872, 1. These picnics brought out both local residents and those drawn from across the metropolitan area. The parochial nature of other Fourth of July celebrations is exhibited in the North Shore celebrations in both Lake Bluff and Winnetka. There parades, speeches, baseball games, music, and fireworks drew primarily local residents. See Michael H. Ebner, *Creating Chicago's North Shore: A Suburban History* (Chicago, 1988), 39, 215.

Willow Springs, to the southwest of downtown Chicago, became a favorite picnic spot after the Joliet and Chicago Railroad arrived in 1854. A 500-foot widening of the Des Plaines River was called Lake Willow Springs.

According to one source, picnickers toted "multitudinous kegs of beer." This widening disappeared with the construction of the Sanitary and Ship Canal in the 1890s. Ronald S. Vasile, "Willow Springs," *Encyclopedia of Chicago* (Chicago, 2004).

To the east of Willow Springs, picnickers were drawn to Oak Lawn Lake—a part of Stony Creek. Picnicking along the creek was unregulated until area residents incorporated in 1909 as Oak Lawn. Betsy Gurlacz, "Oak Lawn," *Encyclopedia of Chicago* (Chicago, 2004).

10. Norwegian immigrants helped organize the first Scandinavian Rifle Club in 1882. A decade later, the Norwegian Sharpshooters purchased land for a shooting range at Willow Springs not far from the German sharpshooters in Palos Park. See Odd S. Lovoll, *A Century of Urban Life: The Norwegians in Chicago before 1930* (Urbana, 1988), 132–33.

11. Along the west bank of the Fox River in McHenry County, family-run resorts developed at the end of the nineteenth century. Run for profit, these resorts catered to middle-class families who could rent the cottages for varying periods of time. Businessmen could travel back and forth to the city during the week, or come out to stay with their families on weekends. Similar cabin resorts developed at Fox Lake and Antioch. While workers could not generally afford the cabins, some did make day trips to this area.

12. Duis, 390.

13. Document 60, "The Desplaines Hall Workers Club Picnics in Ogden's Grove," *Der Westen*, July 22, 1869, in Hartmut Keil and John B. Jentz, *German Workers in Chicago: A Documentary History of Working-Class Culture from 1850 to World War I* (Urbana, 1988), 206–8.

14. Duis, 210–11; and Marilyn Elizabeth Perry, "Dunning," *Encyclopedia of Chicago* (Chicago, 2004).

15. Dominic A. Pacyga and Ellen Skerrett, *Chicago: City of Neighborhoods* (Chicago, 1986), 43.

16. Duis, 212–13.

17. Ebner, 179–84.

18. Ravinia is one of the few which remains in operation.

19. Private piers, beer gardens, beaches, and restaurants sporadically dotted the shoreline of Lake Michigan by 1880. The completion of the Sanitary and Ship Canal in 1901 made the reversal of the Chicago River permanent and made the Lake Michigan shoreline even more attractive.

20. Harold M. Mayer and Richard C. Wade, *Chicago: Growth of a Metropolis* (Chicago, 1969), 334–35.

21. By 1900, a colony of summer cottages belonging to Chicago businessmen comprised the Riverside Holiness Association. Their cottages, built between Des Plaines Avenue and the river, abutted onion farms. Like the early suburban experiments outside Manchester, England, in the late eighteenth century, in this case like-minded people sought each other out for leisure-time activities. Robert Fishman, *Bourgeois Utopias: The Rise and Fall of Suburbia* (New York, 1987).

22. John H. Long, "Flossmoor," *Encyclopedia of Chicago* (Chicago, 2004).

23. Ebner, 221–23.

Discrimination at area golf clubs continued across the twentieth century. Only near the end of the century, was there movement toward the integration of some golf clubs in Chicagoland, and most of the most integrated clubs were the newest. Race, religion and gender remain the basic means of discrimination. See Ed Sherman and Greg Burns, "Fairways barriers fall slowly," *Chicago Tribune*, Sunday, February 2, 2003, Section 3, 1.

24. Edith E. Back, "Wheaton," in *DuPage Roots*, ed. Richard A. Thompson (Wheaton, 1985), 250–51. Wheaton and Evanston were early railroad towns platted on the grid. There was some dedicated public space, but the siting of a college provided a parklike area within the grid in both communities. Wheaton and Evanston

residents could take advantage of the college grounds and other activities. Just after the Civil War, a Naperville businessman donated land for North Central College in the center of a subdivision which he then marketed to commuters and local businessmen. In the late twentieth century, this subdivision became the Naperville Historic District. Everett C. Chamberlin noted that Evanston's streets "run at right angles, and show no suspicion of a curve either to the right or left . . . the curved lines which form the distinguishing traits of some suburbs met with no approval . . . of its devoutly-inclined founders." See *Chicago and Its Suburbs* (Chicago, 1874), 381.

25. Woodstock's public square is perhaps most familiar as the setting for the movie *Groundhog Day*.

26. As county government grew in importance, these courthouses grew from small structures to some of the most substantial in the region. The initial courthouses for Cook, Lake, and DuPage counties were relatively modest Greek Revival-styled structures. All were replaced by larger stone buildings by 1860. The courthouses were designed by some of the region's first architects and were among the most costly early buildings. Their cost was borne largely through taxes paid by area farmers.

27. Over the nineteenth century the Woodstock Square saw the addition of stores, other public offices, a hotel, and restaurants. In 1873, the Spring House, a large ornamental gazebo, was built in the center of the square over a mineral spring. Visitors came to drink these waters, which were thought to have special medicinal properties. In the closing years of the nineteenth century, an opera house challenged the dominance of the courthouse on the square with its taller spire and two-tone brick and stone design.

By the 1870s, Woodstock had a regular railroad stop to the north of the square connecting it to Chicago. This connection, along with the courthouse and opera house, kept the square a busy, lively place long after other crossroads towns had either disappeared or been subsumed by rail towns. Today the courthouse houses a museum, restaurant, and other facilities; county functions moved to a larger campus on the outskirts of Woodstock in 1972.

28. Robert Bruegmann, *The Architects and the City: Holabird & Roche of Chicago, 1880–1918* (Chicago, 1997), 49–63.

29. "The Trail of the Trolley, I: Chicago to Kenilworth and Fort Sheridan," *Chicago Daily News*, July 30, 1908.

Chapter 7

1. A good number of these buildings remain, although they now contain shops and businesses catering to area suburbanites.

2. Wilmette Historical Museum, *Historic Ridge Road Walking Tour*, pamphlet (Wilmette, 1997). Michael H. Ebner explores the history of Gross Point in *Creating Chicago's North Shore* (Chicago, 1988), esp. 134–37.

3. Ebner traces the histories of these geographically proximate places which are not part of the North Shore, as well as developments in the city itself. He makes the important point that "[w]ithout fair discussion of such places as Highwood, Gross Point or North Chicago, a history of the North Shore, or any comparable system of suburbs is incomplete"(xxix).

4. I have commented that Kenilworth grew up as an isolated retreat. *Building Chicago: Suburban Developers and the Creation of a Divided Metropolis* (Urbana, 2002), 28.

5. For instance, an Evanston minister was concerned about young men from Evanston frequenting Gross Point's taverns. See "Four Mile Limit: What the Law Really Is," *Evanston Press*, February 15, 1896, 1. Temperance was a contentious issue not just on the North Shore. Other Chicagoland communities that fought

over this issue included River Forest and Harlem (Forest Park); Phoenix, Harvey, and Posen; LaGrange Park and LaGrange.

6. Ibid.

7. Wilmette also used annexation to control an unruly neighbor to the north, not Kenilworth, but an area known as "No Man's Land" because of its unincorporated status. This was one of the few places on the North Shore where nonresidents had access to the lakefront. Hotdog stands, fireworks concessions, and private beach clubs provided water access for a fee. Gambling, bootlegging, and Sunday movies also attracted outsiders. Hundreds of Chicagoans crowded this area on warm summer days until Wilmette annexed the property in 1942 and then encouraged development of the high-rise apartments which now claim the lakeshore. Wilmette Historical Museum, *Guide to Wilmette's Historic Lake Front*, pamphlet(Wilmette, 2000).

8. "Announcement," *Lake Shore News*, May 8, 1912, 1; "What People Are Doing in Gross Point," *Lake Shore News*, June 20, 1912, 10.

9. Only a few Gross Point teenagers attended the new high school before 1910, even though their parents supported it with their tax dollars. But over time, more and more attended New Trier. Ebner, 163–65.

10. Robert Fishman describes it as a "bourgeois utopia" in *Bourgeois Utopias: The Rise and Fall of Suburbia* (New York, 1987). Kenneth Jackson describes it as a quintessential "romantic suburb" in *Crabgrass Frontier: The Suburbanization of the United States* (New York, 1985), 79–81.

11. Harold M. Mayer and Richard C. Wade, *Chicago: Growth of a Metropolis* (Chicago, 1969),330–32: "A native observed the changes brought by the twenties: 'From Cicero, Berwyn, and the great West Side came the Bohemians and the Poles and other non-Anglo-Saxon Americans. They are good thrifty citizens, mostly wealthy enough to build good homes and keep up a front in Riverside, but not after all, according to the Old Timers, filled with "the Riverside Traditions."' Moreover, 'modern apartment buildings crowd in and shadow the great twelve-room frame houses of the eighties.' Over the bitter protest that 'those who live in Riverside know where everyone lives, anyhow, and the others we don't care about,' the streets were marked and residences numbered for the first time. The old Riverside Hotel once described as a 'sumptuous palace on the lovely, gondola-laden Des Plaines,' wasted away. Metropolitan expansion had reached an old suburban outpost. In spite of these pressures, the old core of Riverside, platted by Olmsted in 1869 retained much of its charm and character."

12. Bonnie Lindstrom, "Berwyn," *Local Community Fact Book, Chicago Metropolitan Area, 1990* (Chicago, 1995), 225.

13. The flat roofed one-story homes were a legacy of developers who envisioned homeowners adding a second floor when they had the funds.

14. Mary Green Kircher, ed., *Brookfield, Illinois: A History* (Brookfield, 1994).

15. Patricia Krone Rose, "North Riverside," *Encyclopedia of Chicago* (Chicago, 2004).

16. Hoffman's park closed after the passage of Prohibition in 1919, but the last amusement parks did not close until the 1970s. In 1904, a site in Plainfield along a new interurban line became a successful leisure site called Electric Park, which included gardens on the banks of the DuPage River, athletic fields, bandstands, dancing pavilions, and an auditorium.

17. "Against Boat Landings," *Riverside News*, June 15, 1912. Riverside residents were most disgruntled with the way Fourth of July celebrations had gone since 1910. Residents of Chicago and neighboring suburbs could take the new electric streetcar to Riverside, where the many empty lots along the banks of the Des Plaines River were ideal sites for picnics and swimming. Some industrious businessmen also rented boats in the area. Local

residents decried the noise, the drinking, and the danger of nonswimmers using their river, and found their own celebrations were overrun by nonresidents.

In 1914, village officials chose to organize a local celebration rather than be subject to the arrival of outside revelers, and Riverside celebrated its first "Sane Fourth, with community residents—not outsiders." First, the village strongly discouraged local businessmen from renting boats. Then, a committee carefully planned a host of activities which would keep Riverside's public spaces squarely in the hands of residents. The day was carefully orchestrated, from the early morning parade of schoolchildren waving American flags to a reenactment of the signing of the Declaration of Independence, to games and races, to evening fireworks. All was designed for Riverside residents and their families, not for the scores of visitors who came to Lyons that same day. "Riverside's Greatest Fourth," *Riverside News*, July 9, 1914.

18. "Bridge Is Nearly Finished," *Riverside News*, October 16, 1913.

19. Kircher, 130–31.

20. Joel Garreau included Naperville as a part of an edge city running in a corridor along Interstate 88. Michael Ebner, using the term coined by Robert Fishman, describes it as a technoburb. See Joel Garreau, *Edge City: Life on the New Frontier* (New York, 1988); and Michael H. Ebner, "Technoburb: The Growth of Naperville, Illinois, from a Small Town to a Midwest Technological Center," *Inland Architect* 37, no. 1 (January 1, 1993).

21. William Julius Wilson, *The Truly Disadvantaged: The Inner City, the Underclass, and Public Policy* (Chicago, 1987).

22. The Naper Settlement "living village" was begun by the first twelve charter members of the Naperville Heritage Society, who moved St. John's Episcopal Church from the top of the hill on East Jefferson Avenue to the grounds of their history museum in 1969. During the 1970s, ten more historical structures in Naperville were moved to the site. In 1979, the society received a contract from the city to develop and administer what has become Naper Settlement. Operating continuously into the twentieth century, the Pre-Emption House had been torn down in 1946. However, Naper Settlement built a replica of the structure to serve as a visitors' center at the close of the twentieth century.

23. Helen Fraser, "Naperville," in *DuPage Roots*, ed. Richard A. Thompson (DuPage County, 1985), 204, 205. See also Ann Durkin Keating and B. Pierre Lebeau, *North Central College and Naperville: A Shared History* (Naperville, 1995).

Furniture was a major industry in Chicago, but not one of the largest. Furniture factories provide an interesting counterpoint to the state-of-the-art techniques employed at the Western Wheel Works or the Elgin Watch Company. Despite production for a national market, most furniture companies maintained older craft methods into the twentieth century. They were also specialty factories that manufactured only goods after they had been ordered. The size of orders could range from single piece to many thousands, but production was determined by orders, unlike production of watches in Elgin or bicycles on the Near North Side where a standard product was marketed after production.

In 1924, the American Furniture Mart was built at 680 N. Lake Shore Drive. Around 3000 furniture manufacturers exhibited here each year during the 1920s. Loss of lumber in Great Lakes led to ultimate decline in the industry.

Philip Scranton, *Endless Novelty: Specialty Production and American Industrialization, 1865–1925* (Princeton, 1997), 170–76 focuses on specialty manufacturers, especially furniture manufacturing.

24. Joseph C. Bigott, *From Cottage to Bungalow: Houses and the Working Class in Metropolitan Chicago, 1869–1929* (Chicago, 2001), especially 19–53.

25. Sources on Douglas include Christopher R. Reed, "CA 35—Douglas," *Local Community Fact Book: Chicago Metropolitan Area, 1990* (Chicago, 1995), 122; Dominic A. Pacyga and Ellen Skerrett, *Chicago: City of Neighborhoods* (Chicago, 1986), 300–21; and Daniel Bluestone, "Chicago's Mecca Flat Blues," *Journal of the Society of Architectural Historians* 57, no. 4 (December 1998): 382–403.

26. Reed, 122.

27. Arnold R. Hirsch, *Making the Second Ghetto: Race and Housing in Chicago, 1940–1960* (Chicago, 1998), describes this transformation at length in chapter 4.

Chapter 8

1. Everett Chamberlin, *Chicago and Its Suburbs* (Chicago, 1874), 102.

2. Carl Sandburg, "Chicago," in *Selected Poems*, ed. George and Willene Hendrick (San Diego, 1996), 3–4.

3. Daniel Bluestone, "Chicago's Mecca Flat Blues," *Journal of the Society of Architectural Historians* 57, no. 4 (December 1998): 382–403. Dolores Hayden titled a book *The Power of Place: Urban Landscapes as Public History* (Cambridge, 1995). Historian Perry Duis has used a variation in his overview of the history of the built environment in Chicago in "The Shaping of Chicago," in the *AIA Guide to Chicago*, ed. Alice Sinkevitch (New York, 1993), 3. Duis subtitles the initial subsection in his essay "The Power of Place."

4. But urban historians are often unwilling to move out across urban regions. Robert Bruegmann has captured the field neatly: "Historians of the city have been especially keen on identifying and exploring what is specifically 'urban' in the development of our metropolitan regions. They have concerned themselves with what they felt were the most fundamental elements that generated America's great cities in the late nineteenth and early twentieth centuries, then left them vulnerable in the postwar years. Because of this interest, their focus was largely on the city center and on the elements in it that survived from the traditional industrial city. They have been less interested in what happened at the periphery of the metropolitan area." In *The Architects and the City: Holabird & Roche of Chicago, 1880–1918* (Chicago, 1997), xi–xii.

5. Perhaps the first structure which was deliberately preserved in Chicagoland after its initial usefulness had passed is the Water Tower. Built in 1869 on N. Michigan Avenue, the building was one of the few in the path of the 1871 fire that withstood its flames. The 154-foot yellow stone tower was built in a style reminiscent of elaborate castle turrets and towers. After the fire, the Water Tower was restored to working order and continued to serve the city's needs into the twentieth century. By the time that the tower was no longer in active use, it had already become a historic icon. When redevelopment swept through N. Michigan Avenue in the 1960s, the Water Tower was not only spared, but became the center for new redevelopment, including Chicago's first downtown indoor shopping mall, Water Tower Place.

6. In 1960, the Chicago Heritage Committee was founded as part of the advocacy for preserving Adler & Sullivan's Garrick Theatre (known originally as the Schiller Building). While the drive to preserve the Garrick was unsuccessful, "the preservation movement in Chicago had been born." For more on early preservation efforts in Chicago, see Theodore W. Hild, "The Demolition of the Garrick Theatre and the Birth of the Preservation Movement in Chicago," *Illinois Historical Journal* 88, no. 2 (Summer 1995): 79–100; and Daniel Bluestone, "Preservation and Renewal in Post-World War II Chicago," *Journal of Architectural Education* 47, no. 4 (May 1994): 210–23. See also Perry R. Duis, "The Shaping of Chicago," in *AIA Guide to Chicago*, ed. Alice Sinkevitch (New York, 1993), 21–22; and Daniel Bluestone, "Academics in Tennis Shoes: Historic Preservation and the Academy," *Journal of the Society of Architectural History* 58, no. 3 (September 1999): 299–307. See

David Lowe, *Lost Chicago* (Boston, 1975), for many examples of buildings demolished in downtown Chicago, largely in the mid-twentieth century.

In 1957, Frank Lloyd Wright's Robie House was the target of one of the very first successful attempts at historic preservation in Chicagoland. Owned by the University of Chicago, it is currently undergoing a massive rehabilitation. See Paul Kruty, "Frederick C. Robie House," in Sinkevitch, 433–34.

7. From 1984 to 1992 the Commission on Chicago Historical and Architectural Landmarks conducted a citywide Historic Resources Survey of pre-1940 buildings. For more on demolished buildings see, Lowe, *Lost Chicago.*

8. On the Near West Side, activists, including Florence Scala, unsuccessfully fought the demolition of their neighborhood after it was designated as the site for the Chicago campus of the University of Illinois in 1961. Only Hull House was saved from the wrecker's ball, standing as a memorial to a neighborhood destroyed, a small link to a lost past. Residents of the Douglas neighborhood on Chicago's South Side were no more successful in saving their neighborhood in the face of the urban renewal and building plans of the Illinois Institute of Technology, the Chicago Housing Authority, and area hospitals. See Bluestone, "Chicago's Mecca Flat Blues."

9. The Chicago Historical Society dates its foundation to the 1850s. A few suburban historical societies date to the 1920s, including Evanston's. These societies were generally supported by wealthy and influential residents who wanted to preserve the legacy of their community (and through it their own).

10. Beyond local historical societies, preservation has been taken up by a few wider organizations. The forest preserve districts of the counties within the region have to varying degrees preserved sites within their boundaries. The National Park Service is involved in two areas of preservation in this region: at the Indiana Dunes National Lakeshore and at the Illinois and Michigan Canal National Historic Corridor.

11. Recent efforts to highlight and preserve the bungalow with the support of the City of Chicago provide a model for wide, but private, support of preservation. See also Camilo José Vergara and Timothy J. Samuelson, *Unexpected Chicagoland* (New York, 2001).

12. Chicagoland is in line with other parts of the United States with regard to this emphasis on rural and small-scale structures. They are easier to preserve. They may also be more attractive for interpretation as well. Interpretation can emphasize independence, self-reliance, and isolation from the wider region far more easily within the context of a house than within that of an industrial site on acres of land. See Hayden, 30.

13. In the 1970s, the National Park Service designated the first industrial heritage sites. Lowell, Massachusetts, was among the first in which preservation work took hold. The Society for Industrial Archeology is a national organization committed to preserving these landscapes. The National Park Service in the last fifteen years has also developed a list of sites important to labor history.

14. Dominic A. Pacyga and Ellen Skerrett, *Chicago: City of Neighborhoods* (Chicago, 1986), 408–49; and David Bensman, "South Chicago," in *The Encyclopedia of Chicago* (Chicago, 2004). City planners and independent urbanists have suggested numerous plans for the site, including architect Walter Netsch who envisions park and residential development on the site's north end. Walter Netsch, "The North Site of the South Works: A 21st Century Solution," lecture presented at the 2003 Chicago Humanities Festival.

15. In 1991, I prepared a guidebook of historical industrial sites in Chicagoland as part of a conference for the Society for Industrial Archeology. See *Chicago: An Industrial Guide* (Chicago, 1991).

16. David Hamer, *History in Urban Places: The Historic Districts of the United States* (Columbus, 1998), 29: "The survival of a building or a district is also usually dependent on adaptability to contemporary needs."

17. Ibid.

18. Dolores Hayden found this to be the case: "Like work on the cultural landscape, much scholarship on ordinary (or vernacular) buildings has focused on rural or small town subjects, on agriculture or craft industries. More has been written about farmhouses and barns than urban boardinghouses or saloons, more about rural one-room schools than urban public high schools. See Hayden, 30.

19. See Ellen Skerrett, "It's More Than a Bungalow: Portage Park and the Making of the Bungalow Belt," in *The Chicago Bungalow*, ed. Dominic A. Pacyga and Charles Shanabruch (Chicago, 2003), 97–116; as well as Joseph C. Bigott, *From Cottage to Bungalow: Houses and the Working Class in Metropolitan Chicago, 1869–1929* (Chicago, 2001).

20. Mary Corbin Sies, "Paradise Retained: An Analysis of Persistence in Planned, Exclusive Suburbs, 1880–1980," *Planning Perspectives* 12, no. 2 (April 1997): 165–91.

21. Lizabeth Cohen, *A Consumers' Republic: The Politics of Mass Consumption in Postwar America* (Cambridge, 2003), 14, uses "mass suburbia" to distinguish the suburbanization of the second half of the twentieth century from the suburbs that had preceded them.

22. Flour was produced and distributed nationally by the closing decades of the nineteenth century. Refrigerated rail cars moved meat (and then fruits and vegetables) onto a national market. But dairy and vegetables and fruits remained locally produced well into the twentieth century. The network of farms and farm centers which have been described in chapter 4 were as vital to the maintenance of Chicagoland as trade or manufacturing. William Cronon provides a model for integrating the agricultural view into a regional one in *Nature's Metropolis: Chicago and the Great West* (New York, 1991).

23. Gregory D. Squires, Larry Bennett, Kathleen McCourt, and Philip Nyden, *Chicago: Race, Class, and the Response to Urban Decline* (Philadelphia, 1987), 26.

24. James R. Grossman, *Land of Hope: Chicago, Black Southerners, and the Great Migration* (Chicago, 1989), 183–84, 197.

25. Joel Garreau, in *Edge City: Life on the New Frontier* (New York, 1988), is among the recent commentators to explore regional landscapes, and suggests that work is a recent addition to suburban areas. His "edge cities" are places with more jobs than housing. However, the suburban location of jobs is not what is new. Industrial suburbs (as well as farmers and farm center business people) long offered many jobs. Instead, the movement of white-collar jobs from central business districts and the evolution of auto commuting have reshaped landscape patterns.

Robert Lewis, a geographer at the University of Toronto, has explored the transformation of worker suburbs to industrial neighborhoods. See "The Industrial Suburb Is Dead, Long Live the Industrial Slum: Suburbs and Slums in Chicago and Montreal, 1850–1950," *Planning Perspectives* 17, no. 2 (April 2002): 123–44.

26. Without question, one of the most frequently referenced geographic distinctions in Chicagoland is between the North Side and the South Side. Fueled in the twentieth century by competition between two major league ball clubs, the White Sox on the South Side and the Cubs on the North, the nineteenth-century settlement patterns varied enough to suggest at least some roots of differential development.

27. This book is both a call for local historians to see a regional interpretation for the structures that they have preserved, and a call for urban historians to use the built environment to craft regional history. The interpretation and reinterpretation of sites is a central role for urban historians in a scene already crowded with architectural historians, preservationists, and local historians. Historians have knowledge and perspective that can shape these sites into stories that can help residents, as well as actual and virtual visitors, to better understand the public past of the region.

Figure Credits

Chapter One: Regionalism of the Railroad Era

1.1   Dearborn Street Station (Leslie Schwartz)
1.2   Monadnock Building (Chicago Historical Society, ICHi 18909; CHS Permission
        no. 39893-3)
1.3   Aurora Roundhouse (Leslie Schwartz)
1.4   Grossdale train station (Jack Keating)
1.5   Norwood Park station (Chicago Historical Society, ICHi-22681; CHS Permission
        no. 39893-14)
1.6   Composite map (Dennis McClendon)
1.7   Rees 1851 map (Chicago Historical Society, ICHi-13574; CHS Permission no. 41912-1)
1.8   Chamberlin 1874 map (Chicago Historical Society, ICHi-36142; Engraver: Rufus Blanchard;
        CHS Permission nos. 41041-4, 41899-4
1.9   Burnham and Bennett 1909 *Plan of Chicago* (Chicago Historical Society ICHi-13284; CHS
        Permission no. 39893-15)

Chapter Two: Chicagoland before the Railroad

2.1   Potawatomi men's clothing (Chicago Historical Society ICHi-36141; Illustration: Field
        Museum of Natural History; CHS Permission nos. 41041-3, 41899-3)
2.2   Contemporary Mettawa (Leslie Schwartz)
2.3   The Chicago Portage National Historic Site (Leslie Schwartz)
2.4 & 2.5 Joseph and Marie Bailly Homestead (Indiana Dunes National Lakeshore, National
        Park Service)

2.6   1820 sketch by Henry Rowe Schoolcraft (Chicago Historical Society, ICHi-05626; CHS Permission no. 41912-2)

2.7   Kennicott's Grove National Historic Landmark (Glenview Park District)

2.8   1830 plat (*Industrial Chicago*, vol. 2, *Building Interests* [Chicago, 1891], following p. 26)

2.9   The Illinois and Michigan Canal map (Dennis McClendon)

2.10   Illinois and Michigan Canal (Leslie Schwartz)

2.11   The Gaylord Building, Lockport, (Leslie Schwartz)

2.12   Sauganash Hotel (A. T. Andreas, *History of Cook County* [Chicago, 1884])

2.13   Beaubien Tavern (Leslie Schwartz)

2.14   Noble-Seymour-Crippen House (Betsy Keating)

2.15   Clarke House (Chicago Historical Society, ICHi-01166; CHS Permission no. 39893-10)

Chapter Three: Farm Centers of the Railroad Age

3.1   The Prairie Crossing Charter School (Leslie Schwartz)

3.2   Farm center map (Dennis McClendon)

3.3   1845 engraving of Chicago (A. T. Andreas, *History of Cook County* [Chicago, 1884])

3.4   The Sheldon Peck House (Leslie Schwartz)

3.5 & 3.6 Garfield Farm (Leslie Schwartz)

3.7 & 3.8 The Chellberg Farm (Indiana Dunes National Lakeshore, National Park Service)

3.9   Stacy's Tavern Museum (Leslie Schwartz)

3.10   Frederick Graue Mill (Leslie Schwartz)

3.11   Itasca train station (*1874 Atlas and History of DuPage County*)

3.12   The Lisle Depot Museum (Leslie Schwartz)

3.13   St. James at Sag Roman Catholic Church (Leslie Schwartz)

3.14   St. Peter's Evangelical Lutheran Church, Skokie (Skokie Historical Society)

3.15   Contemporary view of St. Peter's Evangelical Lutheran Church, Skokie (Leslie Schwartz)

3.16   St. Peter's Catholic Church, Skokie (Skokie Historical Society)

3.17   Contemporary view of St. Peter's Catholic Church, Skokie (Leslie Schwartz)

Chapter Four: Industrial Towns of the Railroad Age

4.1   Union Stock Yards Gate (Leslie Schwartz)

4.2   Union Stock Yards in the late 1860s (Chicago Historical Society, ICHi-32213; CHS Permission no. 41897-10)

4.3   Union Stock Yards Gate, 1890 (Chicago Historical Society, J. W. Taylor, ICHi-04048; CHS Permission no. 41897-2)

4.4   Union Stock Yards Gate, 1954 (Chicago Historical Society, ICHi-04101; photographer: Sherwin Murphy; CHS Permission no. 41898-4)

4.5   Union Stock Yards, 1971 (Chicago Historical Society, photographer: Casey Prunchunas, ICHi-24563; CHS Permission no. 41898-5)

4.6   Back of the Yards (Leslie Schwartz)

4.7   Holy Cross Roman Catholic Church (Chicago Historical Society, ICHi-22788; photographer: Clarence W. Hines; CHS Permission no. 39893-11)

4.8   St. Joseph Roman Catholic Church (Leslie Schwartz)

4.9   Sts. Cyril and Methodius (Chicago Historical Society, ICHi-10302; CHS Permission no. 39893-16)

4.10   Industrial towns map (Dennis McClendon)

4.11   Western Wheel Works (Chicago Historical Society, ICHi-36140; CHS Permission no. 41041-2, 41899-2)

4.12   Cobbler Square (Leslie Schwartz)

4.13   Exterior view of the Joliet Iron Works (Chicago Historical Society, Illinois Steel Company Photograph Album, ICHi-35519; CHS Permission no. 39893-2)

4.14   Remains of stoves and cleaners at the Joliet Iron Works (Leslie Schwartz)

4.15   Bessemer converter at the Joliet Steel Works (Chicago Historical Society, Illinois Steel Company Photograph Album, ICHi-35520; CHS Permission no. 39893-4)

4.16   Gross Park (Leslie Schwartz)

4.17   Back of the Yards stores (Leslie Schwartz)

4.18   Saloons, Back of the Yards (Leslie Schwartz)

4.19   Pullman Administration Building (Chicago Historical Society, ICHi-24181; CHS Permission no. 41898-9)

4.20   The Pullman Administration Building (Leslie Schwartz)

4.21   St. Lawrence south of 111th Street in Pullman in 1908 (Chicago Historical Society, DN-0006818; *Chicago Daily News* photographer; CHS Permission no. 39893-21)

4.22   St. Lawrence south of 111th Street in Pullman in 2003 (Leslie Schwartz)

4.23   Greenstone Church, Pullman (Chicago Historical Society, DN-0006894; *Chicago Daily News* photographer; CHS Permission no. 39893-22)

4.24   The Elgin National Watch Company (Chicago Historical Society, ICHi-26799; photographer Bill Brown; CHS Permission no. 41898-8)

4.25   The Elgin Watch Company Observatory (Leslie Schwartz)

4.26   Elgin National Watch Company housing (Chicago Historical Society, ICHi-20416; photographer John Manly Adams; CHS Permission no. 41897-12)

4.27   St. Alphonsus Roman Catholic Church (Chicago Historical Society, ICHi 24537; photographer John McCarthy; CHS Permission no. 39893-5)

4.28   West Fletcher Avenue worker housing (Leslie Schwartz)

4.29   Best Brewery (Chicago Historical Society, ICHi-23887; CHS Permission no. 41897-11)

4.30   Best Brewery (Leslie Schwartz)

4.31   Schuba's (Leslie Schwartz)

Chapter Five: Commuter Suburbs of the Railroad Age

5.1   Olmsted plan for Riverside (Chicago Historical Society, ICHi-14189; CHS Permission no. 39893-17)

5.2   Riverside train station (Leslie Schwartz)

5.3   The Riverside water tower (Joseph C. Bigott)

5.4   The Riverside Improvement Company Building (Joseph C. Bigott)

5.5   The Riverside Hotel (Chicago Historical Society, DN-0006799; *Chicago Daily News* photographer; CHS Permission no. 41901-3)

5.6   Riverside houses (Joseph C. Bigott)

5.7   Commuter suburbs map (Dennis McClendon)

5.8   Kenilworth train station (Leslie Schwartz)

5.9   The Groveland Park Cottage (Leslie Schwartz)

5.10   Groveland Park (Chicago Historical Society, DN-0065216; *Chicago Daily News* photographer; CHS Permission no. 39893-34)

5.11   Plan for Lake Forest (Chicago Historical Society, ICHi-16261; CHS Permission no. 39893-6)

5.12   The Hyde Park House (Chicago Historical Society, ICHi-00727; CHS Permission no. 39893-1)

5.13   Hinsdale map (1874 *Atlas of DuPage County*)

5.14   Immanuel Evangelical Church, Hinsdale (Leslie Schwartz)

5.15   Housing near Immanuel Church (Leslie Schwartz)

5.16   122 N. Grant Street, Hinsdale, 1910 (Chicago Historical Society, DN-0056000; *Chicago Daily News* photographer; CHS Permission no. 39893-27)

5.17   306 N. Grant Street, Hinsdale (Leslie Schwartz)

5.18   The Hinsdale Historical Society (Ann Keating)

5.19   Kenilworth Village Hall (Chicago Historical Society, DN-0008570; *Chicago Daily News* photographer; CHS Permission no. 41902-2)

5.20   Market Square in Lake Forest (Leslie Schwartz)

5.21   The Kenilworth Union Church (Leslie Schwartz)

Chapter Six: Recreational and Institutional Centers of the Railroad Age

6.1   Cottages at the Des Plaines Methodist Camp Ground (Chicago Historical Society, DN-0007496; *Chicago Daily News* photographer; CHS Permission no. 41042-7; 41900-7)

6.2   Cottages, the Des Plaines Methodist Camp Ground (Leslie Schwartz)

6.3   Breakfast at the Des Plaines Methodist Camp Ground (Chicago Historical Society, DN-0079224; *Chicago Daily News* photographer; CHS Permission no. 39893-26)

6.4   The Waldorf Tabernacle, Des Plaines Methodist Camp Ground (Leslie Schwartz)

6.5   Institutional and recreational centers map (Dennis McClendon)

6.6   Libertyville Station in 1908 (Chicago Historical Society, DN-0006822; *Chicago Daily News* photographer; CHS Permission no. 39893-23)

6.7   Kurz & Allen lithograph (Chicago Historical Society, ICHi-14830; CHS Permission no. 39893-7)

6.8   Grüsse vom Cannstatter Volksfest (Chicago Historical Society, ICHi-21431; CHS Permission no. 39893-13)

6.9   Funeral procession, 1915 (Chicago Historical Society, DN-0064964; *Chicago Daily News* photographer; CHS Permission no. 39893-25)

6.10   Forest Park Amusement Park (Chicago Historical Society, DN-0064698; *Chicago Daily News* photographer; CHS Permission no. 39893-25)

6.11   Harlem Race Track, Forest Park, 1901 (Chicago Historical Society, SDN-000513; *Chicago Daily News* photographer; CHS Permission no. 41042-6; 41900-6)

6.12   "Pair-o-chutes" at Riverview Park in 1939 (Chicago Historical Society, ICHi-20038; CHS Permission no. 41898-6)

6.13   1908 Riverview Merry Go Round (Chicago Historical Society, ICHi-19797; CHS Permission no. 41041-1; 41899-1)

6.14   Ravinia Park (Leslie Schwartz)

6.15   The Homewood Country Club (Chicago Historical Society, SDN-003638; *Chicago Daily News* photographer; CHS Permission no. 39893-36)

6.16   Salvation Army Camp (Chicago Historical Society, DN-0066686; *Chicago Daily News* photographer; CHS Permission no. 39893-29)

6.17   Wheaton College (*1874 Atlas of DuPage County*)

6.18   The old McHenry County Courthouse (Leslie Schwartz)

6.19   Cook County Courthouse (Chicago Historical Society, ICHi-00430; from a daguerreotype by Alexander Hesler; CHS Permission no. 41898-7)

6.20   Chicago State Hospital (Chicago Historical Society, DN-0053716; *Chicago Daily News* photographer; CHS Permission no. 39893-30)

6.21   Grounds around the Chicago State Hospital (Chicago Historical Society, DN-0006807; *Chicago Daily News* photographer; CHS Permission no. 41042-5; 41900-5)

6.22   Fort Sheridan station in 1910 (Chicago Historical Society, DN-0008738; *Chicago Daily News* photographer; CHS Permission no. 39893-35)

6.23   Fort Sheridan (Leslie Schwartz)

6.24   Fort Sheridan (Leslie Schwartz)

Chapter Seven: Regionalism through Neighbors and Over Time

7.1   "Greetings from Gross Point" (Wilmette Historical Society)

7.2   St. Joseph's Roman Catholic Church (Chicago Historical Society, DN-0054492; *Chicago Daily News* photographer; CHS Permission no. 41900-8; 41042-8; 41902-4)

7.3   Gross Point tavern (Chicago Historical Society, DN-0054490; *Chicago Daily News* photographer; CHS Permission no. 4441042-9; 41902-3; 41900-9)

7.4   Brandt Interiors, Wilmette (John J. Keating)

7.5   Interior of a Gross Point tavern (Wilmette Historical Society)

7.6   Topographical map, 1897, from the U.S. Department of the Interior (Joseph C. Bigott)

7.7   Mrs. Vibe K. Spicer (Chicago Historical Society, DN-0067895; *Chicago Daily News* photographer; CHS Permission no. 41902-1)

7.8   University Hall, Northwestern University (Ann Keating)

7.9   Gross Point Village Hall (John J. Keating)

7.10   New Trier Township High School (Wilmette Historical Society)

7.11   Riverside Quadrangle of the topography map published in 1901 by the U.S. Department of the Interior (Joseph C. Bigott)

7.12   Canoes and rowboats on the Des Plaines River (Chicago Historical Society, DN-0006816; *Chicago Daily News* photographer; CHS Permission no. 41901-1)

7.13   Cream City Amusement Park (Chicago Historical Society, DN-0006805; *Chicago Daily News* photographer; CHS Permission no. 41041-10; 41901-5; 41899-10)

7.14   Hoffman Tower, Lyons (Chicago Historical Society, DN-0006804; *Chicago Daily News* photographer; CHS Permission no. 41901-2)

7.15   Hoffman Tower (Joseph C. Bigott)

7.16   Bridge between Riverside and Lyons (Chicago Historical Society, DN-0006795; *Chicago Daily News* photographer; CHS Permission 41041-11; 41899-11; 41901-4)

7.17   Plat of Naperville (*1874 Atlas of DuPage County*)

7.18   Pre-Emption House (Joseph C. Bigott)

7.19   Old Main, North Central College (Joseph C. Bigott)

7.20   Kroehler Manufacturing Company (Joseph C. Bigott)

7.21   Stephen A. Douglas cottage (Chicago Historical Society, DN-005331; *Chicago Daily News* photographer; CHS Permission no. 39893-31)

7.22   First University of Chicago (Chicago Historical Society, ICHi-01517; CHS Permission no. 39893-9)

7.23   Camp Douglas (Chicago Historical Society, DN-0086695; *Chicago Daily News* photographer; CHS Permission no. 39893-18)

7.24   Armour Institute (Chicago Historical Society, DN-0007561; *Chicago Daily News* photographer; CHS Permission no. 398393-33)

7.25   3724 South Michigan Avenue (Chicago Historical Society, DN-0067674; *Chicago Daily News* photographer; CHS Permission no. 39893-32)

7.26   Kehilath Anshe Ma'ariv Synagogue (Chicago Historical Society, ICHi-21603; CHS Permission no. 39893-12)

7.27   Pilgrim Baptist Church (Leslie Schwartz)

7.28   35th and S. State during the 1919 race riots (Chicago Historical Society, DN-0071297; *Chicago Daily News* photographer; CHS Permission no. 39893-19)

7.29   Eighth Regiment Infantry (Chicago Historical Society, DN-0064686; *Chicago Daily News* photographer; CHS Permission no. 39893-20)

7.30   Stateway Gardens (Chicago Historical Society, Clarence W. Hines, ICHi-23483; CHS Permission no. 39893-8)

Appendix: Regional Tours and Selected Sites

Tour maps (Dennis McClendon)

Index